PENGUIN BOOKS
TO MISS WITH LOVE

'This gripping, occasionally shocking and surprisingly moving book is a must-read for anyone who wishes to understand what life in Britain's inner-city schools is really like. Katharine Birbalsingh's important, clear-sighted and utterly refreshing account exposes the terrible failings of our current education system and points the way to how they might be fixed' Kate Hoey, MP

'Remarkable . . . If education in Britain is turned around, it will be the extraordinary teachers like [Katharine Birbalsingh] who manage it' *Spectator*

'Katharine is truly a breath of fresh air. She writes passionately and persuasively about education in London' Boris Johnson

'The most exciting voice on education since Chris Woodhead' Quentin Letts

'Katharine Birbalsingh should play centre-forward for England. In a book that exposes the real plight of inner-city students in our schools, she is right on target' Tony Sewell

'Love it or hate it, this is a book that will enthral or enrage. No one, but no one, will be left less than fired up. Buy it and read it!' Anthony Seldon

'A passionate and outspoken challenge to Britain's education establishment' David Lammy, MP

'Describes in eloquent, despairing voice how schools suffer from high levels of disruption and underachievement' *Telegraph*

'Birbalsingh does not pull her punches' *Guardian*

ABOUT THE AUTHOR

Katharine Birbalsingh is Britain's most outspoken and controversial teacher. Educated at a comprehensive school, she earned a degree in philosophy and modern languages at Oxford University and has taught for over a decade in inner-city schools. *To Miss with Love* was for several years an anonymous blog that exposed the reality of inner-city schools and the problems with the education system. Katharine Birbalsingh now writes regularly for the *Telegraph* and has given evidence at the Commons select committee for education. Her views have sparked a national debate.

www.katharinebirbalsingh.com

To Miss with Love

KATHARINE BIRBALSINGH

PENGUIN BOOKS

PENGUIN BOOKS

Published by the Penguin Group
Penguin Books Ltd, 80 Strand, London WC2R ORL, England
Penguin Group (USA) Inc., 375 Hudson Street, New York, New York 10014, USA
Penguin Group (Canada), 90 Eglinton Avenue East, Suite 700, Toronto, Ontario, Canada M4P 2Y3
(a division of Pearson Penguin Canada Inc.)
Penguin Ireland, 25 St Stephen's Green, Dublin 2, Ireland
(a division of Penguin Books Ltd)
Penguin Group (Australia), 250 Camberwell Road,
Camberwell, Victoria 3124, Australia (a division of Pearson Australia Group Pty Ltd)
Penguin Books India Pvt Ltd, 11 Community Centre,
Panchsheel Park, New Delhi – 110 017, India
Penguin Group (NZ), 67 Apollo Drive, Rosedale, Auckland 0632, New Zealand
(a division of Pearson New Zealand Ltd)
Penguin Books (South Africa) (Pty) Ltd, 24 Sturdee Avenue,
Rosebank, Johannesburg 2196, South Africa

Penguin Books Ltd, Registered Offices: 80 Strand, London WC2R ORL, England

www.penguin.com

First published 2011
1

Typeset by Jouve (UK), Milton Keynes
Printed in Great Britain by Clays Ltd, St Ives plc

ISBN: 978-0-670-91899-7

www.greenpenguin.co.uk

MIX
Paper from
responsible sources
FSC
www.fsc.org   FSC™ C018179

Penguin Books is committed to a sustainable
future for our business, our readers and our
planet. This book is made from paper certified
by the Forest Stewardship Council.

This book is dedicated to the children who inspired it, and to M, and teachers like her, who taught us how to teach.

And to remember the children who have dropped through the net and to inspire change, so that no more should slip through.

Acknowledgements

There are those who must remain nameless to whom I owe a debt of gratitude. I especially want to thank the teachers who read the manuscript and gave me feedback.

Thank you to the blogger Archbishop Cranmer. I have no idea who he is. His Grace has shown me that strangers can show each other kindness and that those who disagree can find harmony in their discourse. There are others who have been kind to me in my recent struggle. A big thank you to Kevin Freeman, Daniel Hind, Adrian Huston, Chris Mounsey, Sebastian Nokes, Lundi Nyoni, Nick Seaton, Benjamin Uduje, Alex Wheatle, Toby Young and my flatmate Richard Stern, who has tolerated much disruption. I would never have survived without you.

Thank you to Venetia Butterfield, Will Hammond and the team at Viking, without whom this book would not exist.

Thank you to Frank, Norma and Christine Birbalsingh, who have stood by me and have become experts at thinking outside the box.

Finally, a sincere thank you to all who have supported me but in particular to Patrick Green, who has shown me extraordinary generosity, and to Dawn Metcalfe, who is a teacher and a half.

Foreword

This book was born in an internet café near Tottenham Court Road. It began as a blog under the pseudonym Snuffleupagus, Big Bird's woolly mammoth friend in the 1970s children's television programme *Sesame Street*, who was invisible to everyone except Big Bird. My name is Ms Snuffleupagus, which gradually became Snuffy on the blog, because I believe education in Britain to be filled with many unseen elephants. Just as no one can see Snuffleupagus on Sesame Street, so many of us cannot see the very obvious problems ingrained in our education system.

Some people, including the parents of children at any one of the five schools where I have taught, will read *To Miss with Love* and believe that I teach at a school far away from theirs. But the majority of children across England's cities are in schools like the one in this book, and some are in schools that are far worse. Ordinary School, as I have called it, was given its name for a reason.

In order not to bore the reader, I have omitted from this diary the fights that happen every week or, indeed, every day. And to protect real individuals, I have kept some of the worst horror stories of our education system to myself. While the characters and situations are my creations, there is nothing in *To Miss with Love* that hasn't happened during my ten years as a teacher.

I worry about losing my job for having written this book. As a profession, we are strongly discouraged from speaking out against the system. But I believe the greatest betrayal of our children is our silence. As a friend of mine said upon reading it, *To Miss with Love* dares to say what we teachers are always thinking but no one ever says. She teaches in a small town in central England. The experiences of Ordinary School are not confined to our inner cities.

I teach because I love children and I want to improve their lives at school. I have written this book with that same intention at heart.

— Snuffy, August 2010

The passage above was written two months before I gave a speech at the Conservative Party conference on 5 October 2010, where I described what I believe to be the failings of the state education system: themes that I explore in this book.

Just over a week later, I was no longer in my job. And in the publicity that followed, my identity as Snuffy – and as the author of this book – was exposed.

Despite everything that has happened since, I believe that I was right to speak out about teaching in Britain's schools as I and many others have experienced it. I hope that others may follow and that some real change may be effected.

Unfortunately, this may not happen. The public is only likely to hear from those teachers who defend the current education system. Many of them are doing so with good intentions. Unlike me, and those like me, they can speak without fearing for their jobs. But while I understand the desire to pretend things are better than they are, I believe that hiding the truth and suppressing any open debate serves neither our children nor our country.

— Katharine Birbalsingh, December 2010

Summer Holidays

I'm walking through Hyde Park in the sunshine when I see some young men, three black and one white, laughing and walking together in the distance. They're wearing hoodies and they bop as they walk. They're big and muscular. They're so solid, you wonder how the ground doesn't give way as they stomp along.

A middle-aged white couple in front of me slows down, the woman guiding her husband on to the grass so as to be out of their way. The young men don't flinch at her clever tactic; they're too busy yelling and laughing.

I suppose, to some, a group of young hooded men is intimidating. I look straight at them. 'Miss! Miss!' They rush towards me. I peer closer. Oh my goodness. They're *my* boys. I remember them as spindly little things, with gangling arms and broken glasses. Now they're proud and built like iron. One of them hugs me. Another jumps around me in excitement. 'Do you remember me, Miss?' Their eyes twinkle.

'Of course I remember you, boys.' I smile. They were in my first ever tutor group, about eight years ago, when I was twenty-four. They aren't boys any more. 'How are you all? I mean, what are you doing now?'

They tell me about college, about their jobs, about how much fun it is. They're shy and excited at the same time. They look up and down as they speak, at everything but me.

One of them frowns. 'Why didn't you come back, Miss?'

'Yeah! You promised us you would come back. You never did.'

I smile. 'I couldn't, boys. I just couldn't. It would have made me too sad. I missed you.'

The tallest of them, Scraper, is bashful. He was mean to me. He knows it. He was always in trouble. I was permanently putting him in detention. And I was so young then, so inexperienced. Scraper used to pull me in every direction. I was an emotional

3

wreck. Once, he even reduced me to tears in the staff room – not that he knows that. I used to worry he would end up in prison. He smiles.

'You know, Miss, I'm working round the corner from school now. At the car place. I fix the cars.'

'Really?' My eyes open wide and I hold my hand out to him. He takes it, shaking awkwardly. 'That's fantastic, Scraper. How brilliant. Well done!'

He looks up from the ground at me as if to say sorry. There's a smile on his face. 'You still watching *Ally McBeal*, Miss?'

I shake my head.

They nudge each other. 'Remember how Miss *had* to watch it? Remember how she'd work all the time, but when it came to *Ally McBeal*, it was *over*, man!'

They howl with laughter. 'Damn Miss, man! English just wasn't the same after you left. Mr Waitingtodie couldn't control us.'

They all join in. 'Yeah, yeah, yeah . . .'

The white one cackles, whipping his fingers together, doubling over. 'Rah! Yeah, man! Ha! Mr Waitingtodie, I forgot 'bout him.' He pauses. 'So where you at now, Miss? Still teaching English?'

I nod, as one of the others whacks him on the back. 'You *ideeott*! 'Course she's still teaching English, man. What else she meant to be teaching?'

'Hmm, yes, but . . . I've moved now. I'm head of department at Ordinary School. You know?'

They grin. 'Not bad, Miss, not bad. Promotion – it could be worse.

So you still have that foot thing we gave you?' Their eyes shine.

I have to think for a moment. 'Oh yes, that foot-massage thing. Yes, of course I still have it,' I lie. 'I use it all the time. And I have photos of all of you. I still have that photo of you in the playground where you're all jumping on each other. It's on my kitchen wall. Do you remember?' This time, I'm telling the truth.

'Yeah,' they snigger. 'Yeah, Miss, 'course we remember.' They throw their arms about as if they're in a music video.

I wince. 'So how old are you now?'

'Twenty-three.'

I put my head in my hands. 'Oh my goodness, I can't believe it. Twenty-*three*? I feel so old . . .'

'Nah Miss, man! You still looking *good*, Miss.'

'Thanks, boys.' I can feel myself blushing. 'Anyway, I must go. But it was such a pleasure to see you all again. Makes me proud. Really.'

'Yeah, Miss, us too.'

They begin to walk away. 'You stay safe now, yuh hear?' they shout back, a couple of them with an arm in the air, gangster style.

'You too, boys.'

Strolling away, I feel guilty for having thrown away that foot thing. Poor kids had clubbed together to buy it. Off I go down the lane, thinking nostalgically of a time when I was young and inexperienced. Sometimes I envy the innocence of that time, that naivety. Sometimes I wish I'd kept my mind shut to what experience has taught me. Sometimes I wonder, if I had done so, how different my life might have been.

Saturday 24 August

'What exactly is it that you *need*, Snuffy?' Bank leans across the dinner table and raises his eyebrows. The others look at me for an answer.

'Need? What do you mean, need?'

'State schools. You and these kids you love. What do you want from us?'

I look at Liberal, my husband of three years, black, in his thirties, cute, with a shaved head, wishing he would invent an excuse for us to leave. Blasted dinner party. We're in a posh house in South Kensington with rich Ghanaian friends. Bank is a banker, tall and slim, and next to him is his lovely wife Compassionate. She is my friend, has dark-brown skin, and wears beautiful head-wraps with African prints. She teaches at the local private school, Wineaton.

'Is it just money?' Bank asks, leaning back on his chair.

Liberal is irritated. 'It isn't *just* about money. Snuffy's kids are disadvantaged. Snuffy's black, educated and committed, and even *she* can't always get through to her kids.' He turns to Compassionate. 'How much are the tuition fees at your school?'

'Well, over ten grand, but what's that got to do with anything? My kids are –'

'*Rich*. They're rich,' shouts Liberal. 'And their parents discuss their homework with them every evening around the dinner table.' They do? 'The problem is the very existence of private schools. If we had only state schools, then Snuffy wouldn't have the nightmares she has, because you lot wouldn't steal all the good kids,' he continues.

Bank's eyes flash. 'You mean I should be forced to send my children to *her* school?'

Compassionate rolls her eyes at me, patting Bank's arm. 'Bank, Bank. Don't be so rude. Snuffy went to Cambridge. You couldn't ask for a better teacher. Her kids have it good!'

'Yeah, I'm looking forward to seeing our results tomorrow. We're hoping for lots of "C"s.' I smile, slightly embarrassed, realizing what I've said. Schools are judged on how many 'A★' to 'C' grades they get. A 'C' grade constitutes a pass; 'C's are our bread and butter. Get ten 'B's or ten 'C's, it makes little difference. But get ten 'D's . . .

'How about we have lunch together tomorrow, Snuffy?' says Compassionate. 'I can drop by your school and pick you up.'

'Oh no, really, I'd love to, but, well, how about we meet at *your* school? I'd love to see Wineaton. I've heard so much about it.'

'Tomorrow at two then?'

I say yes and fold my napkin several times over. Thankfully, the conversation turns from education to the NHS and I'm able to stop feeling so frustrated. I wonder how Crazy and Firecracker have done in their GCSEs? Did Mishap get her 'C'? And our bright stars, Smartie and Diligent . . . ? Under the table, I cross my fingers in my lap.

Monday 26 August

I hand Smartie his envelope and he walks to the other side of the room and tears it open nervously, surrounded by his friends. We're in the canteen but the long lunch tables have been pushed to the side of the room. Smartie is a white middle-class boy whose mother, Mrs Well-Meaning, is one of our governors. As he reads through his results, I can see that he is pleased, and I'm thrilled.

I hand out a few more envelopes and then overhear Mr Good-heart, our head, talking to Smartie. 'Well done, Smartie. Excellent results.' Mr Goodheart smiles proudly, patting the boy on the back. Mr Goodheart is a fattish man, in his fifties and rapidly greying. 'You're staying with us for the sixth form in September, of course?'

'Oh yes, Sir, certainly, Sir.'

I approach. 'So, Smartie, how did you do?'

He grins from ear to ear. 'Well, Miss, I got four "A★"s, five "A"s, two "B"s and one "C".'

'That's great news. Really well done.' I pause, winking. 'And English? How'd you do?'

' "A★" of course, Miss.' He makes a fist in the air. 'Couldn't let you down, Miss.'

'Good for you! Glad to hear it!' I already knew he had the 'A★', but wanted to give him the glory of telling me.

Mishap has just come in. She's a black working-class girl, dark-skinned and overweight, who always refuses to take out her earrings. She got her 'C' grade. I can't wait to see her face when she opens that envelope.

When she does she leaps for joy. 'Hey, Miss,' she calls, having spotted me. She points to her big loop earrings. 'You can't tell me to take these out *now*, can you?' She dances about in victory.

I shake my head. 'No, Mishap. Those earrings are all yours now. How are you?'

'Yeah, yeah, really good, Miss.' The loops in her ears jangle up and down as she speaks. 'I told you I was gonna get it, didn't I?'

'You did indeed.'

'Yeah, yeah, and you never believed me.'

'Well, you proved me wrong, didn't you? Well done. Proof that hard work pays off. So what will you do now?'

'I'll go college, innit. Doing business.'

'That's fantastic, Mishap. Well done.'

I do love coming in on exam-results days. Nothing quite like watching your kids succeed and seeing their faces shine with delight. And this year, our school got 57 per cent 'A★' to 'C' passes, which is up from last year, so we're really happy. That's about average for Britain, so we figure we're doing pretty well, and we're graded 'good' by Ofsted.

As I get on the bus to go towards Wineaton, I think about Smartie's results and how happy we are for him. He's one of our best and brightest. Yet, he only got four 'A★'s. What is Smartie doing with 'B's and 'C's in his results?

I get off the bus and walk towards Wineaton. It's baking hot today so I try to avoid the sun by walking in the shade of its old arches. It's an imposing building. I wonder how many 'A★'s their best kids will have achieved.

The reception area is immaculate, with a pristine office and comfy chairs for visitors. I help myself to a glass of water from their water cooler, give my name at the office and sit and wait.

Compassionate is taking a while to arrive, and as the ladies in the office are not taking any notice of what I'm doing, I decide to go for a stroll through the school. On the walls are lots of old wooden boards with the names of head boys and girls carved into them. Beautiful framed pieces of artwork line the corridors. I wonder if the students painted them.

I think of our corridors, grey and empty except for the bulletin boards we teachers have covered with colourful paper and on which we've pasted up display work by the students. Next to these pieces of artwork, the stuff we have up looks like it might have been done by five-year-olds.

I go to walk through a set of doors and a bunch of boys who must have been playing sport – they look dressed for rugby, in shorts and long socks – are coming through the other way. As I push open the door, the boy in front immediately stops to allow me the room to move through. He pulls up so suddenly that the other boys all pile into each other like dominoes. As if on cue, they all step back to the side of the wall, heads bowed, smiling slightly. 'Sorry, Miss.'

'Thank you, boys.' I walk through and come face to face with a courtyard with fountains and an extraordinary array of flowers. It's stunning.

'Snuffy, there you are! I've been looking for you.'

Compassionate rushes over. She's in a suit and headwrap and looking very glamorous. I instantly feel underdressed. I point towards the doors. 'Those boys, they all stopped to let me through the door – I can't believe it! They actually stopped, they nearly fell over themselves, and then they apologized.'

'Well, of course they stopped. What did you expect them to do? Push through and knock you over?'

Something moves in the gardens, grabbing my attention. 'Is that a peacock?'

'Yes, we have two of them. That one's Sylvester.' Compassionate laughs.

They have *peacocks*? Thank goodness I didn't let Compassionate meet me at my school. I look around at all the greenness and the colours of the flowers and think of our playground: grey asphalt with a few square metres of grass, now turned to mud. I think of the huts outside: three classrooms on wheels, always freezing or boiling hot, because there isn't enough room in the main building for all the kids. *Peacocks?*

Compassionate takes me by the arm. The shock must show on my face. 'Don't worry about this place. I know it's a bit much. These kids have it all. Let's go and get some lunch.'

'How were your results?' I ask tentatively as we walk towards the front entrance.

'Really good. We're pleased.'

'So what percentage passed?'

'Well, you know that independent schools don't judge their performance by the same criteria as state schools, right?'

'Still, you must know what percentage of your students got five GCSE passes?'

'Well, that's just it.' Compassionate makes a face. '*All* our students do. So we judge ourselves on how many got ten "A★"s, and so on.'

I stop dead in my tracks and turn to face her. '*All* your students do?'

My mind is spinning as we head out of the school towards the nearest café.

Sunday 1 September

I'm sitting on the sofa eating ice cream when the phone rings. I get up to answer it. 'Hello?'

'Hello, Snuffy. You all set for the first day of school tomorrow?'

'Hi, Daddy. Yes, Liberal is going to give me a lift in the morning because we'll be starting a little later than usual.'

'Later? Oh yes, the children won't be there, will they?'

'No, they come on Wednesday. We have two days to prepare.'

My father chuckles. 'That's not much time, is it?'

We chat for a while. I ask after my mother, and she immediately jumps on to the other extension mid-conversation.

'Hello, Snuffy. Good luck for tomorrow.'

I smile. 'Thanks, Mum.'

'We can't wait to hear your stories. Reminds us of the joys of teaching.'

We make plans for Liberal and me to visit them in Jamaica during my February half-term holiday. Since retiring, they spend three months of the winter 'back home'. When I hang up, Liberal comes to sit on the sofa next to me.

'You gonna get out the Malcolm X book, like you always do?'

I shake my head. 'Nah. Seems a bit silly, and I have work to finish.'

Liberal makes a fist. 'Awwhh, come on, babe. Where's my soldier girl gone? "By any means necessary!" Remember?'

I laugh. 'Yeah, yeah. Kiss me for good luck.'

'You got it, babe.'

Monday 2 September

Staff gather in the dining hall, sitting on the kids' hard plastic chairs, excited to be back, at our first meeting of the year. One of the deputies, Ms Sensible, a black woman who is always in a suit with her hair tied in a bun, stands and reveals her first PowerPoint slide: 'OFSTED'. The hundred or so people in the room tense together. Some of us let out a gasp. The last thing on our minds is an inspection.

'They'll be coming this year,' she says. 'We can count on it. It's been three years. We're due.' Ms Sensible sighs. 'The only question is: when?'

There is absolute silence. It's as if the devil's arrival has been announced. Ofsted is the enemy. Ofsted is what we fear. A good report from Ofsted is crucial if we are to remain a successful school. And we are indeed a successful school. In fact, we are considered to be a 'good' school. Parents fight to get their children a place here. Some six to eight children apply for each one. We're a shining example of excellence in the inner city. We're what so many other schools wish they could be.

But a bad Ofsted report could ruin all that. Middle-class parents would withdraw their children. We might even lose funding. So Ms Sensible starts to explain the various hoops we will have to jump through. There are so many I can't take them all in. The key thing for staff, Ms Sensible says, is our 'teaching and learning'. That's where we must 'perform' for Ofsted.

With Mr Goodheart and Mr Cajole, the deputy head, by her side, Ms Sensible explains how, over the next few months, the school will support teachers in coming to understand the new Ofsted criteria for 'good' lessons and will help them to learn how to hoop-jump. Ms Sensible explains that preparation for Ofsted has to be our priority.

Staff are not happy. I turn around and spot Ms Alternative, our head of sixth form, shaking her head and sighing. She's in her mid-thirties and likes to wear long, flowing dresses. She shakes her head and sighs. Mr Sporty, the PE teacher, stares at the ground.

After the meeting, I shut myself in my office. Jesus. We have to deliver a certain number of 'outstanding' lessons if we are to hold on to our current 'good with outstanding features' status. Management will direct the inspectors and tell them where they'll find 'outstanding' teaching, 'good' teaching, 'satisfactory' teaching and 'inadequate' teaching. The idea is that the inspectors' judgements match what management says.

Gulp. Management will tell them that I'm 'outstanding'. What if I can't deliver?

Autumn Term Part One

Wednesday 4 September

It is 7.30 a.m. and I'm in the staff room. It is half full. By 8 a.m., everyone will be here. Some of us are in every day at 7 a.m. and most of us won't get out until 6 p.m., dragging a pile of marking home with us. For now, the staff room is buzzing with excitement. The kids arrive today.

People are sat amongst the old armchairs and wooden coffee tables. The notice boards are clear of the usual thousand notices and the room is free of clutter. Give it a few weeks, though, and the place will look like a box room.

Mr Hadenough, one of our maths teachers, grabs my arm. He's twenty-eight and has been teaching here three years. 'Hey, Snuffy. Same old nightmare last night.'

'The one where you're taking assembly in nothing but stockings, suspenders and a pair of fairy wings?'

Hadenough chokes with laughter. 'Worse. I was with 8.4 and they were going *crazy*. I just couldn't get them to stop. A few of them jumped out of the window, and then a fight broke out and I couldn't pull them apart.'

I laugh out loud. 'Come on, we're going to be fine. In two hours, it'll be as if we never left. We won't remember the holidays at all.'

'Yeah, that's what I'm afraid of. I just hope I get a good night's sleep tonight. Maybe I'll take some sleeping pills.'

As I push open the staff-room door, I think about the countless teachers I've known over the years who've had trouble sleeping. What are we? War veterans?

I march down the dimly lit corridor, the displays from the previous school year peeling off the notice boards, my chin up, pulling my shoulders back. God, I'm scared. Bloody hell. How can I still be scared after so many years? 'Right,' I whisper to myself. 'Nobody's going to *fuck* with me today.' I put a smile on my face and pull my papers in tightly to my chest. 'Go get 'em.'

My first lesson is with the new Year 8s. Usually, at the start of a new year, I begin with inspirational speeches of 'Yes we can!' and my students respond positively. As I talk, I can see them sitting up straighter in their chairs, wanting to do well. Well, at least some of them do. But my Year 8s are a different story. They're a 'challenging' group, most of them boys, and most of them missing a few tools from their toolboxes.

This time I take a rather different approach: 'You all know how you did in your end-of-year exams. Some of you failed a lot of those exams, didn't you?' The class shuffles uncomfortably. 'Yet you've been moved into Year 8, no questions asked.' I pause. 'And I suppose you think this is a good thing?'

The class nods. Cent, a pretty dark-skinned black boy with a shaved head, joins in vigorously, shouting 'Yeah!' over and over.

'But did you know that in European countries like France or Italy, or in North American countries like America or Canada, at the end of the year, students have to pass exams in order to move up to the next year? Failing these exams means repeating the year.'

'I'm glad *I* don't live in France,' shouts little red-headed Adorable.

'Yeah! I'm glad I live in England,' shouts Fifty. 'Imagine if we lived in France, we might have to do Year 7 all over again!' Fifty is a light-skinned black boy with a massive Afro; he's smooth and super-naughty.

'Wouldn't you work harder if you knew that failing your end-of-year exams would hold you back?' More noises of agreement. 'So why don't you work hard now?'

'Because it doesn't matter.'

''Cause we want to play!'

''Cause we have too much other stuff to do.'

I laugh. 'Would you want to do Year 7 again this year?'

They twist their faces in disgust. 'No way!' they yell in horror.

'Hmm, so you see? You'd be doing a lot better if you had exams at the end of the year that mattered, wouldn't you?'

Munchkin, a little light-skinned black boy with fat cheeks and glasses, frowns, confused. He's so cute you want to wrap him up and take him home with you. He pipes up, 'But they don't matter, Miss. What difference does it make? Who cares?'

'Well, I care. I care because I know that some of you will go from Year 8 through to 9, and then through to 10 and finally 11, and then you'll fail your GCSEs. Because nothing in our system will stop you from doing this. You can't fail until you get to the end.' I pause, annoyed, wishing that our system were different. 'The governments in France and Italy insist that their children reach certain standards. Their governments make their children work.'

My kids are silent, listening to me rant. The penny is starting to drop.

Munchkin blinks at me behind his round glasses. His eyes draw wide. 'But Miss, why doesn't our government do that for *us*?' His voice squeaks with disappointment.

I look down at lovely Munchkin and sigh. 'You know what, Munchkin? I have no idea.'

Monday 9 September

'This is rubbish! We can't do this,' shouts Dreamer. 'Man, it's too hard! How can you expect us to do all this stuff, Miss?' Dreamer folds his arms across his chest, while a series of 'yeah's comes from the others. Dreamer is originally from Afghanistan, not very clever, a nice enough boy, and like so many boys, he loves to live his life in a fantasy world. He's in my Year 11 GCSE class.

'Well, it isn't me who decides what you have to do. It's the exam board. And thousands of students have gone before you and done well at these exams.' I grit my teeth. 'You have to *try*. You can do this. Of course you can.'

They groan, throwing their heads back. Some of them thump the desks. Dopey looks around at Dreamer and then back at me. 'Tell them the story, Miss. Tell them the story about the train.' Dopey is a tall dark-skinned black boy with little twists in his hair. He grins. 'You know, Miss – "Choo choo!"' He sings it. '"Choo choo!"' Dopey claps his hands. 'Tell them. Tell them!'

Dopey spins his head round, looking to the others for support. Deranged, a working-class white girl, laughs. 'Rahh! You're so dumb, Dopey! Miss told us that story in Year 8.'

Dopey gazes at me and hits the desk. 'Tell them then. Tell them. Not everyone here was in our class in Year 8. They haven't heard the story. Tell them, Miss, tell them.'

I turn to the class. 'OK, it's called *The Little Engine that Could*, and it's about . . .' I turn to Dopey. 'I tell you what, why don't you tell them?'

Dopey quickly turns around to face the class. 'Yeah, yeah, OK, OK, Miss. So yeah, there's this train, right, Miss?' He looks back at me.

'Yes, a little engine.'

'And the little engine is climbing this hill . . .' Dopey stops himself. 'Nah, nah, it's this big mountain. This *really big* mountain, and he's only this little engine. But he still climbs it, see.'

'And what does he say, Dopey? What does he say to help him get up that hill?'

'He says, "I think I can. I think I can. Choo choo! Choo choo!"'

The class starts to laugh. Inspired by Dopey's enthusiasm, Dreamer throws his arm into the air. 'Yeah! "Choo choo!"'

'And what does the little engine say when he finally gets to the top?'

It's Dopey who answers. '"I thought I could. I thought I could."' He's dancing about now. 'The little engine gets to the top because he thought he could, Miss.' Dopey claps his hands and jigs around, making the others giggle.

I look at the class again. 'So what do we think about these exams, then?'

They sit up straight in their chairs. 'I think I can!' They're in stitches. 'I think I can!'

There are two and a half terms left before those GCSEs. We've got time to do it yet. Nothing's impossible. So what if their CAT scores predict 'G' grades? I'll be damned if any kid of mine is getting a 'G'. We have to get them 'C's. Or I guess *I* just have to. Right?

Jesus. Can I do it?

In today's state schools, children are not allowed to know how they're doing in comparison to their peers. Instead, education is 'personalized', with individual targets which will tell a child how to move up the baffling national curriculum level ladder. If parents are lucky, they might have the opportunity to compare their child's results with the national expectation, if their school provides it.

But when one remembers that the national expectation is that children should get five 'C' grades at GCSE, it becomes clear that the national expectation is not something one would ever want for one's child.

So Ms Sensible puts forward a proposal to 'bring benchmarking back' at a middle and senior management meeting after school. Ms Alternative tosses her head in disagreement, tucking her blond hair behind her ear. 'Frankly, I can't believe the school is even considering this,' she says.

Mr Sporty breaks in. 'Yeah, I mean, this is a real step backwards.'

Ms Alternative continues. 'How can we do such a disservice to our kids? How can we make them feel so ashamed?'

There are lots of 'um's and 'ah's in the room. There is general support for what Ms Alternative is saying.

Ms Sensible's cheeks heat up. She sticks her head forward. 'Well, it's only a proposal, of course. It isn't so much for the sake of the pupils –'

'Sorry, Ms Sensible,' interrupts the head of science. 'I think you mean "students". As Mr Goodheart has explained, "pupils" is far too patronizing a term.'

'Of course. It isn't so much for the sake of the *students*, it's for the sake of the parents. Some parents want to be more informed.'

'More informed? But we give everyone personal targets! What more could they want?' shouts the head of geography.

Ms Alternative agrees vehemently. 'It's a step *backwards*, as Mr Sporty said. We're going *backwards* with this!'

Amongst all the growling, our head of history manages to make herself heard. She's furious. 'Look, it's simply outrageous that we're even thinking about this. Imagine telling poor Deranged that she's at the bottom of your class. What would she do? Why would she ever want to try again? How could we demotivate our kids like that?'

I scan the teachers' faces and decide to raise my hand and speak. 'But can I just say, not that I'm necessarily in favour of bench-marking of course, because I understand all of the concerns raised here, but we keep saying that the reason we might tell pupils – sorry, *students* – how they're doing is only for the sake of the parents. But haven't you ever had children ask how they're doing in comparison to the rest of the class? I know I have. Every time I hand back homework, do a test, they always ask for the top score, the bottom score, and what most of the others got. They always want to know how they're doing in comparison to the others.' I point to the head of history. 'And you talk about Deranged, but she's *always* wanting to know how the others have done.'

It takes only a few minutes for my point to be dismissed.

Thursday 12 September

It's the end of the day. Mr Hadenough is walking past. He's a good guy and a good teacher. I notice he's got a nasty bruise on his head and stop him to ask how things are going. 'I've had a shit day,' he says.

'Really? What happened?'

'Well, you know Furious?' Furious is a nightmare. He's a mixed-race Year 10 boy with a different pattern in his hair every week. He's in care, has been since he was a small child. He's bright and can be extremely polite if you catch him on the right day. He could do so much with his life. But as it is, he disrupts lessons, regularly gets into fights and, at the age of fifteen, is on the brink of permanent exclusion. He threw a stone at me today.'

'What?'

'He threw a stone at me. I was with a bunch of kids in the

playground, and we were playing about and they knocked me by accident. So I fell backwards, and I accidentally knocked him.'

'And?'

'So he went mad in his usual way. He began shouting at me. I told him I hadn't done it on purpose and to calm down. He got angrier and angrier. That boy is crazy. He kept screaming, "Stupid teacher! Stupid teacher!"'

'He called you *that*?'

'And then I turned around to talk to the kids again. Suddenly, this stone hits me.'

'Furious threw it?'

'Yeah. The stone came from there' – he points in a certain direction – 'and Furious was the only one standing there.'

'Did you see him?'

Evidence. We always need evidence.

'No. So apparently that means we can't punish him. The deputies are asking the other kids that were there if they saw anything. It's totally ridiculous. What is the world coming to when a teacher's word isn't enough?' Hadenough shakes his head.

'That's awful. I'm sorry.'

'Well. It isn't your fault.'

I give Hadenough a consoling tap on the arm. As I walk away, I remember the one-to-one chat I had with Furious last year, trying to persuade him to stop his dreadful behaviour, asking him whether he wanted to end up at a PRU – Pupil Referral Unit – where children go when they have been excluded from mainstream education. It was clear to me then, as it is clear to me now, that all he needs is some strict discipline. As it is, Furious won't be punished at all. What does this say to him – and to all the other children?

Friday 13 September

Mr Cajole, our deputy, a white man in his mid-forties with a pot-belly, has suggested that Furious go on report to me. He said something about the senior team being over-burdened with kids on report, so it was up to me to try to turn him around. It is after school on Friday, so Furious will start his report on Monday.

Furious turns up at my office after school and plops himself down on a chair, pouting. 'I didn' do not'in', Miss. Why am I here?' He's slouched so far down on the chair it's almost as if he's lying down on it.

'Sit up properly, please. And do up that tie. And the shirt: tuck it in.' Furious does as I ask. 'This isn't the first time we've had this conversation. We've been here a million times.'

'Dunno wha' you mean.' He casts his eyes down to the floor and kicks the table leg.

'You see all these books in here?' I indicate my bookshelves, and Furious raises his head. 'Half these books are about why black kids underachieve.' I stand up and raise my voice. 'Do you want to be another statistic written up in these books?' I sit back down.

Furious moves his head from side to side in slow motion. 'Nah, nah, I dun wanna be a statistic.'

'So I need you to change your behaviour.' I sigh. 'Why do you do what you do when you're so bright and could be top of your year group?' Furious glances up at me as if he knows something but he doesn't want to say anything to me about it. I lean in. 'Come on, Furious, you can tell me. What is it?'

Furious directs his gaze to the ground once more. 'Miss, you don't know what it's like. I can't be like you want me to be.'

'Why not?'

Again he shakes his head, as if he's disappointed this time. 'You teachers don' know not'in'. You don' know. Look, Miss, I can't be seen to be working. I don' wanna be a *neek*.'

'But why? You mean you need to look cool, like some rapper on MTV?' Furious puts all his weight into the back of his chair as if he's some kind of gangster, his head bobbing up and down, exactly the way the rappers do in MTV music videos. I grab his hand and his eyes are forced to meet mine. He's taken aback. I hold his hand in between mine. I feel like I might cry. 'Look at me. You can't throw your life away because of some stupid peer pressure. You're a bright boy. You have to try. You have to try to turn this around. Please, Furious. You have to listen to me.'

Furious pulls his hand out from my clasp and sits up. 'Yeah, yeah, OK Miss, man.' He squeezes his chin as gangsters do. 'Yeah, so I'm on report to you, right?'

'Yes.' I explain the details: he's to see me twice a day; have the report signed and commented in after every lesson. I explain the punishments and rewards. Furious nods as if he isn't really interested but is doing so because he has to. When I've finished explaining, he stands up. 'Will you at least *try*, Furious?'

'Yeah, yeah, Miss, I'll try.' He moves towards the door and opens it. 'Thanks, Miss.'

Saturday 14 September

The weekend is finally here and I'm waiting for Liberal outside the cinema. I'm beginning to wonder what's taking him so long when I notice some kids taking a close look at my gleaming new electric bicycle, which is locked to the bike rack. Mostly black boys, with the odd white one, they're about fifteen years old, with hoods covering most of their faces, and are clearly fascinated by the bike and its battery. I walk over to them and one boy turns to face me. 'Is that your bike?' he asks.

'Yes, it is. Would you like to see it?' The boys make way, shifting about in that gangster manner. I unlock the bike and push it out into the open space in front of us. I explain how it works, where to turn it on, how it charges up at home, plugged in, like a mobile phone. One boy jumps forward and pokes his head out of his hood.

'Can I have a go?'

I hesitate. I may be naïve, but I'm not an idiot. If I hand my bike over, the boy will disappear around the corner, the remaining boys will scarper, and I'll be left looking a fool. Imagine what the police would say: 'Madam, how did they get the bike away from you?' 'Erm, Officer, I kind of gave it to them.'

I smile and hand him the bike. 'Now don't go running off with it,' I say.

The boys laugh. Now who told me to go and give them that idea?

The boy, who has long, skinny legs, climbs on to the bike, and away he goes. He cycles down the street and I look to the heavens, hoping he is going to return. All of us stand in silence, watching as he rides further and further down the street. I look at the other boys. I start to wonder at what point they'll make a break for it. But then, just when I'm imagining spending my weekend buying a new bike, the boy circles the square and makes his way back to us. He skids to a stop. As he jumps off the bike, another boy steps forward. 'Can I have a go too?' he asks.

So I hand him the bike. One by one, they leap on the saddle and sail my bike around the circuit, each one giving it back to me, each one with the opportunity to steal it but each more concerned with placing it safely back in my hands.

Everyone has a ride, and they wave as they turn to go: 'Thanks a lot'; 'It's a great bike'; 'Yeah, thanks for letting us try it out.'

'No problem, boys,' I say, beaming at them. I can see my husband walking towards me. My heart surges with delight. How lovely – for once I have a story to tell which will make us smile.

Tuesday 17 September

I charge towards the overexcited, wound-up group of children in the playground. Seething is shouting at Furious, who is angrily arguing back. Seething is one year older than him, in Year 11. She is Mishap's little sister, a sixteen-year-old dark-skinned black girl with a snazzy short haircut who wears one pink glass earring. Furious often hangs out with the Year 11s. Normally, the girls fall at his feet. But Seething is no ordinary girl. She only dates boys who are much older.

I can see there is about to be a fight. 'Seething,' I call. She ignores me. 'Seething, come here.' Why have I called for her instead of

Furious? I suppose because she is closer to me. She behaves as if I am invisible, despite the fact that she and I have had in-depth conversations about her boyfriend, who deals drugs and treats her badly; about the use of condoms; about her mother, who never pays her attention; and about her father, who doesn't know she's alive. Her refusal to acknowledge my presence tells everyone that she has nothing but contempt for me.

I'm surrounded on all sides by screeching youths egging Seething and Furious on. Furious's girlfriend, Beautiful, is screaming at the top of her voice, as if she's frightened. Seething's best friend, Psycho, looks about ready to throw someone a serious punch.

'Get him! Get him!'

'Nah, man, that ain't right. That ain't right, man.'

'Get her!'

'Raaah!'

I need another teacher here. I need someone to break up the crowd. But no one's around. It's me, or no one.

Furious and Seething have their eyes locked on each other, ready to attack at any moment. The others are desperate for some entertaining blood and gore. 'Seething! Seething, you need to look at me when I call your name.'

She turns away from Furious and eyeballs me instead. 'Why you calling my name?' she screams in my face. 'Why you only interested in *me*? I swear Furious is on report to you! Why you calling *my* name?'

Her face is twisted so severely I barely recognize her. She moves towards me, shrieking. I wonder whether she might hit me. 'There will be consequences for this,' I say calmly. She continues her barrage of abuse.

'Why you calling *my* name? Why you calling *my* name?'

'Seething, you have to stop this. There will be consequences for this behaviour,' I repeat.

She doesn't stop. The other children look on, waiting to see what I will do. My reputation amongst them as a teacher who can control them is in question. I have to hold it together. I have to win this. If I don't, no one will ever listen to me again. But how do you win when you're absolutely terrified?

The children have now lost interest in Furious. A fight between students is good, but a fight between student and teacher is infinitely better. I stand my ground as she runs around me: 'Why you calling *my* name?'

Judging it safe to leave the situation, I back off and march into the building to tell Mr Cajole that Seething needs dealing with. I'm shaking. I grab an incident report form from the office, but I pick up the wrong one. I sit down on one of the office chairs. I have only a few minutes to compose myself before I have to teach. The office staff take no notice of me as I shake on the edge of the chair. This is nothing out of the ordinary. I want to cry, but I get up and brush myself off, my heart still racing.

As I run to my classroom, I think about Seething and wonder how – after everything we've shared together, after all the times I've helped her, listened to her, held her hand when she has cried – she could speak to me in that manner. And what about Furious? Third day on report, and already he's been involved in a serious incident.

Thursday 19 September

Non-contact time is like gold dust to a teacher. Depending on your responsibilities, you might get anywhere from five to eight 'free' lessons per week. That's out of a standard thirty-lesson week. The idea is that one uses that time for planning. The reality is that all of that time and more is taken filling in incident forms, chasing behaviour issues, informing students they have detention, telling off students for being late, noticing that a computer or an interactive whiteboard is broken and reporting it to the computer technician, chasing a student who forgot to give you a letter from home, sending good letters home for the hard-working kids, photocopying, giving a pep-talk to another teacher, listening to a student tell you how miserable he is at home, organizing an extracurricular class or trip, or sending countless emails to other teachers about work matters.

A supply teacher is running late, says Ms Sensible. She needs me to cover part of a geography lesson for my usual Year 8 class. There goes one of my non-contact periods.

The cover-lesson instructions say we should look at 'immigration'. OK then. I hand out the textbooks. The sea of faces in front of me is made up of a variety of colours: we look like the United Nations. A third are black; a quarter are brown, either brown as in Asian brown, or brown as in mixed-race brown; then there are the white kids, some of whom are Eastern European or Portuguese; and a few Chinese kids too.

'So, everyone, we're discussing immigration today. Look around at the class. Looks like lots of us are from somewhere else, or perhaps our parents are.' The children nod, turning their heads to survey each other. 'OK, everyone, out of interest, tell me how many of you were not born in this country.'

Eight children put up their hands. When I ask, they tell me they were born in Poland, Guyana, Nigeria, Lithuania. Very interesting, I think, because, frankly, I had no idea it would be so many. 'OK, OK. Now put up your hand if your parents were not born in England.'

So many hands go up. Silly me. Teachers know always to ask the question in such a way that it gives you the fewer hands to count. I tell them to put their hands down. I rephrase. 'OK – only put your hand up if both your parents *were* born in England.'

Eight children do so. What is interesting is that most of these children are black or brown. Most of the white children are not English at all, and often speak with strong accents. 'OK,' I say, now really quite curious to see the response to my next question. 'Put your hand up if all four of your grandparents were born in England.'

No one. It's hard to believe. Not one child in the class has all four grandparents born in England? Wow. That's immigration for you. Feeling genuinely excited, I tell everyone to turn to the required page of the textbook, and I start to read. ' "Everyone in England is an 'immigrant'." '

Whuuaa? I pause and read that bit again.

' "Everyone in England is an 'immigrant'. The Normans and the Saxons were immigrants. So if you are descended from them, then you too are an immigrant. Essentially, all people in Britain, whatever your background, however many generations, even if your parents, your grandparents, etc., were born in England, you are still an immigrant." '

I look at Adorable, who has red hair and freckles and whose grandmother was Scottish and her other grandparents English, and whose parents before them were English, and then I look across the room to Polish, who is from Poland, has blond hair and speaks English with a heavy accent. Surely there is a difference between them? Surely Polish is an immigrant and Adorable is not?

As I'm reading, Adorable sees the expression on my face. 'What's wrong, Miss?' she asks.

'Nothing, nothing,' I respond. The door swings open and in walks the supply teacher. 'Hello, Miss.' I smile, turning around. 'We've just been talking about immigration, and we've discovered that all of us in the last couple of generations are from somewhere else. Where are you from, Miss?'

The white, mousy woman laughs. 'I'm from South Africa.'

I say to the class, 'You see – Miss is an immigrant too.'

As I turn to go, I look back. 'Miss, just a moment. Can I ask the class a quick question?'

'Of course.'

'Out of interest, everyone, how many of you would like to know, when you have a test or a piece of homework marked, where you came in the class? You know, so that you would know the highest marks and the lowest marks, and everyone would know how you did and you would know how everyone else did?'

Out of thirty students, I count twenty-seven who raise their hands. Munchkin's shoots up and I look at him as he pushes his glasses up his nose. 'It's like you said, Miss. If we never have any end-of-year exams, if we never know how we're doing, then how can we improve?' Munchkin scans the class for approval, and the rest of them tilt their heads in agreement. Even Cent and Fifty, two of the naughtiest and least-achieving kids I have ever known, have their hands high in the air.

As I walk down the corridor, I wonder about the madness of we teachers refusing to benchmark kids, and the madness of modern geography textbooks telling children that all of us are immigrants, equating Adorable and Polish and saying that they are also 'the same'. I think about the last conversation I had with this class and the lack of meaningful end-of-year exams and all of us pretending that everyone is still 'the same'. The deception mystifies me.

Who is the loser in all this? Who is paying the ultimate price? Once all is said and done, the answer will always be: the children.

Friday 20 September

To miss S. I am really sorry that I walked out of your detention normally I never do that and I am really sorry. Normally I always go to your detentions but this time I did'nt and tommorrow I will come back far an hour and I will tell my mum. I was justed angery to day and miss can you not fone my parents please. I am sorry that I was speaking to you rudely I really hope you can forgive miss S. next lesson I will be perfect and again please dont fone my parents really miss s. I am sorry. I write this because you was not in your office I wanted to say this in person but you was not there so I write it see you Monday for an hour.

Dopey

Dopey always makes me go 'Awhh.' And he did it again with this note. He also always drives me round the bend. Dopey is nearly sixteen, and his standard of writing is pretty much par for the course for about 20 to 30 per cent of our kids. Dopey tends to hang out in fried-chicken shops. He also bops instead of walking. He is nearly at the end of his education.

In a few months, when these kids leave school to look for jobs, they won't know much more than they know right now. They'll find it difficult to get a job and, for that reason, they will return to full-time education. They'll also return to full-time education because we pay kids some £30 a week to go to college.

We're trying to teach these kids motivation, the value of hard work and a sense of responsibility. We want our children growing up knowing that perseverance, diligence and a desire to do well for the sake of doing well are what count in life. But if you only ever do anything because it's going to earn you a quid or two, doesn't it suck the very meaning of life out of one's soul?

Saturday 21 September

Liberal and I sit down to breakfast. I pick up the newspaper and see a picture that triggers a memory. 'Hey, this boy in the paper – he looks just like this kid I once knew at school.'

Liberal looks up from his plate. 'At school? You mean, when you were at school as a kid?'

'Yeah. There was this boy, looked just like him.' I point at the picture in the paper. 'His name was Lost. I'll never forget him. He was blond with pretty blue eyes. We were at primary school together and then at secondary, and when we were about thirteen, one day, in maths, he turned to me and he said, "You know, Snuffy, you're really lucky."' I place my hands against my chest and frown. 'And I said, "Lucky? What do you mean, lucky?"' Liberal chomps on his food as he listens. 'And, you know, he told me I was lucky because I could understand this stuff.'

'What stuff?'

'The maths, whatever it was . . . school stuff. He told me that I was bright, that I *got* it, that I could understand what the teachers were teaching us, that I was . . . well . . . *lucky*.'

'How old was this kid?'

'We were thirteen.'

'Sounds like he was pretty bright to me. I mean, understanding that at that age.'

'Yeah, exactly. And that's what I told him. I told him that if only he'd listen to the teacher instead of always messing about, he would *get it* too.'

'What did he say?'

'He said no way would he ever understand this stuff. That I had some kind of gift which I should never take for granted.'

'He used the words "take for granted"?'

'Yeah. He said I should always be grateful for what I had, because it was something he would love to have, but that he knew he would never have.' I shrug. 'I tried to persuade him that if he just worked, it would all be different, that he'd get it, if he'd just do some work, but he –'

Liberal leans across the table and kisses me on the forehead. 'That's what you do all day now, babe.' He moves to the sofa.

I smile. Liberal spreads himself out and opens up the newspaper. 'Come join me over here when you're done eating.'

I gaze over at him. Is that really what I do all day? And if I couldn't persuade Lost, why on earth do I think I'm going to have any more luck with the kids I teach now?

Monday 23 September

Monday morning, and Munchkin, the lovely boy with the fat squidgy cheeks, is in tears, holding his glasses in his hands, sitting on a large rock in the asphalt playground. A cold wind blows through the few trees in the playground as I approach him. 'Hey, Munchkin. You OK? What's happened?'

He wipes his face and points to a bunch of Year 10s on the other side of the playground. 'They took my lunch money.'

'Who did?'

Tears stream down Munchkin's face. 'I don't know. There was a whole lot of them. And they surrounded me. And then my money was gone.'

I squeeze his shoulder. 'You sure you don't have any idea who it could be?' Munchkin shakes his head. Does he know and he's too scared to say? Or does he really not know? 'You can tell me, Munchkin, if you have any idea who it might have been.'

He shakes his head violently. 'No! I don't know who it was.'

I notice a group of Year 10s hanging around by the wire-fence enclosure known as the 'cage' where they play football. I get up and move towards them. Cavalier, one of the nicer boys, looks up and smiles. He's white with sandy hair. 'Cavalier,' I say. 'Do you know about this business of Munchkin and his money being taken?' I point over to where we had been sitting, but Munchkin has disappeared.

Cavalier looks dumb. 'Who, Miss?'

'He was just there a minute ago. A little Year 8 boy, black, really small.'

Cavalier shrugs his shoulders. The other Year 10s are looking over suspiciously. 'Dunno, Miss, dunno,' he says.

OK, silly me. I don't know why I'm bothering to ask. I spot some of my Year 11 GCSE boys eyeing me from the other side of the playground: Dopey, Dreamer (the Afghan boy) – oh, and Furious too. They'll have seen everything. I start to walk over to them, and they turn around and move in the opposite direction. So instead, I run over to the canteen, and find Munchkin by the entrance.

'Hey, Munchkin, there you are – I was looking for you. Let's get you some lunch.'

'But I don't have any money.'

'That's OK. I do.' I smile and help him up.

'Thank you, Miss.'

As Munchkin is gobbling up his food, I go to find Ms Sensible, who is on the other side of the canteen. I tell her what has just happened.

'Do you have any idea who it was?' she asks.

'No.'

'Is Munchkin going to tell us?'

'No.'

Ms Sensible hunches her shoulders then lets them drop. 'Nothing we can do then. But well done on sorting it out.' She touches me sympathetically on the arm. 'Gotta run. Sorry. I have another incident to deal with.'

I return to Munchkin, bend over the table and whisper to him. 'You sure you don't want to tell me who took your money?'

Munchkin shakes his head. 'I don't know.'

Hmm. I glance at my watch. 'Yikes! Come on, Munchkin, it's nearly the end of lunch and I have to get upstairs to teach.'

Munchkin gazes up, blinking behind his round glasses, as ever. 'Thanks for my food, Miss.'

'No problem, sweetie.' I touch his head affectionately. Poor thing. Here he is thanking me when I have totally failed him. What happens the next time they take his lunch money? And the time after that? I look at his cute face and feel so bloody impotent. Sometimes I hate this job. I feel like screaming at the top of my lungs. And then off I run to teach the very Year 11s who just took Munchkin's money.

Thursday 26 September

I plop myself down in the staff room on one of the ageing armchairs that looks like it should be tossed in a skip and grab the *Times Educational Supplement* from the coffee table, which has about a ton of papers scattered across it. The whole room is a pigsty. It is 5.30 p.m. and the sun is still shining outside. For once, most of the staff have gone home. Across the room, Ms Magical is fretting. She's originally from Barbados, in her fifties and walks with a bit of a limp. Ms Magical has been teaching in inner-city London for more than twenty years. Her exam results are outstanding and her classroom is an oasis of calm but at the same time full of excitement. Inspiration, discipline and charisma are her tools, and the children tremble at the thought of disappointing her. It's strange to see her looking so uneasy.

'Hey there, Ms Magical, you OK?' I call.

She looks up from her papers, stressed. 'I don't know what time

I'll get out of here tonight. This Ofsted thing has got me so worked up I can't sleep at night.'

'But you've got nothing to worry about, you're an excellent teacher. The kids love you. Besides, we haven't even got a date – it could be months away.' But Ms Magical casts me a cynical glance. I know why.

Sure, she's a great teacher with fantastic results, but Ofsted isn't interested in that. She's too 'old-school' for them. Today, teachers are forced to plan their lessons according to a certain formula, which demands the inclusion of interactive whiteboards, amongst other things. The regular use of Information Technology, we are promised, helps children achieve a whole grade higher in their exams. Objectives, starters (introductions to the lesson), plenaries (recap of the lesson), timers, games, group work . . . Just master an interactive whiteboard, start lessons with objectives, and shazam! You're an excellent teacher. But what does Ms Magical know about computers? Nothing.

She's a teacher who ignores the new fads in education and continues to teach and adapt her methods according to *choice* rather than the orders of some bureaucrat or politician. If only we could all be brave enough to do the same, brave enough to be different. My guess is that, by 2020, many of the Ms Magicals of today will have vanished from our classrooms.

The eradication of the old-school teacher is the single most destructive 'improvement' that is taking place in our schools today. Teacher-training institutions churn out teachers who have had any ounce of creativity and ingenuity squeezed from them. State-school staff rooms are filled with teachers complaining about the bureaucratic strangulation of our profession, and some eventually flee to the private sector, not for the money, but for the freedom.

'Don't let them get to you, Ms Magical. Who cares what the Ofsted inspector thinks, anyway?'

Ms Magical looks me straight in the eye. 'Snuffy, *I* do. I'm good at my job, but if someone official comes into my classroom and tells me I'm not, I don't think I could take it.' She's ruffled and angry. She slams her books shut. 'I've had enough of this. I'm going home.' She marches towards the door.

'I know exactly how you feel.'

Ms Magical turns back abruptly. 'No you don't. You're young and flash, and you know exactly how to impress the Ofsted inspectors. Mr Goodheart loves you. You'll be just fine.'

I listen quietly, nodding, wondering whether she's right, whether I will in fact be fine, smiling at her absolute belief in me and wondering whether it is justified. 'Well, I think you're great.'

She smiles back as she swings the staff-room door open. 'Thanks, Snuffy. But you know, what *you* think doesn't really matter.'

Monday 30 September

Monday-morning briefings: every school has them. It's the moment when a head stands in front of their staff and gives them that 'umph' to do more than survive the week. Any head worth their salt gives their staff what they need to shine. We're standing in the staff room because there isn't enough room to cram everyone in sitting down. The door is propped open by the bin to allow those standing in the doorway and outside to hear what's going on.

'Morning! I hope everyone managed to enjoy the sunshine this weekend.' Mr Goodheart beams and indicates the sun pouring through the window. 'Lots on this week, as usual. We need to say thank you to Mr Sporty and the PE department, who took our Year 9 football team to compete against Basic School —'

'And we won!' Mr Sporty interrupts. 'Two–nil,' he shouts, throwing his fist into the air. 'And Furious scored the winning goal. You can imagine his face. I don't know if he's ever got anything right before . . .'

There is spontaneous applause. 'You go get 'em, Mr Sporty,' Ms Magical calls out.

Mr Goodheart claps with his hands held high in the air. He mouths the words 'Well done' to Mr Sporty. Some of the staff whistle. One of them pats Mr Sporty on the back. We're all thrilled for him, and for the kids. This is the kind of stuff great briefings are made of.

Various teachers have announcements: new student in Year 7 starting this week; languages department taking a trip out on Thursday; Ms Sensible still waiting for feedback on ideas for our next training day . . . blah blah blah.

Then Ms Joyful, our young, dynamic head of maths, announces that this week's maths challenge was won by Munchkin. My heart leaps. Cute little Munchkin! Well done him.

'Right.' Mr Goodheart reclaims everyone's attention. 'I'd like to remind everyone about our push on independent learning. Remember that this is what Ofsted will be looking for, when they finally get here.' He smiles in a way that suggests he doesn't really believe what he is saying. 'We simply cannot have a situation where teachers are teaching and children are listening.'

I sit up in my chair, not entirely sure if I've heard correctly.

'Group work, pair work.' Mr Goodheart smiles again. 'We need to see more of it. We need to see more *fun* in lessons. Games are always a good idea.'

Oh my God. I can't bear it: games, games, games.

I whisper to Mr Hadenough, 'Why don't we just tell them to take out their PSPs and get on with that instead of learning any-thing at all?'

Ms Sensible moves towards Mr Goodheart and tugs at his arm. She whispers something in his ear. Mr Goodheart gulps slightly. 'Oh! I nearly forgot: Ms Pregnant gave birth. I am told it is a baby girl, both mum and baby are doing very well.' Again he puts his hands together. Again the room erupts into applause.

'We'll be sending flowers from the school, of course, but do let us know if you want to send your own personal message.' Mr Goodheart waves as if to signal the end of the briefing. 'Have a very good and productive week.'

As we get up to go, Mr Hadenough grabs my arm and hisses in my ear: ' "We simply cannot have a situation where teachers are teaching and children are listening." I mean, *what the hell is that?*'

I burst into laughter. 'Shh! I know – who the hell knows what that means?' We giggle uncontrollably as we stumble out of the hall. I nearly bump into Mr Cajole.

'Oops! Sorry, Sir.' I'm still laughing inside.

Right. Must remember what Mr Goodheart said. *We cannot have teachers teaching and children listening.* That's my motto for the week. Whatever I do . . . just be sure not to *teach*.

Tuesday 1 October

Seething and Deranged rush past me at lunchtime, Seething chasing Deranged. I assume they're playing a game. But then Seething grabs Deranged and punches her hard in the back. Deranged's mousy ponytail soars in the air. She has her hair scraped hard against her head in the way the black girls do. If Deranged had it her way, she would have been born black.

The thumps are flying. I realize they aren't playing. Seething is steaming with anger. Without thinking, I leap between them. But Seething takes no notice and keeps throwing punches over and around me as I somehow get tangled up amongst her and Deranged, my books falling from my hands, my bag barely holding on to my shoulder. I flail back and forth, stumbling, lurching.

Being caught between two students fighting feels, I imagine, like being on a sailboat caught in a storm. I have no control and am knocked from side to side, and just as every gust of wind makes the boat keel, so with every lurch I wonder whether, this time, I'll capsize.

Where are the other teachers? I need someone to pull Deranged away. She's too close, and Seething is managing to reach her with her punches. 'You little *bitch*! You'll fuck anything.'

A crowd of kids gathers quickly, watching the commotion, shouting, egging on the girls. Beautiful, Furious's girlfriend and also Deranged's best friend, is screaming. Psycho, Seething's best friend, is growling, all set to jump in. All I can hear is screeching and howling: 'Fight! Fight! Fight!'

'Stop! Stop!' I hear from the sidelines. Cavalier is standing near us, but I can't see him in all the commotion, I just recognize his voice. 'Stop, I said! Can't you see what you're doing? You're hitting Miss! Stop!' I fly to the side, still latched on to Seething, who's clutching my bag in her anger but without any real sense of what she is doing. Cavalier raises his game. '*Stop, man!* You're hitting Miss. You gotta stop, man!'

Finally, Ms Alternative comes to my rescue and pulls Deranged away. Now that she is out of reach, Seething stops and I march her to the office to hand her over to Mr Cajole.

Later, I look for Cavalier in the playground. I find him playing football. He looks a little like a young David Beckham. 'Thank you for your help, Cavalier.'

'That's all right, Miss. They were well out of order.'

'Yes, Cavalier. Thank you. You're a real gentleman.'

Cavalier blushes. 'Yeah, maybe.' And then he nods to me with his chin, in the way that gangsters do.

Thursday 3 October

I'm staring out of my office window, noticing the colour of the leaves, when it strikes me that I haven't been outside in daylight this whole week. It is 7.30 a.m. and dark outside. By the time I get out of here tonight, it will be dark again. I pull my coat around my shoulders and kick the broken radiator. Damn heating. Why are schools always so freezing cold? Other, normal, human beings work in environments where heating is a given. Stupid radiator.

Looking outside, I spot Cavalier and open the window. 'Hey, Cavalier! What you doing here so early?'

'Hi, Miss. I have a maths-revision session with Mr Hadenough.'

Revision session this early? Gosh, Mr Hadenough is doing well. Good for him. Here I am complaining about the heating, when he's already working with the kids. I hold my thumb out to Cavalier. 'Good for you! Get the most out of it.'

I turn back to my work. Three weeks till half-term. I'll go and get a coffee from the staff room. That'll warm me up. On my way, I run into Munchkin. 'Hey there, Munchkin,' I call. 'What are you doing here so early?'

Munchkin looks at the ground. 'Morning, Miss. I like to get the earlier bus, and I live kind of far, so I want to make sure I'm on time, Miss.'

I keep walking towards the staff room and shout back, 'That's great to hear, Munchkin, fantastic. You keep being that way – responsible.'

Munchkin nods. 'Yes, Miss.'

'Oh, and congratulations on that maths thing – well done.'

'Thanks, Miss.'

I push the staff-room door open. Fingers crossed there's some milk in the fridge . . .

Friday 4 October

Furious sits himself down on a chair in my office. His foster parents sit next to him. From what I understand, Furious's white mother had him very young. Mr Inevitable and Ms Desperate have been looking after Furious now for the last six or seven years. So they feel like his real parents. Ms Desperate is an attractive Nigerian woman, always in heels, with masses of curls. Mr Inevitable is built, jet black, about 6 foot 4, and a little intimidating.

I smile and clasp my hands. 'Good morning, Mr Inevitable and Ms Desperate. Thank you for coming today. I suppose you've had to take time off work?'

They nod, forcing a smile. Mr Inevitable points at Furious. 'He's got himself into trouble again, hasn't he?'

'Yes, well, there was the incident with Seething last week, which could easily have been a fight. And then there was the

39

incident with Mr Hadenough with the stone, which, well' – I fix Furious with a look – 'well, it was just appalling.'

Furious jumps up. 'It wasn't me, man! What you accusing me for?' He pulls his face into a grimace, staring at me.

Mr Inevitable's eyes follow his son as the boy starts out of his chair. He rises too. 'Sit down, Furious. What do you think you're doing?' He points to the chair. 'Sit down, *boy*.'

Furious sits back down. I curl my hair around my ear. 'As I was saying, there have been several incidents, in particular towards the end of last year.' I cough. 'And, well, Furious's report so far is not going as well as we would have hoped.' I lift the report in my hands, indicating all the negative comments written by his teachers.

Ms Desperate gulps. 'Oh God!' She grabs Mr Inevitable's arm. 'What are we going to do?' I start to wonder whether she might cry. I look at Furious, who is staring at the floor in silence.

'Of course, there is the football match that Ordinary won.' I smile once more. 'Furious scored the winning goal.' He continues to scrutinize the floor, but a grin breaks out on his face.

'Football?' Mr Inevitable is disgusted. 'What does it matter if this boy can kick a football?' He sighs. 'It's his report that matters.'

'Indeed, Sir, well, let me show you . . .' I bend closer towards them.

We go through the report, which details Furious's lack of attention, rudeness, truancy, fighting and general defiance at school. Mr Inevitable and Ms Desperate make the appropriate listening noises; Furious's gaze continues to be pinned to the floor. I keep calling for his attention, and from time to time he deigns to give it to us. I suggest various ways of disciplining the boy at home: taking away his mobile phone, his television rights, his football on Saturday mornings. The two of them indicate their agreement.

I look them straight in the eye. 'You know that we're on our last legs here, right?'

Mr Inevitable bends forward, grabs his son by the collar and drags him halfway across the table. I move back, out of the way.

'Yuh hear what she said? Yuh hearing her?' Furious is half across the desk with his face up against Mr Inevitable's. He bobs his head up and down like a clockwork toy. The only man he has ever known as a father lets go and the boy slips back on to his chair.

I fiddle with my hair again. 'Right, so as I was saying, we really need to get this right this time, Furious.' I tap the report in front of me. 'I hope you understand what is at stake.'

He nods.

'Oh my Lord,' Ms Desperate cries out. 'What this boy is doing to me!' She places her hand across her chest.

'Don't worry,' I say to both of them. 'If you do as we discussed, and punish and praise him at home in the way we talked about, I'm sure we'll get Furious back on the straight and narrow.' I stand, holding out my hand. They take their turns at shaking it – all but Furious of course. Furious has his hands stuffed in his pockets, his eyes once more riveted on the floor. 'Good to see you again. Hopefully, next time, the news will be better.' I pat Furious on the back as he walks out of my office. 'Right, Furious?'

'Yeah, yeah, right, Miss,' he says without looking up.

I watch Furious and his foster parents walk down the corridor, and when they turn the corner I return to my desk. I've only just sat down when my door bursts open. I look up. It's Ms Desperate. She approaches my desk and grabs my hand. 'Please, Ms Snuffle-upagus, please, please help him. He doesn't know what he's doing. I don't want him to throw away his life.' I blink at her, a little startled. 'Please, Ms Snuffleupagus. I don't trust the school. I don't trust them people. But you, Furious says you're different. Please, I'm begging you . . . save him.'

I gape at this woman, who is nearly in tears, at her wits' end, and wonder what can be done. I wonder what on earth I can do. 'Yes, Ms Desperate, I'll do my best. I promise.' I lightly touch the back of her hand. Then I make the ultimate mistake. I smile. 'We'll save him,' I say.

What the bloody hell am I thinking?

My phone rings. It's Inspirational. Inspirational left Ordinary School this year and has started teaching at Basic School, down the road, which has mixed-ability classes. He's been working all summer developing schemes of work to take into account the nature of mixed-ability classes. I have never known any teacher in my teaching career who is more interested in how children learn than he is. He's in his early thirties, white, talented, went to Oxford and works every moment he is awake.

'Snuffy, I know you go under when term starts, but we're already in October. Come on, we need to meet.'

'Yeah, yeah, we will. Soon, I promise. How's it going at Basic? How's the mixed-ability situation?'

'Good, good . . . I think. Well, it's too early to tell.'

'How did Basic School do? You know, results-wise?'

'Really good. Seventy-five per cent.'

'*What?* How is that possible?'

'BTEC science for everyone and health and social care for the bottom ones.' Inspirational laughs. 'All that matters is that final number – who cares if the qualifications these kids are taking mean anything.'

I have to agree. 'Yeah. And, of course, standards aren't dropping. No, of course not. They're still the same, year after year.'

'Yeah. You know, I met this woman who works for one of the exam boards, and she was telling me how they get promoted if they manage to come up with qualifications which the schools like and take on.'

'Oh my goodness! But that makes sense. That's how exam boards make their money: they sell their exams to schools.' I slap my forehead in frustration. 'And as we're under so much pressure to produce results, heads of department will always choose the easiest exam board for their subjects.'

Inspirational lets out a gasp. 'Yeah. BTECs count for four

GCSEs, remember, and they're so bloody *easy* ... why would anyone do physics, for example, which is only worth one GCSE?'

'Anyway, have you established yourself with the kids yet?'

'Yeah, getting there. They just about all respect me now. Except for Year 9 of course.'

'Give it till half-term, then you'll have 'em.'

'How's Mr Goodheart? And the rest of them? Mr Cajole? Ms Sensible?'

I give him all the news from school, and any gossip I've heard. 'Poor Hadenough's been banished to a classroom off the gym corridor.' The gym corridor is the worst: there's no light, no space and no possible way of getting support from other teachers.

Inspirational sighs loudly. 'Why are they so stupid sometimes? Poor Hadenough.'

'I know. He's really fed up. I'm worried about him.'

'Get him to observe you.'

'Do you really think that would help?'

'I found it really useful that time I observed you last year.'

'Well, if you say so.'

'And tell him that we should all get together and have a drink sometime – if you can stop working for a moment.'

I laugh. 'Sure, I'll tell him. See ya.'

Monday 7 October

I'm standing in a large hall in Kensington Olympia. I have a day off from school. I've been invited to speak at an event put on by the Teaching Development Agency, which is designed to encourage people to go into teaching. I scan the audience: lots of women, a mixture of races, though perhaps the majority white, age range between twenty-five and fifty-five. All these people are considering a career change.

'My name is Snuffy,' I start, 'and I'm a teacher in one of the comprehensives in London. It's great to see so many of you here today. There's nothing I like more than telling lots of people all about the fantastic job of being a teacher.'

The crowd waits patiently to hear. They've just heard a talk from a head of a London school, but now they want to hear from someone who is on the battlefield, day in, day out. I gesture with my hand to catch their attention and launch in: 'Look, I'm not going to lie to you. It ain't easy. It's damn hard. It's so hard you're going to find yourselves working every hour that God gives you. If you want an easy life, then teaching isn't for you. I work anywhere from sixty to seventy hours a week. I'd say some teachers manage to get away with maybe fifty hours a week, if they're lucky.'

I can see the audience beginning to twitch. Maybe teaching isn't for them after all? I wag my finger at the crowd. 'But that doesn't mean teaching isn't worth doing. I'm just telling you: be prepared to work hard. And you have to be prepared for the kind of work it is: it's exhausting; it's challenging; it's all-consuming.' I pause, watching them twist in their seats. 'But the thing is: there is no better job in the world than being a teacher.'

I raise my voice. 'The reason you'll find yourselves working so hard is not necessarily because you have to. You'll do it because you want to. You'll do it because the more you give in teaching, the more you get out of it. When people say that teaching is rewarding, they're not just saying it. It really is the most satisfying job on the planet. Those same friends of mine who don't understand how I can work so hard for so little pay, they always say to me, "You may not earn much money, Snuffy, but I don't know anyone who loves their job the way you do." There is never a Monday when I think, Gosh, I don't want to go to work. Sure, sometimes I get tired and I think, I need a break, I need some time off – but if I won the lottery tomorrow, I assure you, there is no way I'd give up on school.'

A man in the audience puts up his hand and I nod in his direction.

'Yes, but what about all the horror stories of bad behaviour? Do you get insulted by the kids a lot?'

I laugh. 'Yeah, yeah, sometimes the children's behaviour is a problem. But that's what makes teaching so fascinating. Changing their behaviour is a *challenge*.' I grin. 'And it can be done. Of course, you don't have to teach in an inner-city school. You can teach in the private sector, or in a "good" state school. There's a lot of choice in teaching. So don't let the stories of bad behaviour on the part of the children put you off. Look, just yesterday, some of the kids were practising how to bowl a cricket ball and they showed me how. I was so rubbish. I was bending my arm. And Dreamer kept saying, "Keep your arm straight, Miss." But I couldn't do it. And then another one, Dopey, as if defending me, said, "Yeah, well, Miss is too much of a glamorous lady to be able to throw balls properly." It was so cute, I tell you. Every day, they make my day. Every day.'

A woman raises her hand. 'Yes, but what about the money issues? Do you struggle on a teacher's salary?'

I shake my head. 'No, no, it's fine. I mean, I'm never going to be rich. But then I don't want to be. And I'm guessing none of you want to be either, or you wouldn't be here today. Teachers' salaries have gone up a lot recently and, if you're good, you can earn a lot more than you did as a teacher before, so no, I never hear colleagues complaining about their pay. I think we're all pretty happy with our salaries.'

I point at another woman with her hand up. 'So why did you go into teaching then?' she asks.

'Well, a very long time ago, when I was at university – I was at Cambridge – we did these outings to inner-city schools in London, Manchester, Leeds, and so on, trying to encourage working-class kids, black kids, underprivileged kids to apply to Oxbridge. The idea was to take black Oxbridge students who had been educated in the comprehensive-school system and send them to talk to kids who might identify with them. So I was the perfect choice.' I make a fist. 'We were trying to change the world, I guess. You know, alter the intake at these universities. I was a revolutionary.' I chortle. 'Now I'm too busy to be a revolutionary . . . No, but seriously, I found that, in doing this, I really made a difference to these kids. That when I arrived, they were all saying "No way" to the idea of applying to Oxbridge, and then, when I left, they had changed their minds.' I interlace my fingers. 'I liked the way that made me feel. Like I was making a difference. So that's why I teach. That's what I love about the job. We make a difference every day. We change the world every day. And what better way to live is there than that?'

I answer a few more questions, and eventually we break up and everyone heads towards the refreshments bar. As I grab an orange juice, a young black woman of about twenty-six or twenty-seven approaches.

'Hi, Snuffy. I thought I'd introduce myself, as I'm sure you won't remember me. My name is Inspired.'

She holds out her hand. I take it. I study her face, trying hard to remember, but I can't. How embarrassing. Who on earth is she? 'I'm terrible at remembering people,' I say awkwardly. 'I'm sorry. How do we know each other?'

'Well, I was at one of the schools you came to speak to. And you know, I was having a hard time then, and I didn't know what to do with my life, and then you came. So I applied to Oxford, and I got in and I did my degree in English there.'

'Really? Oh my God, I can't believe it!' I'm practically jumping up and down with excitement. 'That's amazing!' I'm so astounded I grab her and hug her. When I pull back I say, 'You know, I've never met anyone before — I mean, after talking to them at their schools — to hear what happened next. I can't believe it! We really *did* make a difference. So what happened after your degree? What are you doing now?'

'Well, I'm working for a bank in the City. But I'm not really enjoying it. I don't feel fulfilled. So I thought maybe I'd become a teacher.'

Wow. I step back. We seem to have come full circle.

Tuesday 8 October

I'm sitting in the canteen looking out of the window when Munchkin comes up to me. He's been crying. 'They took my phone, Miss,' he gulps. 'They took it.'

'Who took your phone?'

Munchkin shakes his head. 'I dunno. It just went. I had my bag over there.' He points to the table where he was sitting. 'And I got up to empty my tray, and they must have took it then. It's gone.'

I leave my plate of food and go over to where Munchkin was sitting. I ask him to talk me through it again. We search his bag. No phone. I ask the kids sitting around the table. Did they see anything? Does anyone know anything? No one knows a thing. At least, no one will admit to knowing.

'Miss' – Munchkin swallows hard, trying not to let the tears out again – 'I got that phone for my birthday last week.'

I run outside and find Ms Sensible, who is on duty in the playground. I explain what's happened. Her mouth curls up. 'Anybody see anything?'

'No.'

'Does Munchkin have any idea who it might have been?'

'No.'

Ms Sensible lets out a sigh. 'What can we do? I can mention it at assembly. But we have nothing to go on here.'

'I know, I know,' I say helplessly.

Back I head towards the canteen. Through the window I can see little Munchkin waiting for me, waiting for some good news, waiting for me to come and tell him that I've fixed it, that I've got his phone back. My heart sinks lower and lower the closer I get to him. As I approach, I shake my head, as if to warn him of the bad news. He instantly understands and his face drops, bottom lip sticking out. And the tears which he was doing so well at holding back begin to trickle down his cheeks.

The wind is blowing hard outside. The air has developed that cold winter's edge. Wind always makes the kids misbehave. Don't know why. It just does.

Deranged marches into my Year 11 lesson and parks herself on a chair, tie undone, bag on the desk (when she knows the rules are to have it on the floor), and puts her head flat on it too, as if she is going to sleep. She is wearing her favourite big hoop earrings and I ask her to take them out, which she does, with her head still glued to the desk. She's fifteen years old now, but at eleven she was the loveliest little darling. I've watched her, as I have watched so many, descend into the depths of street culture: the walk, the talk, the bling, the defiance, the rudeness, the pride. But Deranged is by no means as bad as some. She's just nothing like the sweet girl I once knew.

I suppose she's annoyed with me because that fight between her and Seething last week got her excluded for two days. She missed our lesson on Monday, so here she is, finally, irritated and rude. Dreamer and Dopey look over at her, surprised by her behaviour, and wait to see my response.

'Deranged, please put your bag on the floor. And your tie, please' – I point to my collar – 'you know what to do.' Deranged casts her eyes up to heaven, looks at me as if I've killed her pet dog and kisses her teeth. Seething and Psycho are so interested they stop chatting and look on, keen to see what will happen next. Will Deranged do as I have asked? 'If you continue in this manner,' I go on, 'I'll have to ask you to leave the room.'

She throws her head back and stares at me in such a threatening way that, if I were in the street, I would be positively terrified. 'I don't want to be here anyway,' she snarls. She stands up. 'Gimme some work. I'm going.'

'Right then.' I hand her some work, and keep talking. 'Go to the office and explain the situation. I'll expect to see you back here at the end of the lesson.' Deranged grabs the work from my hand and strides out.

Beautiful, Deranged's friend, a Pakistani Muslim girl who wears her skirts as short as they'll go, waves her arm around in the air. 'Miss! Just ignore her. She's mash-up today.'

I take her advice and continue with the lesson. Come the end, Deranged reappears, and I take her to see Mr Cajole. Mr Cajole begins quite well. He talks of how teachers are not paid to take abuse. He talks of how hard we work to teach our lessons and how all we expect in exchange is some respect.

Deranged's response? 'But she annoys me.' Then she sighs and looks at her watch. 'I can't stay, you know. I have places to be. I shouldn't be here.'

It's fifteen minutes after the end of the school day. Mr Cajole explains that he isn't asking Deranged to like me. He simply wants her to pretend. And I agree with him. I explain that she is welcome to hate me but that, when addressing me, she must show respect. Deranged sucks in her breath between her teeth. 'But she annoys me,' she repeats.

'Do you understand what we are saying?' Mr Cajole is speaking an octave higher than usual, in an attempt to 'persuade'. Deranged nods, looking at the clock up on the wall. 'So what needs to be said to Miss, then?'

'Sorry.' She grits her teeth as she says it.

'Thank you,' I say, smiling. 'I hope we can return to the excellent behaviour we all know you are capable of.'

Deranged checks the time once more. Twenty minutes have now passed since the end of the school day. Mr Cajole notices this and, as she turns to go, he calls out, 'Thank you, Deranged. Thank you for waiting. That was very good of you.'

'That's OK, Sir.' She smiles as she leaves.

Deranged is back on side. She doesn't hate him. Mr Cajole got what he wanted. But I can't help but wonder: at what price?

Seething saunters towards me. She is wearing a nose ring, and students are not allowed facial piercings. It matches her pink glass earring, and stands out against her dark skin. I ask her how she is. She responds with a kind of grunt, just acknowledging my presence. I point to my own nose, indicating that I want her to remove the nose piercing. She sneers, 'Nah, man,' and throws her hand in the air as she marches off. She perches herself against the radiator with Deranged, Beautiful, Psycho and a few other girls. I go after her.

'Seething, come on now. Please could you remove the nose piercing?' I ask several times, politely, but each time more insistently.

She continues to ignore me. The other girls look on: 'It's so extra, man'; 'She's only just had it done, she *can't* take it out'; 'What you picking on *her* for?'

The girls are annoyed because, often, teachers look the other way when it comes to uniform. Teachers are generally too stressed to enforce the school rules on dress and appearance, and there is no personal payback for them in the classroom. Why make life difficult for yourself? Far easier, if you see Seething coming down the corridor, to turn around and go the other way.

I insist. Seething refuses. So I ask her to follow me to the office. She gets up and stomps away from me, towards the office but in deliberate defiance, while the other girls chant, 'Go, Seething!'; 'Do it, Seething!' I walk up to her.

'Seething, come on, make the right decision here. Go to the office. Do as I ask.' She eyeballs me as if I'm dirt under her feet. 'Come on, Seething. You know there'll be consequences if you don't do as I ask, so come on.' I hold my arm out in a sweeping gesture, moving towards the office. Seething lets out a cackle and heads off in the opposite direction. The other girls scramble together and follow.

The result? I tell Ms Sensible, and she keeps Seething out of a sports event that she wanted to attend. When Ms Sensible asks her to apologize to me for her behaviour, she refuses.

To pick children up on things which are 'school rules', as

opposed to your own rules for your classroom, is one of those areas where so many of us fall short. For some of us, it is because we are liberals and secretly believe it is silly not to allow children to dress as they wish for school. For others, it is simply too much trouble. We care more about ourselves than we do about the children. Much easier to placate Seething than to insist she reach certain standards which she will kick back against. I don't pull the children up every time. I can't. It's too exhausting, especially when so many other teachers never do it.

And every time I don't, I fail them.

Friday 11 October

I'm crossing the playground when I see little Munchkin with two of the Year 10 boys, Cavalier and Wholesome. Wholesome is a Nigerian boy whose mother has him under her thumb. They are nice boys, so I'm not worried. But they're being a little rough with Munchkin, tapping him on the head a little too vigorously, so I approach. 'Hey boys, what are you up to?' I interrupt. 'Go pick on someone your own size!'

Cavalier laughs, tapping Munchkin on the head again. 'Don't worry, Miss, we like Munchkin. He's a cool dude.'

'You *like* him? But he's in Year 8!'

'So? Aren't we allowed to have friends in Year 8? He's cool.'

'Yeah, I know what you mean. Munchkin is great. He's so small, isn't he?'

Munchkin makes a face. So do Cavalier and Wholesome. Cavalier carves a shape in the air with his arm. 'Small? What difference does that make? Who likes someone 'cause they're *small*?' The three boys fall about with laughter.

Hmm. Well, I do. That's what makes Munchkin so cute – 'cause he's so small. But, too embarrassed to say what I think, I quickly rush past them. 'Gotta go, boys. See you later.'

'Yeah, see ya, Miss.'

And they get back to their roughhousing.

Having just read an email from Ms Sensible explaining that Seething is refusing to apologize but that she hopes we can resolve this on Monday, I decide to ring her home. Often, it's an efficient way of dealing with an issue.

I tell Mrs Nutter about the incident and explain to her that we need to move on from this: Seething needs to apologize, assure me that in the future she will do as I ask, and that will be that.

'Yeah? What does she have to apologize for? What about all dem other girls with nose piercings? What about dem, eh? You ain't asking dem to take out their piercings!'

'Well, I had just come from dealing with another girl over her nose ring when I saw Seething. I only asked her to take it out.'

'You made her miss her sports thing! And she went to the office like you said, so what's your problem anyway?' Mrs Nutter yells furiously down the phone.

I explain that while Seething eventually ended up at the office, the instruction had been for her to follow me there. I explain that there are consequences for bad behaviour and that I had made this clear to Seething when she chose to walk away from me.

'You teachers are always victimizing these kids. I know what you teachers do. It's illegal what you do. It's illegal!' It's a Saturday, I think, as she continues to rant down the phone at me. I really should be doing something other than this. 'I've taught Seething how to stand up against you teachers. I've told her how to stand up for her rights.'

Yes, Madam, you have. I think of my own mother, who would have shot me dead if I had dared to get my nose pierced as a teenager. And suddenly I feel terribly sorry for Seething. What chance at life does she have with a mother like this?

Sunday 13 October

Having a husband like Liberal has its ups and downs. One of the ups is that he is the perfect twenty-first-century man. He always says he doesn't want a wife, he wants a woman who does her own thing. So he doesn't mind me working all hours and he is happy to cook dinner. One of the downs is that he doesn't believe a word I say and, while he never says it, he probably thinks I'm a lunatic. We sit down to dinner. Liberal looks at me sheepishly.

'What's wrong?' I ask, frowning.

'Well, I haven't told you, but you know how I went to that new bar across the way from the cinema last night?'

'Yes?'

'Well, we were leaving, and I was standing outside waiting for Bank and the other guys when these black kids on bikes, wearing balaclavas, ride past, looking happy, and they wave hello to me.' Liberal shrugs. 'So I wave back.'

'And?' I raise my eyebrows, waiting for the punch line.

'Well, we went on to this bar, and anyway, the point is, later we discover that another black kid has been knifed up the road. So those guys had to be responsible.' Liberal drops his head into his hands. 'Snuffy, what I don't understand is why are they all killing each other.'

I sit up in my chair. 'Ah, babe, look, I'll tell you why. When your family is failing you and cannot give you discipline and order, you look to school to help you. But the majority of black children in this country are in chaotic schools where there is no order whatsoever.'

'But that doesn't explain —'

'Hang on,' I say. 'I have a point. There is no order because the teachers are scared of being accused of racism and so there's a refusal to exclude black kids who deserve it.' I can already tell from his reaction: he's heard it all before. 'These black kids leave school without anything: no learning, no order, no discipline. They can't even write English properly. But notice: it isn't the girls who are killing each other. It's the boys. Why? Because a man has to feel like a man.'

Liberal's features take on a new shape. 'What? You're not serious.'

53

'I certainly am. Normally, men – whatever their colour – get to feel like men by going out, getting a job and bringing home the bacon. Normally, they achieve something at school, they're good at a particular subject and are able to stand at the top of the Empire State Building and bang on their chests and feel proud. But when you cannot take that route because you have nothing, and you know that you have nothing, the only way you can feel like a man is to kill another man. That's easy. That, you can do.'

Liberal looks deflated. He moves his head from side to side as if trying to shake water from his ears.

I smile. 'Hey, how come you didn't tell me this when you got in last night?'

'You really need me to tell you why?'

I get up from the table. 'OK, yeah, I get it. I'm too much, I know. What d'you say to a DVD?'

Liberal grins. 'Sure, but I get to choose which one.'

I smirk. 'The choice is all yours, babe.' If only being allowed to choose which DVD was enough to give every boy a sense of manhood!

Monday 14 October

Kids lie. They all lie. Even the good ones. They lie to get out of trouble. It's instinctive. They do it without thinking, in order to survive. I'm not bitter. I just know kids.

'Right, that's it! That's enough. Sit down.' I try to restore order in the class. Cent slides on to his chair. 'That's your whole break-time gone now.' I turn towards the whiteboard.

'It's 'cause I is black, innit?'

Fifty starts to howl with laughter, sending reverberations through his Afro. Munchkin puts his hand over his mouth as if he's in shock. I turn down the sides of my mouth and advance towards him with my board pen in hand.

As a teacher, if you show any sign of weakness, any sense of being unsure, any lack of confidence, the child will pounce on it and wring it out for everything it's worth. It's instinctive: survival of the fittest.

The reply 'It wasn't me' is standard when you've just seen the kid throw something at another kid's head. Day after day, I see kids turn purple with outrage, as if they've been accused of something they didn't do. Standard, too, is the conversation which goes something like: 'Look, Johnny, you and I both know that you did it. I saw you do it. I'm not crazy. So let's save everybody a lot of time and energy. Just stop denying it, and say what I need to hear so that we can move on.' And the reply: 'Sorry, Miss. It won't happen again.'

Black kids are no different to white ones. They, too, want to survive. But they have one thing the white kids will never have. Black kids all have that winning ace up their sleeve, which they can play when the going gets really tough – the race card: 'It's 'cause I is black, innit?'; 'Yeah, man, you know she hates us, innit. She hates us 'cause we is black.'

If the black kid has got himself a slightly scared new white teacher, he is in serious business. He has got them running scared. The kid can literally smell the fear. So the teacher starts to back off. Maybe they didn't see what they thought they saw. Ah well, perhaps it is just easier to let the black kids 'chat' at the back of the class. Making them work is so much hassle, and they're going to make me feel bad about being – well, you know . . . Well, for being white.

I point my board pen in Cent's face. 'That's right. It's 'cause you is black. OK? That's your whole breaktime gone.' Fifty and Munchkin double over in laughter. The whole class creases up; even Adorable can't help but giggle.

Breaktime comes and Cent sits there still, fuming, his arms folded over his chest. After about ten minutes, I stop my work and look over at him. 'OK then, Cent, what am I expecting to hear?'

'Sorry, Miss. I won't do it again.' He groans.

'Why not?'

''Cause I don't wanna be a failure. 'Cause I should be listening, innit?'

'Yes, that's right, Cent. Well done. Now get out of here.'

Cent grins. 'Thanks, Miss.' And out the door he runs.

Tuesday 15 October

Hadenough is standing outside the classroom with me. He's decided to watch me with my crazy Year 8s. We're waiting by the door. The kids are on their way.

'So, always meet them at the door, right?' I advise.

'Yeah, sure, I know.'

The kids come tearing down the corridor. They're pushing each other, running, shouting. As they approach, one by one, I catch them by the eye, which sends an electric bolt through them. Some straighten their backs, others visibly slow down, others take a deep breath. 'It's Miss, it's Miss,' they whisper to each other and line up by the door.

I stand in front of them quietly, my finger on my mouth. 'Shhh.' Fifty laughs. 'Fifty!' I say sharply. 'Over there!' I point to the other side of the corridor. He stands to the other side on his own, head down, his Afro pointing out at a 90-degree angle, in silence. The others look terrified as a result. I look at Hadenough. He smiles.

I open the door and let them in, a few at a time, allowing them to chat as they unpack their things. I let Fifty in right at the end. 'I expect top behaviour from you today,' I whisper to him as he enters the room.

Fifty hangs his head. 'Yes, Miss.'

'$5 - 4 - 3 - 2 - 1 - 0$.' And there is silence. 'Look at the sheet in front of you. That's your starter. You have four minutes. Get to it!'

They all start scribbling. I move around the room checking on what they're doing. Hadenough, who is sat at the back, taps me on the shoulder and leans in. 'You do this for every class? One class goes out, and in the two minutes it takes for the next class to arrive, you get sheets out on the desks?'

'For the challenging ones, yeah. And make it super-easy so they don't have to ask you what to do. Just get them settled with something simple,' I murmur.

'5 − 4 − 3 − 2 − 1 − 0. Pens down.' I smile, standing in front of the class. 'OK, everyone, looking this way.' I wait. 'Everyone looking this way, please . . . Fifty! Cent! Looking this way, please.' They look at me. I point at the interactive whiteboard. 'OK, everyone, look at this poem.' I start reading:

> I think that school is
> Heaps of fun
> Almost all of the
> Time, especially when
> Everyone is working like they are
> Supposed to in
> Class and following the
> Head's suggestions,
> Obeying what the teachers say,
> Opening doors for people and
> Looking out for each other.

Fifty groans loudly. 'Oh my God, what is this?'

Cent laughs. 'Poetry, man. So boring, man.'

I look smug. 'Hands up anyone who likes this poem.'

No one puts up their hand. 'OK, OK . . . but what if I told you that there is a secret message in it? What if I told you that you may think this kid loves school but, in fact, it's just the opposite?'

The kids look at me blankly. Even Adorable doesn't have any ideas. 'OK, everyone, in groups now . . . you have four minutes. Try to figure out what the secret code is.' I direct certain kids to move here and there and away they go. I detect that Munchkin and Cent are talking about something else. I walk over to them and put my hand gently on Munchkin's shoulder. They return to the task at hand. I walk around the room. 'Study the poem. The answer is in the poem.'

Suddenly Adorable and Fifty shout out. 'We've got it: he hates school. He hates school!'

I put my finger over my mouth. 'Shhh! We still have a minute left . . . Come on, everyone . . . Are Adorable and Fifty going to be the only ones who get it?'

Finally, I count down. '5 − 4 − 3 − 2 − 1− 0.' I pause. The chat continues. 'I said, silence.' Cent is still talking. '*Cent!*' The class goes dead quiet. 'Stand.' Cent stands awkwardly by his desk and I continue with the lesson.

Lots of hands are up. 'OK, Fifty. Tell us the secret code then. Why don't you come up to the board?' He gets up and runs over. 'Here it is, here it is!' He points down the side of the poem to the first letters of each line. 'It says "I hate school."'

'That's right, Fifty. Well done. Fantastic work today.' Fifty beams and waltzes back to his seat. Some exhale noisily. Others start calling loudly: 'I got it before you did!'; 'I saw it before you did, yeah!'

'OK. OK, everyone. Settle down.' I motion to Cent to sit back down and he does so. 'This is what we call an acrostic poem, and today our objective is to be able to write our own acrostic poems by the end of the lesson.'

And on we go, with me jumping on inattention, leaping around the room to keep that attention, praising good behaviour and setting detention for bad. Towards the end, I take a look at Munchkin and Cent's poem. They have been working together. It's about *The X Factor*. It is pure brilliance.

I'm on my toes, clapping my hands. 'I love it, boys. I love it.'

'Mr Hadenough! Com'ere, you have to look at this.'

Hadenough approaches and reads the poem. 'Great stuff, boys. You wanna be stars?'

They nod. I step forward. 'Well, I tell you what, next lesson, you two are going to perform that poem. Everyone needs to hear it. It's brilliant.'

Munchkin looks worried. 'We have to get up in front of everyone?'

'Yes, Munchkin. Don't worry, you'll be fine.'

We finish up the lesson and I send them off. As they're walking out, I remind Cent he has a five-minute detention with me after school.

Hadenough winks at me. 'Thanks for that. Let's talk later, OK? Teaching now.'

'Yeah, me too. See you later.'

Wednesday 16 October

Hadenough sits down in my office. 'Thanks – you know – for having me in. So yeah, I know, you stamped on Fifty at the start and then you told him what you expected without the others hearing, and then you picked him out later to tell everyone about the poem so you could say, "Well done." I know, I know.'

I'm nodding as Hadenough speaks then add, 'Yeah, yeah. And I have the routines down pat, and they know I'll jump on them for the smallest thing. And the starter, remember, that's key: something simple to get them settled.'

Hadenough frowns. 'Yeah, I know, but I can't spend that kind of time planning one lesson. Sure you can pull that stuff off once in a while, but *every day*?'

'The more difficult the class, the more time you have to put in. That's how it works.'

Hadenough's eyes open wide. 'But *all* my classes are difficult. For you, 'cause you're just better at this, I guess, you don't have so many nightmare classes. But for me, it means practically *all* my classes.'

'But if you put the time in,' I say encouragingly, 'it'll get better. You just need to give up your life for a while and then, with time, you can cut down a bit.'

Hadenough looks at me in disbelief. 'Have *you* cut down?'

'No, but –'

'But what? You work every moment you're awake! My girlfriend has had enough of me already, let alone me saying that I'm now going to put in even more hours.'

'Well, it's not *that* much.'

'Yes it is. You want me making more phone calls home, sending more letters and cards home, marking books more regularly, giving more detailed feedback, making lessons more exciting, changing up the exercises regularly . . . All that takes time, you know.'

I sigh. 'OK, but you need to get across to them that you believe in them. They want to feel loved.'

Hadenough stands up. 'All right. I'll try spending the occasional lesson talking about our lives, building my relationship with them.' He pauses. 'Let's just hope an inspector isn't around when I'm doing it.'

I chuckle. 'Yeah, exactly.'

Thursday 17 October

This afternoon, when I'm not teaching, I decide to follow Mr Sporty, the head of PE, who's taking some Year 8 classes to their games lesson. There is something special about watching kids do what they love. There is a different energy about them. It is incredible to see them enjoy school.

Schools in the inner city generally don't have playing fields on their grounds. So the children have to get on to a coach or train to get to a place with enough grass so that they can play football. This costs the school anywhere from 2 to 4 grand every month.

After our forty-five-minute journey, we arrive at the gates to the sports fields. Munchkin, Cent, Fifty and some of the other boys are so happy it could just as well be Christmas Day. The children are buzzing with excitement. They run to the changing rooms, rushing to put on their PE outfits. Even red-headed Adorable, who is a quiet, shy girl, is giggling with her friends Quiet and Polish.

Once the kids are out on the field in their brightly coloured shorts and tops, Mr Sporty gathers them around. 'Now, everyone, I want you to look out on to those fields.' He points out into the distance, and the children turn to look. 'I want you to think of Didier Drogba or Kelly Holmes. All of the big sports stars had to start somewhere. They all went to school, just like you, and they played football on fields like these.' The children gaze at the grass as if it is made of gold. 'You are going to play football out here and, one day, maybe you too will be Wayne Rooney or Rio Ferdinand.'

Munchkin puts his hand up. 'You really think so, Sir? You really think one of us could be a footballer?' He's so eager, so happy. He always makes me smile.

Mr Sporty winks. 'Not just one of you. I think you could *all* be footballers. And imagine that! You could be earning millions of pounds. You could be living the high life, on TV, known by everyone, chased by the girls – or, girls, I guess the boys will be chasing you!' Adorable, Polish and the other girls snigger. Mr Sporty continues. 'Imagine, you could be like Rio Ferdinand. You could have the second best job in the world.'

The children look puzzled. Munchkin draws his eyebrows together. '*Second* best job, Sir? Then what's the best job in the world?'

Mr Sporty turns up the palms of his hands. 'Well, that's easy. Don't you know?' The children look at each other and mutter. Mr Sporty winks. 'The best job in the world? Well, that's obvious. It's being a *teacher, of course!*'

Friday 18 October

Today, I'm getting a coffee in the staff room when I start chatting to Ms Alternative, the head of the sixth form, and she mentions that she has decided to send her son, who has just started Year 7, to Infamous School.

I'm astonished. At Infamous School, the teachers can't teach, the students certainly don't learn and, frankly, hardly anyone survives. Why on earth Ms Alternative would have her son attend this school is beyond me. She has inside knowledge on what schools are like, she's middle class and therefore articulate and savvy enough to move her child elsewhere, and she's a stickler for detail, as any good teacher is.

'Really?' I venture. 'But aren't you a little worried? I mean, well, Infamous have been given Notice to Improve.'

'Notice to Improve' is the status attributed to some failing schools by Ofsted. It doesn't want to say that they are inadequate or failing, so it tells them they should improve. It means that inspectors have observed a number of lessons that have been judged 'unsatisfactory'. This has nothing to do with the intake (the students). I have known schools to have extremely challenging students and to receive a grade of 'outstanding' from Ofsted, the highest grade there is. 'Notice to Improve' or any of the half-dozen terms Ofsted has for 'failing' usually means that the senior leadership team in the school has been judged incompetent, as giving little or no leadership at all.

'Why would I be worried? Infamous is an *excellent* school. My friend's daughter got Level 7s last year. For her to have got those grades, there must have been some good teaching in the school.'

'Yes, yes, I mean of course. Schools with Notice to Improve will have a variety of lessons going on, and some of them will be excellent. But still . . .'

I have also met students from Infamous School, and they are the worst of the terrors on the buses. They are beyond repair. Infamous is just crap. Everyone knows this. Why the hell doesn't she?

'My son has made wonderful friends there,' she continues. 'He's so happy. Why would I want to move him from somewhere he's happy?'

Inside, I'm thinking that children don't necessarily know what's best for them and that if she moved her son, he would no doubt make friends elsewhere. 'So you're not worried then? Not at all?'

Ms Alternative lets out a breath, and looks me right in the eyes. 'Well, yes, I *am* worried.'

Ah, she's not crazy after all. Finally. No mother could possibly send her child to a school with Notice to Improve and not be worried.

'I'm worried about the plans to open up a Free school nearby.'

Other teachers who have been listening in, including Mr Sporty and Ms Magical, are all nodding their heads in agreement. I, how-ever, nearly fall off my chair. While I might choose to work in a school that has been given Notice to Improve in an effort to make it better, and I might, if I were a head, specifically seek out a school with problems and take on the challenge of turning it around, I would never send my own child to such a school. By all means, choose a state school for one's child, but choose a *failing* state school?

Saturday 19 October

'So how'd it go?' Inspirational chirps on the phone.

'How'd what go?'

'You know, Hadenough observing you. Did it help?'

'Nah. Well, maybe. I dunno. I think he just finds it really tough to put in the ridiculous hours.'

Inspirational sighs. 'Well, I tell you, I'm not willing any more either.'

'What? What do you mean?'

'Nothing really. It's just so goddamn hard. I'm so tired. I can't wait till half-term.'

'Hey, you know, rumour has it that Mr Sporty slept with Ms Alternative.'

'What? *What?* Ms Alternative? But doesn't she have a boy-friend?'

'I don't know. If she did, then maybe she doesn't any more.' I laugh. 'It's all ablaze with action at Ordinary since you left, you know.'

'Aarrggh! Why did I leave? Why did I leave? Tell me more, tell me more!'

Sunday 20 October

Liberal jumps off the ladder, having just been up in the attic. 'Look at these photos I found!' He hands them to me. There I am, on my college grounds, lying around in a very short pair of shorts with Compassionate and Liberal. So much space, such incredible buildings in the background. Liberal squeezes next to me on the sofa, pointing at the photo. 'Look! You're reading Karl Marx. Remember how we were going to change the world?'

'Yeah, well, no time to read that kind of stuff any more. And anyway, I *am* changing the world,' I chortle. 'Look at *you*: you're so *young*!'

'Yeah, I know. Couldn't believe it when I first saw them. Look how thin I am, and you, babe – wow! You looked great. Used to love those shorts.'

I slap him. 'What? What do you mean "looked", in the past tense? I look great right now!'

We both double up. Liberal eyes the photos. 'Yeah, babe, yeah. Sure you look gorgeous now, but youth, man, there's something wonderful about youth.'

I get up off the sofa. 'I'll tell you what's wonderful about it. When you're young, you have all the time in the world to waste. But right now, I have some marking to do.'

Monday 21 October

Dreamer pushes my door open, his earphones in, music blaring. I look up. 'No, no, let's start again. Back up and turn off that music.' Dreamer does as I say, tucking his black, shaggy hair around his ear, and pulls some work out of his bag to hand to me.

'Thank you, Dreamer. Well done. So what do you want to do later, Dreamer?'

'You mean this evening, Miss?'

'No, no. I mean in life. What do you want to do job-wise?'

'Ah, well, that's easy, Miss. I'm gonna be a footballer, you know, for a big, big team . . . say like Arsenal.'

My heart sinks, as it always does in these conversations. 'A footballer? OK, but what if that doesn't work out? What might you want to do then?'

Dreamer's smile grows wider. 'I dunno. Don't need to know. I'm gonna be a footballer. That's what you teachers don't understand. I don't need my English GCSE.' He points to the work he's just handed to me. 'What's the point of *Mice and Men* when I know I'm never going to need it?'

'So yes, maybe you'll be a footballer. Maybe. Do you play for any kind of national league now?'

Dreamer has to admit it: 'No.'

'Do you play for any kind of team at all?'

'Well, I play football for the school team.' He puffs out his chest.

'Don't you think there's a difference, Dreamer? What if, for some reason, you just couldn't have a career in football?'

Dreamer looks confused, as if I've just told him that the sky is purple. I'm talking about a world that could never exist. 'Nah, Miss! I'm gonna be a footballer, you wait and see! People get spotted, you know. They get found. I'm gonna get found.' And then he pauses, as if he feels sorry for me. 'But I'll think about a Plan B if you like.'

I smile. 'Yes, I'd like that very much.'

'OK, Miss.'

'Dreamer, man! What'cha doing?' shouts Dopey from down the hall. 'Ain't you coming to play football?' I pop my head out the door and wave. Dopey waves back.

Wednesday 23 October

Broom, our Polish caretaker, shouted at me to get a life when he threw me out of school at seven thirty tonight. When I tried to explain that it made no difference – going home, that is – because I would just continue working there, he didn't want to hear it. 'Just stop working!' he screamed.

He's right. Back at home, it's 10 p.m. and I've been working since 7.30 a.m. I am bloody well giving up. It's a good thing Liberal is working late tonight or I'd never hear the end of it. Thank goodness this is the last week of this half-term. One week off after Friday. Liberal and I are going to Paris. I can't wait. I can't wait even to be able to pick up my dry cleaning.

Now I have to sleep. 10.30 is my bedtime. Have to be all guns blazing for the little lovelies in the morning.

Thursday 24 October

Damn these stupid computers. I'm fiddling with the wires at the back of the one in class as my Year 11s chat. I turn to them. 'Like I said, everyone, just keep the noise to a minimum. I'll be with you in a second, if this computer manages to come on.'

I plug in the red lead and take out the yellow one. I push all the leads back in. Click, click, click. I move to the projector. On – off – on. What the hell are all these buttons for?

Dopey's arm shoots up, while he twists his hair with his other hand. 'Miss! Miss! I forgot my book today. I need a piece of paper, yeah?'

'You forgot your book? You know how important it is to bring your book in. I'll get you one in just a sec.'

Dopey taps the table. 'No, Miss, I need one now. That way I can write the date and title.'

I push myself up off the floor from where I was playing with the wires, defeated. 'OK. I think I may need to get a technician.' I walk through the desks and the kids towards the massive metal cupboard at the back where the paper is kept. As I move through, the class seems especially quiet. I get to the cupboard and turn back to face them. 'You know, Dopey, I hope this is the first and last time you're going to forget that book. You can't afford to write stuff on paper; you'll lose it.'

The class regards me quietly. Dopey smiles, shaking his head. 'Yes, Miss, sorry, Miss. I won't do it again. Promise.'

I swing back the cupboard door.

'*Raaaaah!*' Dreamer leaps out at me from inside the cupboard, roaring like a lion.

I jump back, screaming. 'What the hell?'

'Rah!' The class bursts into laughter.

I do too. Dreamer finds his balance and stands up straight. 'Got you, Miss!'

'What on earth . . . Dreamer! What *are* you doing?' I grin. 'Now sit down and stop being so silly. You nearly gave me a heart attack!'

'Cool, Miss, yeah, sure.' Dreamer sits.

I grab some paper from the cupboard and look round to Dopey, the smile still on my face. 'Did you really need some paper?'

Dopey waves his book in the air. 'Nah, Miss. Here it is, here it is!' He's in fits.

Friday 25 October

It's 8 a.m. I'm late. I run through the school gates, clutching my bag in one hand and some papers in the other, heading quickly towards my office. Oh well, last day before half-term. Who cares? I pass Stoic, who is sitting on a bench reading a newspaper. Stoic is a tall, slim Guyanese boy with very short hair. He's in Year 13. He's been at the school since Year 7 and is about to go off to university. The teachers love him. He does everything we say.

'Morning, Stoic.'

He looks up, smiling. 'Morning, Miss.'

Geesh. What's he doing reading a newspaper? No wonder the other kids hate him.

I reach a door and stop to reposition my papers. Stoic comes running up to me. 'Let me get that for you, Miss.' He pushes open the door and stands to the side.

'Well, thank you, Sir!' I beam. How lovely. How wonderful that we still manage to have students like Stoic. OK, enough about Stoic. To my office, quickly! What the hell am I going to teach today?

Half-term

OMG. We're back tomorrow. Paris was so lovely – walking by the Seine, eating ice-cream cones and going up the Eiffel Tower. But how'd a week go by so fast? I have a *ton* of marking I didn't get done. What can I tell the kids? Bloody hell. I hate letting them down. The work's due back tomorrow. It's OK, I can get it done tonight. Dinner, and then two hours' marking – yeah. Just have to make sure I don't insist on doing the washing up, I don't suddenly decide to do the household's laundry, and I don't find myself drawn to cleaning the bathroom. Whenever there's marking to do, a million other jobs suddenly become essential.

Ugh. I'm distracted. 'Liberal! Can you get rid of that silly pumpkin that is still hanging up in the window?'

'Yeah, you get on with your work, I'll take it down. Do you want to take it to school?'

'Nah, Halloween is over. But when the Christmas stuff appears in the shops, keep me in mind, will ya?'

Liberal smiles, and I put my red pen to paper.

Autumn Term Part Two

'Hey! Flowers for you at the back, Snuffy,' the school secretary, Ms Reliable, calls cheerily from the office.

'Flowers? Really? For me?' I run to the back of the office and rip open the card: 'Keep up the fight, soldier girl! All my love, Liberal.'

My head walks by as I'm reading the card. 'Does Liberal have some competition here? Ooooh, Ms Snuffleupagus, what *have* you been up to?'

'They're *from* Liberal, actually.' I give a little giggle and disappear down the corridor with my flowers. As I'm entering my office, along come Dreamer, Dopey and Furious.

'Hey Miss, man,' shouts Furious. 'Who gave you dem flowers?'

'Must have been a Frenchman. That's how they do it in France, you know.' Dreamer nudges Furious.

'Hey, yeah, man, what's the difference anyway, you know, between Paris and France?' Dopey shakes his head. 'Yeah, Miss. Serious, Miss, man. 'Cause *bare* people say I'm goin' France and I'm goin' Paris and there ain't no difference.' He turns to his mates for support. 'Innit?'

'Yeah man, yeah man,' they all agree.

'But Miss has been to *bare* places, you know.' Dreamer nods approvingly, as do the others.

'You been Spain, Miss?' I nod.

''Course she's been Spain,' shouts Dreamer. 'Ideeott!' He pauses to think, then, 'You been Miami, Miss?' Again, I nod.

'Rah!!!' they all exclaim, laughing.

Dreamer is impressed. 'If I'd been Miami, I'd have met some babes.' I raise my eyebrows. 'Oh, sorry, Miss. I didn't mean for that to come out.' Then he turns to his mates. 'But it's *true*, innit? *Bare* babes in Miami. It's *sick*, man!'

'Yeah man, yeah man,' they murmur in unison, going on for

what seems like an eternity about the girls in Miami – as if they have any idea what they are talking about. They've completely forgotten about my flowers. I guess that's what thinking about 'babes' will do to boys.

'Furious, don't forget to see me at the end of the day with that report now.'

Furious's face drops suddenly and the smile he was sporting disappears. 'Yeah, yeah, OK, Miss.'

As they run off, I think about how much I like those boys, how much I like my flowers and how some days are as lovely as can be.

Thursday 7 November

I'm standing outside the staff room, having just hauled Dreamer out of his lesson for laughing at his teacher and shouting 'Idiot' in her face, when Mr Hadenough approaches from behind. 'Ms Snuffleupagus, what do you do when you can't get the lesson started, when the class is completely out of control?'

Dreamer can't resist. 'You give up teaching, man.'

I stare at Dreamer. 'I have told you that is *enough*. You're already in plenty of trouble. Now go and sit on that chair over there, please. I'll be with you in just a minute.'

I motion towards the staff-room door with my head and Hadenough follows me in. He looks drained, beaten. The circles under his eyes have deepened. He wipes his brow. 'That 8.4, they're out of control.'

'OK. You get the disruptive ones out. And then, normally, you'd call for your head of department, Ms Joyful, or the second-in-charge. And if they aren't around, just call on anyone in the department for help.'

'Yeah, I did that. Ms Joyful removed the worst two. But that still left about six of them, all shouting at me from different directions. And what's going to happen if an inspector is in the room and I can't get them to shut up?'

'Well, you can have one or two standing in different corners of the room, maybe put one outside, have one stand by your desk. Hmm. You can . . .'

Suddenly I realize that Hadenough is shaking. I ask him if he is OK. Tears start to well in his eyes. OK? No. About to have a nervous breakdown? Yes. I sit down with him. 'Look, we can sort this out,' I say. 'You did all the right things. Try to think about the other lovely classes you teach. Do you want a cup of tea?'

He shakes his head. 'No. I need some whisky. In any case, I have to get back to the class.'

'The class?' I frown. 'What do you mean, "the class"? You mean you're talking about *now*?' I jump up. 'You mean you're teaching 8.4 right now?'

Hadenough's head droops. 'I just wanted them to be quiet. Just to be silent for one lesson, so that they could do their test. They wouldn't stop. They kept on and on: "I don't want to sit there"; "He took my chair"; "Why do we have to do this exam?" . . . I might as well have been invisible.'

I move towards the staff-room door. 'You mean there isn't anyone with the class right now?'

Hadenough slumps even further in response. I tear out of the door and steam down the corridor. Bloody hell. 8.4 *unsupervised*? Anything could happen. Run, Snuffy, run. As I rush past, Dreamer looks up. 'Hey, Miss! You said you'd be back in a minute. Where you going?'

I fly along the corridor, twist round the bend, up the stairs. Come on, Snuffy, hurry up, hurry up. Please God don't let any of them have leapt out the windows. I nearly bang into one of the bins attached to the wall. Two students are sat in the corner of the corridor, chatting. 'Get up!' I shout. 'Get to your lessons! *Now!*' They scamper off. I head up another set of stairs. And just as my foot touches the top floor, I see Deranged down the other end of the corridor.

Dring dring dring dring dring dring dring dring.

Oh God. Fire alarm. It'll have been 8.4. Oh God.

The kids pour out of the classrooms. Some of them are running. I head towards Hadenough's classroom. By the time I get there, it is empty. 8.4 are scattered amongst the crowds. There is no way we'll get the culprit now, not with the whole class having been unsupervised. Kids are swarming everywhere. 'Slow down!' I shout. They ignore me and run even faster. Kids are emerging from every corner.

'*Rah!*' They're laughing and screaming as they charge down the corridors. They love it when the fire alarm gets pulled.

Dring dring dring dring dring dring dring dring.

I head quickly down the stairs. As I pass the staff room, Hadenough comes out. 'I'm sorry, Snuffy. I screwed up, I know.'

I give him a reassuring pat. 'Don't worry about it. They're a hard class. Come on, let's go and get them into order in the playground.'

'Thanks, Snuffy.'

I manage a smile. As we head down the stairs, I think about Hadenough's fear: 'What do I do if there's an inspector in the room?' Indeed. What does one do? Pure and utter humiliation awaits us all. I wonder when Ofsted will come? I wonder how many of us will survive?

Friday 8 November

We have no idea who set off the fire alarm. With 8.4 unsupervised, there's an entire class we cannot account for. I catch Deranged on her way to the canteen at lunch. 'Hey, Deranged, I saw you in the corridor when the fire alarm was set off. Do you have any idea who did it?'

Deranged shakes her head. 'Nah, Miss.'

'It's the third time it's happened this year. Mr Cajole would appreciate any help you could give.'

Deranged looks at me blankly. 'Nah, Miss. I got there after, innit. Sorry. Didn't see nuffin'.'

'OK, OK, forget about the fire alarm. I like the new hairstyle.'

She laughs. Her blondish hair is down for once, not plastered against her skull. 'Yeah? Well, it won't stay like this.' She pulls her hair up on her head. 'It's better up.'

'Anyway, so you know you have a real chance at getting a "C" in English, right? You know that with just a little bit of focus and hard work, you'd get it, right?'

Deranged nods. 'Yeah, yeah, Miss. I know. Just have to do some work, innit.' She tosses her head, looking pleased.

She starts to head off and I call after her. 'So if you need any help, remember you can find me in my office any time after school . . .'

'I know, Miss, I know.'

Monday 11 November

I put the phone to my ear. 7.30 p.m. Bloody hell. I really need to get out of here.

'Hello?' comes the answer.

'Ms Desperate, hello! It's Ms Snuffleupagus here.'

'Oh, hello.' Her voice drops. 'What's Furious done now?'

'No, no, I'm calling with good news actually. Furious has been doing really well on report. He's been getting top scores for behaviour. I promise you, it's fantastic. I'm really pleased. He's been making such an effort recently, so I wanted to let you know.'

'Really?' Ms Desperate sounds like she might cry. 'Really? Ms Snuffleupagus, when I saw it was the school calling, I was bracing myself for what you might say this time, and, well, I can't tell you how happy this makes me.'

'Yes, me too, Ms Desperate, me too,' I say, grinning. 'You have a good evening now.'

'Thank you, Ms Snuffleupagus, thank you so much.'

I hang up the phone and decide that's a good end to an otherwise pretty stressful day. So I pick up my bag and walk straight out the door.

Tuesday 12 November

I stand in front of Year 11 at assembly. Rows of plastic chairs face the front of the canteen, the students on them preparing themselves to be bored by yet another assembly. I have a bunch of photos on a PowerPoint which I took in a favela in Brazil. I was there last year. I trawl through photos of rotting meat amongst piles of rubbish outside broken schools, small children carrying guns bigger than themselves, and makeshift houses which look like they'd blow over in a strong wind.

'As you can see, the poverty of these favelas is similar to the poverty you might find in some parts of Africa.' I point to the children on the screen. 'Children as young as five or six are part of the drug trade because that's how they can bring home money to their families.'

No welfare state to save you there. No dole queues to join. No job centre to find you employment. No social worker to put you in care. No free education where teachers give assemblies about travelling the world.

The students are intrigued. Stories of drug dealers and gun-carrying children have them sitting at the edge of their seats.

'Because of the massive divide between the middle classes and the very poor, the middle classes live behind bars.' I show some more photos. 'Apartment buildings are guarded twenty-four hours a day.'

Again, they're listening intently. Living in what looks like serious wealth behind armed guard seems glamorous. All my kids want to be on MTV.

'So I want you to think about what it must be like to live in this favela and have nothing. And then think about what it's like to live here, in London. Just look at how lucky we are.'

As soon as I say it, I can see some of the children laughing, mocking my words, whispering to each other that I have no idea. I don't know what it is to live 'in the hood'. I don't know how hard their lives are.

Seething has completely switched off, her arms folded in front of her, and she's kissing her teeth quietly. She eventually apologized (without her mother's help) for the nose-piercing incident, but since then things have been less than easy. This assembly of mine is only going to make things stickier between her and me.

'I'm not saying we don't have our problems, but the fact is that people get mugged all the time around here and they manage to survive the mugging. In Brazil, they'd just shoot you in the head.'

A murmur breaks out amongst the kids. Furious nudges Dopey. 'Man, she ain't got no idea. You won' get killed here? Heh! Yeah right . . .'

Seething looks straight at me and screws up her mouth in such a way as to make it clear she hates me. Psycho is playing with her nails. I'm flabbergasted. Some of our kids really do see reality in a totally skewed way. I remember once saying the same thing to a bunch of kids in a school in Harlem, New York. I told them that they were lucky to live in a country which gave them end-of-year exams which counted for something. They too wouldn't have it. They were victims: nothing more, nothing less.

These kids get their sense of self from the belief that their lives are harder than everyone else's. The harder your home situation, the more respect you get. Single mum at home? Unemployed? Council house? Seven brothers and sisters? Living on an estate? You'll be the most popular boy in the school. Oh no, not yet – join a gang and *then* you've got it made. Making something better of your life is a concept completely alien to them.

Wednesday 13 November

When I return to my office after school today, Beautiful is hanging around in the corridor, her skirt hiked high as it can go. Of course she's with Deranged, who has reverted to scraping her mousy hair back up against her skull. Beautiful is crying. They are both in my tutor group as well as in my Year 11 English class. 'Hey, girls,' I greet them. 'Is everything OK?'

Deranged squeezes Beautiful's shoulders. 'She's really upset, Miss. I think we should speak to you.'

Beautiful shakes her head, tears and mascara running down her face, and tugs at Deranged's blazer, wanting to leave. I open my office door. 'Come on, girls. Come in.' I grab a tin of biscuits off my desk. 'Here, have a biscuit.' I hold the tin out towards them.

Wiping her tears away, Beautiful takes a biscuit. The girls lock arms and enter my office. They sit down. I ask Beautiful various questions and get no response. She just munches on her biscuit as Deranged rubs her arm. I figure this has to do with Furious. Furious and Beautiful are the most revered couple in the school, mainly because of Furious's nightmare reputation. 'Nightmare' equals 'cool' and provides one with never-ending and extraordinary fame. All the boys want to be just like Furious. 'Has Furious done something?' I ask tentatively.

Beautiful moves awkwardly on the chair. 'Well, we've broken up, innit.'

Beautiful and Furious have been going out for some months. They break up and make up all the time. Beautiful used to be the loveliest girl in Year 7. She used to carry a novel with her to fill in any moments of boredom. Then she turned pretty in Year 9, and Furious, a year below her, took an interest. Beautiful has long, highlighted straight brown hair and brown skin. She's so lovely to look at that she has been 'chosen' by the 'baddest' boy in school to be his girlfriend.

'So who did the breaking up?'

'He did. He's a jerk. He doesn't listen to me. He says I'm meant to be a Muslim but I don't act like it. He says I don't pay him attention.'

Deranged won't have it. 'He's mash-up, man. I don't know why you stick with him. Tell her, Miss. Tell her she's better off!'

The more I probe, the more I hear about Furious's demands. He demands that Beautiful follow the Qu'ran, whatever that means. Her short skirts are a real problem for him. She isn't even allowed to spend her lunchtimes with her friends. He tells her what to do and how to do it. If only Beautiful's father knew. But he has no idea. Beautiful is a Pakistani Muslim. Her parents are hip enough to let her go about with her hair out for all to see, but they would flip if they knew she had a boyfriend, let alone that he's a black boy who has been considered for exclusion.

'I'm sick of it, Miss, I'm just sick of it!' Beautiful wipes her eyes. 'You don't know all I do to help him. I try and do what he says, but it ain't fair. I can't do this no more.'

'Hmm, yes, I see what you mean,' I murmur. 'Well, then isn't it a good thing that he broke up with you?'

She sobs and sobs. 'No! I love him, see! And now he's going around getting everyone to gang up on me. I don't have any friends any more!'

'But, you know, Beautiful, Furious is a *boy*, after all. He probably doesn't think things through as you do.' Beautiful smiles. And, for a moment, I see the lovely Year 7 girl who used to look up at me from behind her book. 'I mean, I know I shouldn't say this, but boys aren't as clever as us girls. I'm guessing that Furious is nice to you when the two of you are on your own at home, yes?' She nods. 'And I'm guessing that when he's around his friends at school, he acts like an idiot? Right. That's because he's a boy.' I grin. 'And now, he's acting like a robot that's gone berserk because he doesn't know how to deal with feeling sad. I tell you what, I'll speak to Furious, and maybe we can sort all of this out.'

Beautiful looks at me gratefully and gets up to go, Deranged still holding her hand. Inside, I'm thinking, Better speak to Furious and tell him to stop this nonsense. Because I know this won't end here. There's no way they're going to stay apart. I give Beautiful's arm a squeeze as she walks out of the door, saying, 'Don't worry, Beautiful, we'll sort all this out. I promise.'

Boys steal Munchkin's money. Boys throw stones at Mr Hadenough. Boys turn lovely girls like Beautiful into something they're not. We even have girls behaving like boys. Are boys the problem? Or is it that we have no handle on them? Or perhaps it is because we believe that 'boys will be boys' and in Britain in the twenty-first century, 'boys being boys' can mean any number of things? Indeed, in the twenty-first century, 'boys being boys' can mean absolutely anything.

Thursday 14 November

In the twentieth century, being 'bad' was pretending to have sex with a girl in the summer and bragging about it to your friends back at school in September. 'Bad' was smoking and driving a car in some silly race for 'pinks'. In the twenty-first century, it is something else entirely.

Furious is sitting in my office. He hardly says a word. He just looks at the floor, nodding intermittently. I tell him that he's enough of a stud to be nice to his girlfriend and not lose his rep. Furious has a mentor who works in the City and tries to talk some sense into Furious once a month. I ask him how his mentor treats his girlfriend. His shoulders twitch dismissively. 'Nice,' he mutters.

'And is he less of a man for being nice to his girlfriend?'

Furious grunts a 'no'. I tell him that the Snoop Doggs on MTV who rap about their bitches and their hos while slapping them around don't actually treat their girlfriends and wives in that way. That isn't what being a man is about, I say. Be like your father instead. 'You want to be a *man*, Furious?' His big eyes grow even bigger. 'Then be bold enough to show your friends how one should treat a girl. Beautiful needs looking after. She's your girl-friend, not your bitch. And you're behaving like an idiot, not a man.' It looks as if I might have hit a chord. I smile. 'So get out of here, and go and sort it out, OK?'

He scuttles out of my office, a little ashamed, but clearly intending to do good.

Friday 15 November

When students do something I like – give a good answer, do some good work – I give them a star. I simply say to them 'Star' and they draw a star in the back of their exercise book. Today, I say 'Star' to Fifty.

His eyes light up and he turns around to stick his tongue out at Cent. 'Raah! Whaya say to that, eh, Bruv? Miss gave me a star! Yeah, Bruv, whaya say? Whaya say to that? No star for *you*, Bruv!'

I look over at him. He's pushing his chest up, proud as can be, and I'm genuinely amazed at how some stupid hand-drawn star can make this boy react in such a way. Cent's response? He snorts and whacks Fifty in the back.

'Hey!' scowls Fifty.

I leap over to them. 'OK, OK, boys.' I put my hand out. 'We're not really going to have a fight over stars now, are we?'

Munchkin starts to giggle, and Cent and Fifty laugh with him. They both grin. 'Nah Miss, nah.' But I can't help but think: How cute!

Monday 18 November

I'm working in my office when I'm distracted by a sudden noise from downstairs. I run out and tear down the stairs to find a bunch of Year 11 girls doubled up in hysterics. A few are crying, they're so overcome. Deranged is shrieking, Beautiful is hanging on to her in an effort not to topple over, Seething is tossing her head from side to side, grinning, looking at the floor, twiddling her one pink glass earring. Whatever it was, it must have been deeply funny. I shoo them along outside and return to my office. Ten minutes later, Stoic appears at my door. Stoic is fiercely proud and polite, and is top of every top class. 'I'm sorry to have disturbed you, Miss,' he says.

'Sorry?' I look up from my work. 'Oh, hello Stoic, how are you?'

'I'm fine, Miss. Fine, thank you, Miss. I'm sorry about the noise.'

'What noise?' I wonder what he could possibly be talking about.

'The noise, Miss. The girls downstairs, laughing.'

'Oh yes,' I think, having forgotten. 'Yes, the girls.'

'Well, they were laughing at me.'

'Laughing at you, Stoic? Why on earth should they be laughing at you?'

Astonishing. He's apologizing for being laughed at. Well, that's Stoic for you.

'Because I tripped as I was going down the stairs. So they laughed. You know how it is, Miss.' Stoic shrugs his shoulders, as if to say it can't be helped, and moves to leave, but I keep talking.

'Stoic, just a moment. You know, I've been thinking about students like you – you know, the good ones – and I've been wondering about what makes you the way you are.'

'I don't know, Miss,' he answers. 'I just want to do well.'

'Hmm, yes . . . I know. But the question is: *why* you want to do well?'

'I don't know, Miss.' Stoic searches for an answer, trying to please me, but fails.

'Is it your parents? Do they insist you do well?'

Stoic thinks about it. 'I suppose it's training, Miss. I was trained from when I was young.'

'You think they're silly, don't you?' I smile wryly.

'Sorry, Miss?'

'You think they're stupid, don't you? You don't understand why they behave like that, do you?'

'No, Miss. I don't. I used to try to talk to them when I was younger. I would try to tell them to listen to the teachers and to do their work, but now . . .' Stoic looks defeated. 'Well, now, I just get on with my work and ignore them.'

'Don't you mind them laughing at you?' I probe.

'No. They can do what they like.'

Poor Stoic. I've embarrassed him now. 'You know, Stoic, I was once like you.'

'Really, Miss?'

'Yes, just like you. I didn't have many friends at school. I was top of my class and people used to laugh at me all the time. And just like you, I used to wonder why they never did their work. Why they never took anything seriously. I never fit in with the crowd. You stay the way you are – OK, Stoic? There's nothing better in life than being different. How's the Oxford application going? When's your interview?'

'Yes, Miss. It is all going very well. My interview is next week.'

'Good. You're getting all the support you need for that, right? It's history you've applied for, right?' He nods. 'And the history department is giving you mock interviews and so on, yes? Excellent. Well, good luck, Stoic. If anyone deserves a place there, then it's you.'

'Thanks, Miss.' And off Stoic goes, to spend, as he always does, the rest of his lunch hour alone.

A note from Dopey and Dreamer, which I found under my door today:

We comed to your detention but you wasn't in your office or librey.

These boys are leaving us this year. Poor things. I guess Stoic might have ended up just like them. But he chose differently. What on earth is going to happen to *them*?

Wednesday 20 November

Ms Alternative rushes up to me. 'Snuffy! Would you believe that we were all waiting there for Deranged and her family, and they never showed up!' By 'we', she means Deranged's head of year, her form tutor and herself. A meeting had been arranged with Deranged's parents to discuss her deteriorating behaviour. Ms Alternative goes on to tell me that she had arranged the meeting herself, on the phone, and that there was no mistake: they knew the meeting was today. 'So I rang her home, you know, as you do.'

'And?'

'Well, her mum went round and round in circles, first saying she wasn't sure of the date, and then saying she didn't know about the meeting. Then suddenly, she has to run, says she will speak to the dad, and we end the conversation there.'

'So what did Deranged say?'

'Well, she had lots of attitude, saying no meeting had been arranged, didn't know what I was talking about, treated me like I was crazy. And so I rang home – but now, no one is answering.' Ms Alternative exhales dejectedly. 'Next thing you know, the office gives me a message saying that Deranged's father rang. Notice how he just left a message for me – he didn't ask to be put through to me. Oh no. They don't want to talk to me.'

I'm exasperated. 'It's ridiculous. How can a family behave in this way? I mean, Deranged, I kind of understand, she's a kid, but her parents? How can they be complicit in this?'

'I know, I know. I mean, once, a while ago, I rang her home, and I know I had the dad on the phone, and he pretended to be someone else.'

I grimace. 'Huh?'

Ms Alternative leans in, whispering, 'Yes, well, you see, I think they're claiming housing benefit and pretending he doesn't live there, or something like that. I'm not exactly sure. But that's why they try to keep the dad out of the picture.'

At what point does a child who has been schooled in the art of lying by watching their own family abuse the welfare state for personal benefit understand that telling the truth, however unsavoury, is of greater value than any monetary prize the lies may bring? And how do we teachers build robust enough arguments in favour of 'doing it properly', 'having dignity', 'pursuing a sense of personal responsibility', when some of what the welfare state does proves all our arguments wrong? I feel like a very little cog in a massive machine, a machine which is fixed in such a way as to keep my children poor.

Monday 25 November

Mrs Principled is a small blond woman in her forties, middle class, articulate, and believes in the state school system. Four years ago, she chose to send her son Cavalier to my school and, in doing so, put her child in our capable but far from foolproof hands. Four years on, Cavalier is in Year 10, in the middle of his GCSEs, working relatively well. It's Thursday afternoon and I'm teaching my not very bright Year 8s when I notice a bunch of kids running around in the playground.

'*Fight!*' scream some of the kids in my class. '*Fight!*' Everyone jumps up and runs to the window.

I move quickly to the back door. Oh my God. It's Furious and Cavalier. Wait a minute . . . Furious and *Cavalier*? Why would they be fighting? They're surrounded by what looks like a pack of wolves, eager for blood, but who are in fact children.

Damn. I told Furious he had to stay away from school tomorrow, because of another incident last week with Mr Hadenough. Mr Goodheart took ages to make a decision and so I only told Furious this morning that that was his punishment. I knew he was angry, but I never thought this would happen.

In the way that firemen run towards a fire, we teachers instinctively head towards the middle of a fight. As I do, I see blood. Cavalier's forehead is pouring with it. Right in the middle of his forehead is a hole about the size of a ten-pence piece, and blood is shooting out in every direction.

Jesus. My heart skips a beat. Right, Snuffy, focus; pull it together and *go*!

Cavalier has the upper hand and is tearing into the other boy, so I grab hold of him and try to pull him off. By now, the children have stopped their usual shouting and jeering. They're silent, standing stock still contemplating the chaos. The blood scares them. Furious is still swinging punches and Cavalier is too strong for me to hold back alone.

'Dopey!' I shout. 'Dopey, grab Furious! Come on, everyone, grab him! *Help me!*' I'm screaming. My heart is racing. I trip over my feet. I fall backwards, taking Cavalier with me. As I fall, he stumbles and scrambles up. Dopey moves towards Furious and takes hold of him. 'Get Cavalier, man! Cavalier, man!'

Seething and Deranged seize Cavalier from behind. I pick myself up, still holding on to Cavalier's arm. My head is pounding.

And my hands are covered in blood. 'Walk him away,' I yell to Dopey. 'That way!' I turn to Dreamer. 'Go and get me another teacher. Now!' The kids gawp at me. 'I said *now*!' I'm bellowing, my voice cracking. Dreamer scampers towards the main building. With Cavalier still in my grasp, I turn to some of the others: 'Find me the weapon.'

Then I march Cavalier to the office. As we walk, the blood gushes down his face. I rub it off his forehead so that it won't get in his eyes. Cavalier is a nice boy. As far as I know, he's never been in any kind of trouble. We teachers like him. 'Don't worry Cavalier, you'll be OK,' I say softly. 'We'll get you to a hospital and you'll be fine.'

'I'm OK, Miss, really. I'm OK.' He pushes his fingers through his blood-stained hair.

We arrive at the office and I hand him over to Mr Cajole. I wonder whether now, if Mrs Principled could turn back the clock five years to when Cavalier was in Year 6, would she? Would she throw her principles to the wind and send her son to a different school?

I rush back to my abandoned class, still shaking from the ordeal, telling myself to stay calm. 'Whatever you do, Snuffy, don't let the kids see they got to you.' I run in, breathe a sigh of relief that they haven't set the room alight, grab the textbook and say: 'Right, where were we?' They laugh, saying they can't work now, not after that. They notice Ms Sensible, who has been sent to find the weapon, outside. Upset, she brushes a tear from her eye.

'Hey, she's crying!' shouts Adorable. They all turn to check me out.

'Rah!' they scream.

'Miss was right in the middle of the action and she ain't crying!' shouts Fifty. 'Rah! Miss is hard, man!'

Munchkin is shouting the loudest. I look at his squidgy cheeks and remember Cavalier at that age – cute, cuddly and scrumptious. I think of him now, blood running down his face, and wonder whether he's going to be OK. 'I sure am,' I lie, still shaking on the inside. 'Remember: don't mess with me. I'm hard as nails.' I make a fist. 'And now, I say, back to what we were doing.' Reluctantly, they open up their books.

Tuesday 26 November

Liberal slams himself down at the dinner table. 'Look, I'm all for your insistence that you change the world from the ground up and work with these lunatic kids and everything, but I draw the line at you being involved in fights with weapons. Soldier girl, it's dangerous.'

'Dangerous? Half of what I do is dangerous! That's my job. Come on, I've been in these situations before. Fights happen all the time.'

Liberal shakes his head. 'Yeah, but not ones with weapons. All it needs is for you to be in the wrong place at the wrong time and, well . . .'

I put my hand on his. 'I know you're worried. But there's no need to be. It's part of my job. It's just the way it is. We have weapon situations all the time, it's just that I haven't been directly involved in one before.'

Liberal stands up, pushing back his chair. 'Being a teacher shouldn't mean you have to take your life in your hands.' He has a point. 'What was the weapon anyway?'

'A metal bar.'

'A metal bar? Jesus. What kind of animals are they? I swear to God, if I ever get my hands on those kids . . . You know, your father and I spoke about this. He's very worried. What's going to happen to those boys in any case? Isn't one of them in serious trouble already? Isn't he on report to you, or something like that?'

'Yeah. Furious. I don't know what's going to happen. Both boys are out of school, pending an investigation. I was told that Cavalier got patched up in the end. Ms Sensible said she would update me on Monday. We'll have to see.'

Furious – a boy whose parents I had promised we would save – a boy who doesn't know the meaning of the word 'gratitude', who has disrupted the learning of countless other children for years . . . yet, somehow, I want to save him. Cavalier – a boy who has never been in trouble, a boy who has even carried things for me at his own insistence, suddenly to be involved in something so vicious? To go to school one morning expecting to learn and end up in hospital instead – none of it makes sense.

My head sinks, and I concentrate on holding back the very real tears inside, because I can't let Liberal see that I find all this terrifying too.

Thursday 28 November

'Good evening, and welcome to our school.' I smile. I bat my eyes. I am in hell. 'Would you like a guide to show you round? How about Adorable and Munchkin here?'

The two step forward. Her red curls bounce and he pushes his glasses up his nose. She smiles. He grins. She bats her eyes like me. The Year 6 parents clamour for a place in their group. The younger children get pushed forward.

I didn't go into teaching to be a salesperson. And I certainly didn't expect to have to 'pretend' in front of parents in the hope that they choose us. Pick our best kids to show them round, put on a great show: that's how you nab the middle-class parents. And the whole point of becoming a teacher was so that I didn't have to sell my soul.

'Parents have choice' is what we're told. Open evenings are meant to allow parents the opportunity to look around the schools and choose the one they want. But no parent would ever choose a school which is considered 'bad'. Why would they? Clearly, they're all going to choose the school they consider to be 'the best'. This is why some schools have ten children or more applying for every place. That means that nine of those parents are not going to get their choice. In fact, every year, there are parents in London who don't get a place for their child at all. We don't even have enough school places for everyone, let alone parents getting the school of their choice. What kind of choice is that? To get the school that one wants, one either has to have a sibling at the school or live within a radius of a few hundred metres of the place. And then, even supposing you do get in, do you really know what you are getting?

After the crowds have been sent off with our guides (students who have been cherry-picked and drilled to be on their best behaviour), a black man in his forties approaches. 'Hello,' he says. 'Could you spare me a moment to talk to me a bit about the school?'

'Of course, Sir, how can I help?' I smile. I flutter my eyelashes. I'd rather be having root-canal work done.

'Well, you know, we're very keen on this school and I'd very much like my daughter to come here next year.' The man hesitates slightly. 'But I'm very old-fashioned. I like discipline. What's the discipline like here?'

Do I tell this man that sometimes classes are so chaotic that the teacher cannot teach? Do I tell this man that children push and shove each other and fight on a regular basis? Do I tell this man about my own recent experience? No. Of course not. But then, I hate lying. If I'd wanted to perfect my lying skills, I would have gone into PR. So I smile. And flutter my eyelashes once more. 'Well, Sir, we are all very interested in discipline as well. You'll be going to hear the head's speech?' He confirms it and I continue, 'Well then, I'm certain you'll hear him talk about discipline, and you'll know everything you need to know.'

I make my excuses and run off in the direction of a guide I can see has diverted her group from the 'official tour'. The head can do the lying. He's paid more than me. Hell isn't just other people. It is Year 6 parents who think they have some kind of choice.

Saturday 30 November

Compassionate has put on a dinner fit for kings, and I look across the table, eyeing Liberal and wondering if he might leave me now that he's discovered that other women can cook. But he's so engrossed in conversation with Bank that I figure the thought hasn't even crossed his mind.

Finished with the main course, we are about to start on a beautiful homemade apple tart when Compassionate taps her wine glass with her fork. 'OK, listen up, you two, Bank and I have an announcement to make.'

Liberal goes quiet and looks at her expectantly. Bank covers Compassionate's hand with his and smiles. 'So?' I clap my hands. 'Don't keep us in suspense.'

Compassionate sits up. 'I'm pregnant!'

Liberal looks at Bank. 'Congratulations, man!' He shakes Bank's hand across the table.

'Boy or girl?' I ask. 'Or I guess you don't know that yet, do you?'

Compassionate shakes her head. 'Nope. All we know is that I'm pregnant. Baby is due 7 June.'

Liberal rubs his hands together. 'So, now you're gonna have to put your money where your mouth is. What you gonna do? Private or state?'

Compassionate and I look at each other as if Liberal has lost his mind. 'Isn't it a bit early for that conversation?' I say.

But Bank ignores my comment and leans back in his chair. 'Well, there isn't any dilemma as far as I'm concerned. The kid is going private from day one, I tell you. From day *one*.'

Liberal looks at Compassionate. 'You're really going to let your kid go to private school?'

'Well, of course our child's going to private school. What kind of idiot would send their own child to an inner-city state school?' She looks at Bank. 'Wineaton Prep would be perfect.'

Bank nods. Liberal pulls himself up on his chair. 'But what about supporting the state sector? Don't you care about state education? If people like you – *black* people like you – continue to refuse to put your children into mainstream schools, then those schools are never going to succeed.' He pauses, motioning in my direction. 'What about poor Snuffy? How can you abandon her like this?'

'Abandon her?' Compassionate laughs. 'Oh come now.'

'What does she care what we do with our kid?' Bank shouts.

Liberal is fuming. 'It isn't just about Snuffy, it's about all those poor kids out there. Don't you see? If you remove all the good kids from the inner-city schools, then they're done for.'

I look up. 'It's true. Without middle-class kids, we *are* done for . . .'

'Maybe. But I don't care. I care about my kid getting the best education I can give him. What's wrong with that?' He turns his gaze to me. 'If you and Liberal had a kid, where would you send him? Private or state?'

Liberal claps his hands. 'Our kids will go to state schools, of course.' He turns to me. I look down at the table. Bank watches.

'Oh really, Liberal? You sure about that?'

Everyone stares at me. Compassionate raises her eyebrows. 'Well, Snuffy?'

'I would want our child to have the best education possible. I guess it depends on what one thinks that is . . .'

Monday 2 December

'Hey, Snuffy.' Hadenough takes a seat next to me at the long canteen table, placing his spaghetti Bolognese squarely in front of him. 'God, I hate this food. Why can't they cook anything decent in this place?'

I take a bite of my half-filled triangle sandwich. 'How's it going?'

Hadenough grins. 'I hear we've got him.' He nudges me in the side. 'Furious – I hear he brought a metal bar into school. We've got him! That's enough grounds for permanent exclusion, right?'

'Yeah, I suppose so.'

Hadenough squeezes my shoulder. 'Exactly! So why aren't you looking happy? You're free! No more report, no more constant disruption, no more chasing him around the school.' Hadenough winks at me. 'And, more importantly, when Ofsted gets here, Furious won't be here ruining it for us all.'

'Yeah, I guess you're right. He deserves to go. But I just didn't think it would be so soon. He was doing well on report, except for maybe in science.' Hadenough looks at me, drawing his head back. I give in. 'OK, OK! You're right – to hell with him. I guess it *was* a lucky break.'

Tuesday 3 December

My Year 8s are hard to motivate. Today we start talking about the royals. 'What's the point of them?' is what most of them say. But Munchkin thinks otherwise. 'We need the royal family 'cause they're important, 'cause we need . . . hi– . . . hi– hierarchy.' So I get interested, and ask him what he means. ''Cause we need someone up there.' He is struggling to express himself when someone else says 'as a role model', and he lights up. 'Yeah! That's it!'

'Whuuuatt?' screech various members of the class. 'The queen? What's *she* ever done? What's the royal family ever done?'

'She helped people, she did. She did! She helped people in the war,' Munchkin stammers.

'Yeah, yeah, yeah,' grumbles Fifty, 'and what about that Harry, huh? He dressed up as a Nazi!'

We spent the last lesson analysing an article about that particular antic of Harry's. 'So what's wrong with that?' I ask.

'What's wrong with that?' screams Cent. 'Well, he killed all those Jews, didn't he?'

'Well, I'm not sure it was Harry exactly who killed all those Jews,' I venture. But the whole class is up in arms at my tentative sally.

Quiet, a small black girl who rarely speaks, declares that we cannot dress up as Nazis because they fought against England. 'England!' they sing, as if they were on the football terraces. 'England!' Much to my amazement, I can see that not only do they think of England as *their* country but, while they might not be so fond of their queen, they certainly love their country.

Adorable quietly explains to me that Harry wearing the Nazi uniform might offend some Jews. Polish, who also never speaks but only plays with her glasses, which seem to be permanently broken, suddenly pipes up, 'Yeah! It's like, it's like, it's like . . .' We all wait in awe as, frankly, I cannot remember her ever speaking voluntarily before. 'It's like . . . that MP who . . . that MP who . . . parked in that disabled parking space.'

And I simply burst into laughter. I cannot believe Polish has spoken, let alone made sense somewhere in her confused little head of the idea that people in positions of importance, role models for my kids, should behave in such a way that will make them – and me, for that matter – feel proud of our country.

'So should we kill the queen?' I ask. No, they don't like this idea. Adorable points out that it isn't right to kill people. No, we mustn't kill them.

'I know!' one of them exclaims from behind me. 'Let's shove 'em in Rough Estate!'

'Yeah!' They all cheer. 'Yeah, 'cause that way they'd get shot and it'd have nuttin' to do with us.'

My kids are pretty clever. They're thinking like politicians already.

Friday 6 December

Sometimes, the little things remind me of why I do what I do and why I rail so hard at the system. Today, as I was cycling in the rain and slowed down to throw something in the bin on the pavement, I missed. I struggled with my wet bike and dripping helmet, trying to near the pavement so I could pick the item off the ground. A young man walking nearby came to my aid. He picked it up and put it in the bin for me.

When I get home, I run in the door. 'Liberal! You'll never

believe it!' I run up the stairs. I recount the story of the young man and the bin.

Liberal raises an eyebrow. 'So?'

'So? What do you mean, "So?"? My kids, whatever their colour, whatever their class, would never pick something off the ground to put it in the bin for someone else. It was amazing!'

Liberal chortles. 'Snuffy, you've been in that school of yours for too long. What are you talking about? People do that kind of thing all the time.'

I sit on the sofa, thinking, Do they? Is my world so different to the world where Liberal lives? He gets up. 'I've made us some curried goat, you know.' He goes to the kitchen.

'Thanks, that sounds great.' But my mind is still on that young man. I want my kids to grow up to be just like him. I want them to know what true dignity is, to know kindness and consideration, to grow up into decent human beings who will not only be able to tell the difference between right and wrong, but who will fight for it, even if it means standing in the rain and cold a little longer.

Monday 9 December

'Ms Sensible! Ms Sensible! Do you have a moment?' I run up to her in the corridor. It's 7 p.m. and she clearly just wants to make her way home.

She lets out a breath. 'Yes, Snuffy, what can I do for you?'

'Well, I was just wondering about Cavalier and Furious. You know, what's going to happen to them. I mean, it's been two weeks and, well, I was just wondering . . . You said that they were excluded for fifteen days, pending the investigation. Do you know what's going to happen now?'

Ms Sensible puts her books down on the window ledge. 'Snuffy, Furious wasn't the one who brought the metal bar into school. It was Cavalier.'

'Cavalier? What do you mean? Why would he bring a metal bar to school?'

'Seems he was scared. He says he and Furious have been "having issues", whatever that means. Something to do with Beautiful, apparently. Anyway, he brought the metal bar in to protect himself against Furious.'

Oh my goodness. Beautiful. Of course. She said Furious wouldn't let her talk to other boys. And she's always been friends with Cavalier. Oh my goodness, why didn't I realize? Furious must have been threatening Cavalier. 'Poor Cavalier. So Furious managed to get the metal bar off him, and that hole in his head was caused by his own metal bar?' Ms Sensible nods. 'So what's going to happen?'

'Don't know. That's up to Mr Goodheart. But for the moment, both boys are out.' She picks up her books and turns to go.

'Ms Sensible!' She turns back to face me. 'They're going to be allowed to come back, right?'

As I say the words, I wonder what on earth has got into me. Furious is an evil little monster who ruins other children's lives. Why the bloody hell would I want him to come back?

Ms Sensible shrugs her shoulders as she walks off. 'Who knows?'

Who knows indeed. Who knows who deserves not to return to school? The boy who brought the metal bar in to defend himself? Or the boy who inspired such fear in him that he did so?

Tuesday 10 December

I'm walking along the corridor when I see Munchkin standing outside his science class. I raise my eyebrows. 'You been sent out, Munchkin?' He bows his head. 'I saw you outside your technology lesson the other day as well. Why are you suddenly getting kicked out of your lessons?' His eyes are fixed firmly on the floor. 'You know how important it is to behave in lessons so that you don't miss out on your learning, right?' Was that a slight bob of his head? 'I'm getting a little worried about you, Munchkin,' I say, starting to move off.

He looks up, smiling. 'Don't worry, Miss, I'll be fine.'

Our lovely trainee teachers, from a wide variety of teacher-training providers, are coping well. That is, six of them seem to be coping. Two of them have already dropped out. They say something like one third of newly qualified teachers (that will be our lovely trainees next year) drop out in the first term. Well, our two trainees have disappeared before ever really getting their hands dirty. Our second absconder took five days off ill and then didn't return. No explanation, no phone call, nothing.

I grab one of our trainees, Bushytail, who teaches French, and pull him to the side to ask what happened. 'Well, I think Terrified thought it was going to be a bit of a breeze and was a little shocked to find out how difficult it can be,' he explains. I frown, confused. He continues. 'Well, you remember that first day when you were telling us about the projectors that went missing last year?'

'Uh huh . . .' I think back. Oh yes, one breaktime in the staff room I told them that we had had six projectors stolen. We now have six interactive whiteboards which don't work.

Bushytail looks at me, expecting me to recall more. 'Don't you remember what she said?'

'No,' I answer.

'She asked you if the students had stolen them, and you told her yes, and another teacher said, "Reality check: that's what kids do these days."'

Oh, right. I see. Yes, now I remember. Didn't she know? I mean, didn't she know what kids are like these days – especially in the inner city? I suppose we must have scared her away.

'And how are you finding things, Bushytail?' I ask tentatively, dreading the answer.

'Good, good . . . I'm really enjoying it. My Year 8s, 8.4 . . . they're a bit of a handful, but apart from them, I'm doing OK, I think.'

'8.4?' I say. 'I teach them. It's true, they aren't easy. Would you like me to come and observe you sometime? Maybe I could be of some help?'

Bushytail's eyes flare in appreciation. 'Oh yes, that would be wonderful. Please do.'

'OK then,' I say, beaming. 'Email me and we'll set up a time for next term.' As I wander off, I think to myself: what on earth am I doing taking on more work? As if I don't already have enough to do.

Thursday 12 December

'Ms Alternative rang them up asking for an explanation, you know.' My head sighs as he drops his papers on to his desk.

We thought for sure Stoic would get in. If *he* doesn't get in, then who does? 'So what did they say?'

'He was number seven. They took six.' The head shrugs his shoulders.

I wrinkle my nose. 'Unlucky, I guess.'

'Well, no, I just wish I could be like the old boys and ring up someone and say "Hello, this is Mr Contacts here, I'm just wondering, ahem, about, you know . . . Well, I understand there isn't a place for him at your college, but might we not find him a place at another college . . ."' I draw my eyebrows together in disagreement. 'Well, that's what they say in the books about how it's done!'

'Yes, but that was ages ago . . . I don't think that now . . .'

'You know they said that his essays were the *best* they have ever seen from a state-school student. The *best*! What does that mean? He's the best but we won't have him?' I nod, thinking lots of things, and not saying any of them. The head sighs. 'Well, I won't go into it. We all know there are issues with Oxbridge taking state students and, well, I won't waste time talking about it. What was it you came in for again?'

Later, as I am walking away from the head's office, I mull over what he said. Is there an issue with Oxbridge taking students from state schools? I don't think there is. Yet he is convinced of it. Stoic's essays were the best they have ever seen from a state-school student, they said. What does the head hear? That his essays were the best. And of course he's right. If what they say is true, then either Stoic really messed up the interview, or the six students they took are not from state schools. The head has come to the latter conclusion. I tend to agree. That is the most likely of outcomes.

His thinking then takes him to the next step: if his essays were the best, then he should have had a place over those six other students. And if Oxbridge didn't have 'issues' with state-school students, then the lovely Stoic would have a place there next October. Oh how I wish that could be true. But there is one slight slip in his thinking. The point is that Stoic's essays were not the best. They were the best the tutors had ever seen from a *state-school* applicant.

'From a state-school applicant.' The words reverberate around my head as I walk down the hall. If Stoic is the best we can produce and all that means in the grand scheme of things is that his essays are only good by state-school standards, then what on earth are they doing in *private* schools? What must they be teaching? What are they able to do with their kids that we cannot? I guess they aren't chasing loads of bad behaviour. I guess they're actually able to teach for an entire lesson. I guess they plan their lessons according to what would make for good learning, as opposed to what will keep the students in their seats. I guess they can teach their children whatever they want and are not bound by the national curriculum and influenced by the madness that all lessons must be 'fun'. I guess they simply live in a different world.

Friday 13 December

'Beautiful,' I call after her as she scuttles down the corridor during lunchtime. 'Have you heard from Furious?'

''Course I have, I see him every day.' She stuffs her hands in her pockets. For once, she's wearing trousers.

'So how is he?'

She shrugs. 'Yeah, he's OK, innit.'

'And what about Cavalier? Have you seen him too?' Beautiful goes quiet and looks at her feet. 'Beautiful? What's wrong? Is everything OK with Cavalier?'

She looks up. 'Yeah, Miss, yeah, he's fine.'

'Are you sure about everything being fine? I mean, has Furious been threatening either of you?'

She shakes her head. 'Nah Miss, man, it's fine. Yeah, sure, Furious can get a little mad sometimes, but he's OK. And Cavalier too. Yeah, I mean, they ain't best friends or nuffin', but they is fine.'

'OK, Beautiful. Just let me know if you have any problems with Furious, OK? I'd like to help.'

Beautiful chews her gum. 'Yeah, sure, Miss.' She turns to go.

'And put that gum in the bin!' I shout after her.

'Yeah, yeah, Miss. I'm doing it, I'm doing it.'

Deranged appears down the corridor and the two of them lock arms and head towards the canteen. What a funny pair. Deranged, white, working class, with her hair scraped back like a black girl's, and Beautiful, a Pakistani Muslim who doesn't cover her hair and whose father has no idea she is dating the most revered black boy in school. It's amazing to think the two of them could ever be such good friends.

Thursday 19 December

As I pass the head's office, I overhear him talking to Ms Sensible: 'Bloody Cavalier and that metal bar! And Furious . . .'

'Sir, if you don't mind me saying, you know what we need to do.'

Mr Goodheart exhales. 'I know, I know.' He slams what sounds like his fist on the table.

I rush back to my office and quietly close the door. I feel like a thief. What does that mean? Is he going to exclude them?

We teachers like Cavalier. He isn't disruptive, or unkind. He's polite and does his homework. We don't want Cavalier excluded, especially when we know that any given school only has a certain number of 'exclusion places' before the Local Authority or Ofsted starts to raise an eyebrow. Exclude too many and someone will start asking questions.

Choose to exclude and take a stand on weapons: show the other children that weapons will not be tolerated and discourage others from similar paths. Or, choose to ignore the crime and use the 'exclusion space' for someone more deserving of it, and put a smile on the faces of many teachers and students. Choose. And in doing so, choose who should get a chance at life.

Friday 20 December

The kids are gone and the Christmas lunch for staff is over. A sharp wind is blowing hard outside. I've spent the requisite time in the canteen eating my turkey and singing Christmas songs; now, I could go to the staff disco in the gym, but I have too much work to finish up. I've snuck back into my office and closed the curtains. They'll assume I've gone home.

I open up some of the Christmas cards I stashed on my desk earlier. One is from Stoic:

> *Dear Ms Snuffleupagus,*
>
> *Miss, I know I get stressed sometimes and I wanted to say thanks for putting up with me. You have been there for me since the beginning. I know I would not have got an A* in my English GCSE had it not been for you. To have such an inspirational teacher around makes coming to school worthwhile and for that I thank you too, Miss. Good luck with everything and may all your wishes come true at Christmas.*
>
> *From Stoic*

As I am reading, Hadenough rushes into my room carrying a bottle of beer. 'Snuffy, what're you doing? You can't be working *now*. Term is over. We're finished: it's Christmas. Why don't you come to the canteen for a dance?'

'Nah. I have to get this stuff done. They'll kick us out at five. I have to finish. I'm already taking home enough work as it is.'

Hadenough puts his hand in his pocket and pulls out a sheet of paper. 'I've got something here you'd like to see. Promise me a dance and I'll show it to you.'

I look up from my papers. 'How much have you had to drink?'

'Snuffy, I'm being serious. Promise me you'll come and dance, and then I'll show this to you.'

'OK . . . OK. I'll have *one* dance. Now what is it?' Hadenough hands me the scrumpled piece of paper and I open it up. It's a copy of a letter from Mrs Principled to Mr Goodheart. I look up at him suspiciously. 'Where on earth did you get this?'

'Don't worry about it. Just read it. Read it.'

And so I do, out loud.

Dear Mr Goodheart

It is with a heavy heart that I find I write to you now. For four years both Cavalier and I have benefited from all that Ordinary School has to offer. Cavalier has so enjoyed his time at secondary school. When he was in Year 7, he used to run home with stories of the different children, the different religions and cultures, the way the canteen does world food, the way you cater for all of your students with such care and love. As a parent, I have always felt welcome to criticize and I always knew I would be heard. You will remember our long discussions at parents' evenings on how to improve Cavalier's experience at school. How I will miss those days.

I find now that I write to you in desperation to plead for my son's life, which you hold in your hands. If you exclude him from Ordinary, where is he to go? What is he to do? While I understand why you may feel the need to make an example of Cavalier, I wish to suggest that maybe a boy like Cavalier, who has never had a blemish on his record, should be given a second chance.

If you exclude him, you and I both know that no other school will take him. He will be forced to go to the PRU [Pupil Referral Unit], and what kind of education will he get there, with unspecialized teachers teaching children who have been excluded from mainstream schools? Those places are simply stepping stones to prison.

Cavalier knows he has done wrong. If he could take back the stupid decision to carry that metal bar into school, he would do it in a minute. But now, all we can do is beg you to take pity on us and give him a chance to prove to you that he can make Ordinary School proud of him.

Yours sincerely,
Mrs Principled

I look up at Hadenough. 'Yeah, exactly. Pretty hard-core stuff, eh?' he says, grabbing the letter back out of my hands. 'So maybe that'll do it. Maybe the head will let him stay.'

'Nah. That letter won't make a difference. Mr Goodheart *has* to exclude him. What about the other kids? He can't be seen to condone bringing a weapon into school.'

Hadenough frowns. 'I swear, if they kick Cavalier out and let Furious stay . . . I swear . . .'

I jump up. 'Come on, I believe the disco is calling. What's going on with Mr Sporty and Ms Alternative? Are they up to anything on the dance floor? Let's go!' I grab Hadenough's beer out of his hand and take a massive swig.

Saturday 21 December

I'm sitting at my desk, looking at my watch. It's 9.05. Where the hell are they? Revision class in the holidays. Why? Because otherwise they'll fail. But where the hell are they? It's 9.06. Dopey rushes in. He's wearing expensive trainers and a hoodie. 'Miss, man! Miss, man!' He looks around. 'Hey! Where's everyone?'

'I don't know. You tell me. Where are they?' I stand up. 'You know, I'm tired of this. Why am I here? Where are you all?'

Dopey puts his hand up and takes out his phone. 'Yeah, yeah, Miss, gimme a sec. I'll ring 'em.' He dials various numbers while I shuffle through some papers. 'They're comin', they're comin', Miss. Dreamer just got out of bed. He'll be here in fifteen minutes. Beautiful's comin' too.' Dopey smiles. 'And when she gets here she can ring Seething and the girls.'

I look up at Dopey and grin. 'You're pretty good, Dopey. Thank you.'

'That's OK, Miss. They got to be here, we don't wanna fail. Uh uh. Little engine, Miss.' He giggles.

'Yes, Dopey, that's right. The engine . . . Come on then, get out your pen. We have a ton of work to do.'

'Aarggh, Miss.' Dopey winces as if in pain and then, as if he'd swallowed a magic pill, 'OK, Miss. "Choo choo!"'

Wednesday 25 December

Last night, as Liberal and I sat in church, which was mainly filled with people over the age of sixty, we listened to a young girl sing 'Silent Night'. She stood on the steps of the pulpit in exactly the same place I, at a similar age, recited the 23rd psalm, 'The Lord is My Shepherd', many years ago. I remember spending hours learning it. I spent evening after evening practising with my father. Every time I tripped up over the words, I would start again, and my father would listen to me again and again until I got it right. Eventually, I stood tall in front of the congregation and recited the psalm to perfection.

No doubt this young girl who sang on Christmas Eve prepared in a similar way. As I listened to her, I thought of the children at my school and wondered what they would be doing with their Christmas Eves. Had they been preparing for a recital? Had they been learning how to cope with nerves, enhancing the projection of their voice, believing that they *are* something – a part, however small, of the universe? My guess is that most of them will be playing their PSPs, imagining what new games Christmas Day will bring. Not all of them of course, but some, who would call themselves Christians, truly have no idea what Christmas is really about.

Although I must admit that, often, I don't believe wholeheartedly in God, I do wish my kids knew more about Him – whether

'He' is the Christian God, Allah, Vishnu – or simply had some sense of the sacred. I wish they could move away from the materialistic madness that Christmas has become and understand the meaning of a 'Wonderful Life': that life is made wonderful not by gaining another PSP game but because of what we leave behind after us. As Arthur Ashe, the African-American tennis player who died young having contracted AIDS from a blood transfusion, and who lived what can only be described as a wonderful life, said: 'From what we get, we can make a living; what we give, however, makes a life.'

All of us will die. Very few of us will live. Here's wishing that, if not now, then one day, my children are given the chance to really live.

Spring Term Part One

Monday 6 January

I'm sitting on the bus, on my way to school, when four black girls, aged maybe twelve or thirteen, try to board. They stamp on in their boots, which are splattered with snow. The black bus driver, who is in his fifties, tells them to get off because they don't have their travel cards.

'Yuh, prick!'; 'Yuh think you're somethin', eh?' They jeer and stamp about at the front of the bus, shouting insult after insult at this poor bus driver, sucking in through their teeth and gesticulating aggressively. I think of our girls at school and how some of them would behave in the same way. During the holidays I spotted Seething on the high street shouting at a policeman. I toy with the idea of getting up and saying something to these girls, but decide against it.

On the girls go until, finally, the bus driver bangs his plastic window hard. They go quiet. They seem surprised. The bus driver is angry. 'What is wrong with you? Why do you behave like this?' His Caribbean accent shakes with anger. The bus is silent, listening. 'I feel nothing but shame when I look at you, yuh know. When I came to England from Trinidad, no one would take me, yuh know. No one would give me a room.' The girls are standing still, in silence, like the rest of us, listening. 'You all have free bus travel now. *Free* – imagine that! All you have to do is bring your cards, but no . . . you don't have any respect . . . No respect for the system. Yuh get given a flat, yuh get money . . .' His voice is cracking. I wonder whether he might break down into tears. '. . . and all you is going to do is spend it on *knickers*!'

My eyes open wide at the word 'knickers'. I can't quite believe what I'm hearing. The girls purse their lips and step off the bus.

When I get off, I think about this bus driver and how hard it is to carry that sense of shame. How many of us carry it? My feet feel like lead as I wander towards school through the light snow on the pavement.

I'm quickly shaken out of my stupor by the various teachers passing me: 'Hi, Ms Snuffleupagus'; 'Happy New Year!'; 'How was your holiday?'

Mr Hadenough shouts from an upstairs window. 'Hey, Snuffy, all set for Ofsted?'

I wave, smiling. 'You're kidding, right?'

He chuckles, slamming the window shut. Yup. We're back. Spring term. Let's get down to business.

Wednesday 8 January

Some classes are easy to control and some are a real challenge. It all depends on the group dynamics, how many unbalanced children you have and whether they are used to getting away with bad behaviour. Every teacher has a class they dread, and I am no exception. 9.5 is a nightmare. I guess I should be grateful they aren't swearing, fighting or jumping out of the window, as they've been known to do with other teachers.

With Ofsted looming, Mr Goodheart has brought in a behaviour guru to aid us in our 'behaviour management techniques'. I'm keen to have her watch me teach 9.5.

Ms Expert is small with brown hair, a rather round woman who wears too much make-up. She sits down in my office and takes out her notes.

I sit up straight, pen and paper in hand. 'So give it to me then. You saw a very normal scenario when you were observing me. Too much chat, the staring into space, the students spreading themselves out across desks as if they're getting ready for bed . . . And then you saw how reluctant they are to ask questions, or to engage altogether. What do I need to do differently?'

'Well, Snuffy, I noticed that you told them all off for not doing their homework. Well, why do you set homework anyway? It doesn't have any positive cognitive effect on children, you know.

I shouldn't worry about homework with this class: just don't set it. And that game of yours at the end – the noughts and crosses, girls against boys – they didn't like it much, did they?'

She's right. 'No. Like I said, they aren't really at all interested in the lesson.'

'Oh no, you're wrong to think they aren't interested. Your game was *boring*. And what did they get for winning? Nothing!'

'Well, they would get the feeling of satisfaction of having won.'

'Oh, come on, Snuffy. And you only had one game, and that was at the end of the lesson. Why don't you have games throughout the lesson?'

'Because having a game at the end is one thing, but a lesson filled with games is not really a *lesson*, is it?'

'Snuffy, you're far too old-fashioned. These kids need to have incentives to learn. I mean, you don't come to school for nothing, do you?'

I laugh. 'Ms Alternative once said the same thing to me simply about kids attending school – that we should pay kids to be here. And now you're saying we should do the same in lessons!'

'Well, why not? Don't you want them to learn? If they won't learn under the methods we use to teach them, then we must change the way we teach to accommodate the way they learn.'

I nod, studiously taking notes. But how much do we need to change? And at what point do we say this change is too much? I'm already using some games, chopping my lesson into tiny bits to accommodate the students' short attention spans, giving them gold stars for their work and praising them for the slightest thing they get right. Apparently this isn't enough.

Ms Expert goes on to explain that chocolate makes a good prize. Sure, chocolate at the end of term perhaps, but every lesson? I want them learning for learning's sake! When I refuse to indulge in what I see as a farcical attempt to bribe the kids, she compromises: I should give out gold pencils instead.

Ms Expert and I chat for some time. She is a clever and informed woman, and while I fundamentally disagree with most of what she says, I enjoy arguing with her. After a while, though, I agree to give it a go. 'OK, OK. I'll give what you say a go with all my classes, especially as Ofsted is going to be visiting soon. In one of my Year 8s, there is this boy Munchkin who has been losing interest recently. Do you think this would help?'

'Of course it will. You'll see, Snuffy. We can talk again in a few weeks. I'm looking forward to what you'll tell me.'

As Ms Expert leaves my office and closes the door behind her, I can't help but feel like I've just given in, that I've accepted that my kids are not capable of learning in any normal sense, and games and prizes are the only things that will save them. I think of Compassionate's children at Wineaton and wonder whether she has to go to such lengths to get their attention?

But who knows? I've been failing to engage them my way. And engagement is the name of the game with Ofsted. If your children don't seem engaged while an inspector is in the room, it is the teacher's fault – always. So while games will teach them less, perhaps their learning *some*thing and being engaged is better than nothing? Maybe Ms Expert is right . . .

Thursday 9 January

I'm at the whiteboard when I overhear some of my Year 10 boys chatting. This is one of the top sets. These boys are bright, and the class is a joy to teach. Wholesome is tall, muscular and plays basketball like a young Michael Jordan. Cavalier was his best friend. I say 'was' because Cavalier's seat remains empty and his absence hangs heavy in the classroom. Hip, a dark-haired white boy, leans over to Wholesome and whispers. Wholesome's reply is loud enough for me to hear: 'Whaya say? Me nah wannit.'

I'm confused. Sure I hear this type of talk all the time from the kids, but Wholesome's parents are not Jamaican. They're not even from the Caribbean. Wholesome is Nigerian.

Incredibly, the other black boys in the class accept his posturing happily. It makes me think of Deranged, who always does her best to look black. But not just any kind of black is cool. Jamaican is cool; Nigerian is not. Hip, though white, is as cool as the black ones. He puts up his hand. 'Miss, when is Cavalier coming back?'

'I don't know. I'm not sure it's been decided.'

'Yeah, well, that Furious, he's on report to you, isn't he, Miss? Fool. He should be the one who isn't allowed back.' Hip turns around to look at the rest of the class, who nod their agreement. 'Yeah, yeah.'

'Well, it isn't that simple, as you know. Cavalier brought a weapon into school. It complicates things.'

Wholesome bangs his fist on the desk for emphasis. 'Yeah, well, that's 'cause he was scared. And so was I scared.' Wholesome's accent has returned to normal.

The rest of the class goes silent at Wholesome's revelation. I decide not to pursue it, as I know there's no way he'll speak with everyone else listening, and I insist that they all get back to their work. Hip laughs. 'Ah, Miss, you're so *boring*!'

After the lesson, I motion to Wholesome, asking him to stay behind. 'What do you mean, he was *scared*?' I pause. 'And why were *you* scared?'

Wholesome shakes his head. 'Nah, Miss . . . it was nothin'. Forget I said nothin'.'

'No.' I squeeze his arm. 'Come on . . . tell me what's going on. Who knows? Maybe it'll help Cavalier's situation.'

Wholesome reluctantly tells me that both he and Cavalier are friendly with Beautiful. Furious doesn't like it. Furious has banned her from speaking to them altogether. Wholesome has done a better job of obeying the order than Cavalier. Cavalier was outraged and would sometimes meet up with Beautiful in secret. 'In secret?' I echo. 'You mean they were . . . you know . . . I mean . . .'

Wholesome laughs nervously. 'No, no, Miss. They're just friends. But they had to sneak around 'cause Furious wasn't having it.' He wrings his hands. 'And that morning . . . well, Furious found out. I think Dopey spotted Cavalier with Beautiful the day before and then he told Furious. Cavalier knew the fight was coming. And he knew he'd never win. He had to defend himself, Miss, he *had* to!'

'I know, I know. I'm sorry, Wholesome. I'm sorry.' I look up to see Hip through the cracked glass, knocking at the door and motioning to Wholesome to hurry up. Hip and Wholesome are best friends. 'Off you go, Wholesome. Hip is getting impatient.'

As Wholesome wanders off, I look down at my papers, thinking. How come we can't protect these kids? How come Furious seems to rule the world? Since when were the children in charge?

Friday 10 January

Schools are under increasing pressure to get larger numbers of their students passing their maths GCSE. As such, schools often put their students in for the maths GCSE exam a number of times, starting in Year 10.

Hadenough bursts into my office, a smile plastered across his face. His maths GCSE 'D'/'C' group took 'early entry', and their results are out. He launches himself into a chair. 'I did it! Can you believe it? Dreamer got a "C"! And you'll never believe it, but so did Seething – and guess what Psycho got?'

I raise an eyebrow, grinning. ' "C"?'

Hadenough leaps up, heads to the window and gazes out. 'Half the class . . . we did it! They got a "C"! I've made my target!'

'Well done – that's great news, Hadenough. But what will you do with them now?' These kids will have barely scraped those 'C' grades. These kids needed a 'C' so that they could have a life, get into some kind of college and, maybe, one day, to some university that used to be a polytechnic. Work for a 'B' in maths? One might as well tell them to fly to the moon.

Hadenough shrugs his shoulders. 'Who cares? I've made my target!'

'What about all those kids in there who still need to work to get the GCSE and aren't going to be able to because of the chaos that the ones who have passed will cause? Look, I don't mean to be negative. It's great. Really. Well done. God knows those "C"s are all about you and nothing to do with them. But why do you care about your target?'

Hadenough screws up his face. 'I'm gonna get my payrise now. It was dependent on half the class getting "C"s. I'm gonna get my *moneeeey . . .*'

'You mean *threshold* depended on this?' But nothing can take the smile off his face. I leap up out of my chair. 'But can't you see that this is crazy? It's going to be bedlam in that classroom now!'

'Hmm. I see what you mean.'

Feeling like a real killjoy, I try to smile and pep things up a bit. 'It's great news, Hadenough. I mean, who'd ever think that Psycho could get a "C"?'

Hadenough's face relaxes once more. 'Anyway, you heard about Mr Sporty and Ms Alternative at the end-of-term disco, right?'

'No.'

'What? You are *so* out of the loop, Snuffy! How can you not know . . . you must be the only person who doesn't.'

'Doesn't know what?'

'He banged her in the caretaker's office while we were all dancing upstairs.'

'He *banged* her? You mean they had *sex*?'

'Yeah, yeah . . . across the caretaker's desk . . . Ewuuuhh.' Hadenough makes a face. '*Bam!* It was over in five minutes apparently. That's what Ms Joyful said. She saw it all . . .'

'She saw it? How'd she see?'

'She was passing outside . . . you know how those windows are always open.'

I cover my open mouth with my hand. 'That's disgusting. At the disco? Oh my God! Anyway . . . doesn't this woman have a *boyfriend*?' The bell rings. '*Shit.*' I cover my mouth, realizing what I've just said. 'I'm late, I'm on duty.' I throw on my heavy winter coat, and my hat and gloves. Then I push Hadenough out of my office and charge down the corridor as fast as my legs will carry me.

'So how far along are you now?'

Compassionate and I are sitting in a café near her school. It's starting to snow outside. We've both been in school this morning and decided to meet for lunch. Compassionate taps her tummy.

'Nearly five months.' She smiles. 'Bank's really excited.'

'Brilliant. How much maternity leave will you take?' Compassionate explains that, with Bank earning the kind of money he does, she doesn't have to worry about being back at work too quickly. School is very demanding. She's thinking of taking at least a year and possibly returning part time. 'But with everything that's been going on in the financial world, isn't Bank worried about his job? And what about *you*? Aren't there fewer families willing to pay those school fees? Isn't the school suffering?'

'Yeah, that's true. The school is making cutbacks.'

'You should be teaching in the state sector like me, and you'd be just fine.'

Compassionate frowns, not understanding what I mean. 'But you work all the time. I don't know anyone who works harder than you.'

'Yeah, but that's out of *choice*. Most teachers are like me, though. But there's a minority in every inner-city school who sit around and do nothing. And why not? I'm never going to lose my job, am I? If I never mark the kids' homework, never pick them up on their uniform or behaviour, never teach them properly, who's going to care?'

'The parents care.'

'Ha! Yeah, maybe *your* parents care . . . some of ours don't even care when we ring to tell them that something's going on with their kids. Even the middle-class ones don't chase us. They're not paying for their kids' education, remember . . . so they aren't so demanding. The less they hear from us, the better for them.'

Compassionate frowns again. 'That's so the opposite with us . . .'

'I could take a ton of days off work. What can the head do about it? Nothing! Apparently, this academic year, on average, we teachers have taken eight days' sick so far. Well, I haven't taken a single day off sick. I know others who are just like me. That means someone else is taking those eight days for us.'

'Yes, but Snuffy, those teachers are probably exhausted. When I hear the stories you tell . . .'

'I don't blame them for taking the time. But the point is that no one takes any notice of what we do in the inner city. As long as you have the stomach for the rudeness, and the occasional flying chair, if you're lazy and want a decent salary, teaching in the inner city is a good option.'

Compassionate sits up straight. 'Your head could fire you just as mine could fire me.'

'Fire me? No. It's practically impossible. He doesn't have the time to go through all the procedures. It would take him years . . . And as long as I can be seen to be trying to improve, he can't get rid of me. And even if, by some miracle, after years of exhausting battle, he does manage to get rid of me, I can just get a job in another inner-city school. Really, Compassionate, you can't imagine some of the teachers that teach at our school. They're crap, and the head can't do anything about it.'

Compassionate looks concerned. 'But surely . . .'

'The kids can do what they like and so can the staff. NUT: that's all you need. The union will fight for you to be rubbish in the classroom and not get fired – all the way . . . They'll put up such a good fight, the school might even pay you off.'

'So why have any standards at all?'

'I often ask myself why on earth I work as I do. Something drives me inside. I don't know.'

Compassionate dismisses the subject with a wave of her hand. 'Anyway, forget all that, what about the more important stuff like babies? Are you and Liberal going to start a family soon?'

Slowly, my head moves from side to side. 'Oh no, not now, I couldn't possibly, not with all the work I do. And I'm so tired all the time. Perhaps in the future. With things as they are, life is simple. We're going to Jamaica at half-term, you know.'

'Oh yeah, I forgot. That'll be so nice – wish I was going too! Well,' Compassionate says, patting her belly, 'I'll need lots of help when this one gets out. I hope I can count on you.'

I put my hand on hers. 'Of course you can.'

Monday 13 January

We are all gathered in the canteen for a briefing. I can smell the croissants the canteen ladies are making for break.

'Morning, everyone!' Mr Goodheart smiles. 'I hope you all had a good weekend. Cold, but good nevertheless. Lots on this week: Year 7 parents' evening on Wednesday, students performing at the Royal Festival Hall on Thursday evening; anyone wanting to go should speak to Ms Cello. And we have some visiting student teachers on Friday, so expect to have some visits to your lessons.' He looks down at his diary. 'Still no news on Ofsted. We are waiting for the call. So be ready. I hope many of you have been able to take advantage of Ms Expert, who is with us for two weeks. She's a fantastic source of ideas for improving engagement and behaviour. So use her while you can.' Ms Sensible approaches Mr Goodheart from behind and whispers something to him. He continues. 'Finally, some news for you on the Cavalier–Furious incident from last term. Cavalier will *not* be returning to the school. Furious is back in school today.'

The news sends a tremor through the staff. There are whispers everywhere. I turn to Hadenough and catch his eye. There's a defeated expression on his face. I'm only just taking it on board. 'Furious is back today? How can I just be finding that out now?'

Hadenough blows a stream of air out through his teeth. 'That means I have him first period. Ugh.'

At the end of the briefing, Ms Sensible approaches. 'Furious will meet you at the office to get his report. Then he will see you at the end of the day. Things are to return to normal.'

There's nothing I can do. 'OK . . . thanks,' I say.

As I run in the direction of the office in search of the little urchin, I'm baffled by the injustice of it all. Poor Cavalier. As Wholesome said, he had no choice. I'm so angry at Furious I have to pause so as to calm down before I reach the office. I need to be supportive of him. I need to love this boy, whatever he's done. I need to help him: that's my job, after all. I need to help him change his life.

I spot Furious through the glass door chewing on some gum, tie hanging down and shirt untucked. For the first time, the sight of him actually makes me feel ill. Does he know what he's done?

Tuesday 14 January

Furious has been back less than two days and already there's been an incident. He had Wholesome up against a wall at breaktime today. It was over Beautiful. And today it was confirmed to the kids that Cavalier would not be returning. I can only imagine how they all must feel. So I asked Mr Inevitable, Furious's foster father, to come in after school to discuss how to make a success of Furious. I couldn't bear the idea of ringing Ms Desperate, having promised her that we would fix Furious and having so far failed miserably.

Mr Inevitable isn't due for half an hour and I'm hungry so I go in search of a Kit-Kat. As I'm walking down the high street, I see Furious and Mr Inevitable outside a chicken shop. Furious is holding on to his box of chicken and chips and looks terrified. Foster dad is shouting. As I walk towards them, their conversation gets more and more heated. When I arrive, they're standing rigidly, as if they're about to fight, their noses practically pressed against each other.

'I'm gonna fucking knock your block off,' shouts Mr Inevitable.

Furious says not a word. His dad continues shouting at Furious even though I am now standing right next to him. 'You're such a fucking fool. You've got everything! We've done everything you could possibly ever have asked for, you've got everything you want! I'm gonna kill you, you understand? There's nothing more we can do for you. You just don't care! You were nearly out last term after that fight but, by God's mercy, they've let you back in – and already you're looking for more trouble. Would you behave like that if *I* were here? Eh? Would ya? Would ya?' Furious shakes his head in fear. 'Yeah, too fucking right! 'Cause I'd knock your fucking block off!'

The whole time, I'm shifting back and forth from leg to leg, wincing at every swear word that is being bellowed for all and sundry to hear. 'Sir. Please, Sir,' I stammer. 'Please, Mr Inevitable, I mean, I know you're angry, but . . .'

Suddenly I spot Munchkin walking towards us, heading to the chicken shop. I shut my eyes, as if, somehow, doing so will make him disappear.

Munchkin grins. 'Hi, Miss!'

'Hi, Munchkin! You getting some chicken?' He nods and disappears into the shop.

Furious's foster dad turns to his son. 'You think you're coming back here tomorrow, do ya? Well, you've got another think coming. You're a fucking pain in the ass. We're gonna send you away. That's it. You're not coming back here.'

Send Furious away? Does he mean put him back into care? What does he mean?

'Well, Mr Inevitable –' I hesitate. 'We could give Furious one more chance. The plan is for us to put him on a Pastoral Support Plan.'

'*What?* Doesn't that mean you're about to exclude him?'

I wince. 'Well, it's what we do to support children who are really struggling. But yes, if Furious fails it, then he could be in danger of exclusion.'

Inside, I'm thinking I'm not sure if it would ever happen. It is just so difficult to get a kid excluded. They need to burn the school down before you can get them out. Mr Inevitable looks horrified. He looks at Furious.

'Do you see what you're doing? Look at what we've done for you! We've given you everything! Why are you doing this to us?' He's shouting, shaking his head. 'That's it. I'm going to send you to your nan's. That's it. You're fucking well out of here!'

He turns to me. 'Ms Snuffleupagus, I'm pulling Furious out of school. I'll send him to my wife's mother. He needs a firm hand and I've fucking well had enough!'

My heart goes out to Furious, as he stands there looking like a scared little boy. Mr Inevitable points down the road, still screaming. 'Go to the fucking car!'

Furious turns to me, nearly in tears. 'Goodbye, Miss.' And starts to head down the street.

I start to panic. He's telling me *goodbye*? 'Well, Mr Inevitable, hang on a minute. You're angry at the moment. It would be best if we made these decisions when things weren't so heated. Let's give him one more chance, and if he messes up just once, then you send him where you want.'

He marches down the road and grabs hold of Furious, pulling him back towards me. He points his finger in Furious's face and shouts, 'You see that? You are such a fucking idiot! You come home and tell me all these lies and tell me how you think *she* hates you, how *she* picks on you, how *she* lies about you.' He points at me. 'And here is this woman out here begging for you. And you know why? You know why she's begging? 'Cause she fucking believes in you, that's why!' He turns to me. 'I have to go, Ms Snuffleupagus. I'm sorry. I'm just so angry. I have to go.' And he stamps off down the road with Furious in tow, leaving me standing there, not quite sure if what I have just witnessed is real or something from a Hollywood film. I turn around to head towards the corner shop to get that Kit-Kat.

Believe in him? Yes. Believe in my job? Yes. Believe that we can make a difference? Yes. Believe nothing. Believe everything. Believe in it all. If I didn't believe, I'd never survive.

'That's half the class. Where's the coursework from the rest of you?' I look around the room at my GCSE halfwits and can't contain my frustration. 'How on earth do you expect to get this GCSE if you don't do as I say? Today is the deadline.'

Dreamer laughs. 'Yeah, yeah, Miss, we know.'

'Well, if you know, then why haven't you handed me your coursework?'

'Oh, come on, Miss. We came in at the beginning of the Christmas holidays to do work for you, and you turned up late, remember? Isn't that enough?' shouts Dopey. There's a ripple of agreement from Dreamer, Beautiful, Seething and Deranged, among others.

'No! That was so you could catch up on your first piece of coursework; now, this is your second piece. And today is the deadline.' I don't try to hide my annoyance. 'You all know I'm here till 7 p.m. every day. Why don't you just stay behind one day and finish it? It is beyond me why you *choose* to fail like this.'

Dreamer nods in my direction, looking cute, trying to charm his way out of this. 'Oh, come on, Miss.'

'No!' I shout. 'It isn't good enough: today is the deadline.'

Dreamer smirks. 'Oh come on, Miss . . . when's the deadline?'

My eyebrows draw together. 'What do you mean, when is the deadline? The deadline is *today*.'

Dreamer shakes his head. 'Nah, nah, Miss, not that deadline. When's the *real* deadline?'

'What *real* deadline?' I feign confusion. 'I told you, *today* is the deadline.'

I know I'm lying. Dreamer knows I'm lying. In fact, the whole bloody class knows I'm lying. Everyone knows that they could give me the coursework any time up until April, quite frankly, and I'd accept it. Why? Because my results are not their results, they are *my* results, they are *our* results. Dreamer can get a 'C' grade or more. I'd have to be mad to let him fail. Not only would it affect my own results (and possible promotion and pay), but it would affect my school's overall results too. The public would consider us to be a bad school. And then we would become one.

'Dreamer, come *on*. You're driving me crazy. Remember the little engine! We have to climb that mountain.'

'Yeah, yeah, Miss. Stupid engine, man. I'll give it to you on Monday, OK? Now you *know* that I work for you!'

I grin. 'Yes, yes, Dreamer. Monday it will have to be.'

Somewhere inside me, while I hate this system, upon hearing this, all I can feel is relief and gratitude.

Thursday 16 January

I'm listening to a radio programme on gun crime with some of my Year 8s: Munchkin, Fifty, red-headed Adorable, quiet Polish and Cent. David Cameron is speaking on the radio, and one of them says, 'David Cameron!'

Fifty has seven brothers and sisters, a mother who cannot cope and a father who we, at school, have never met. He bangs on the desk. 'He's a neek! What's he know 'bout gun crime? He's just a rich white bwoy.'

'Yeah,' replies Munchkin. 'Yeah, gettin' a gun is easy, man. Just go round the corner and get one.'

Inside, I'm thinking, Munchkin knows where to get a *gun*? Why is Munchkin speaking like that?

'What you talkin' 'bout, man?' shouts Fifty. 'The guns are comin' from the government G!'

'True, true.' Cent nods. I ask what he means. 'Look, Miss, there is about fifteen thousand police in London, and five thousand of police are dodgy. They want a bit of extra dodge, right?' They all laugh.

'But why would you boys need a gun?' I ask naively.

'Miss' – Fifty rolls his eyes – 'if you're on the clip . . .' I frown to show that I don't understand. 'Yeah, I mean, if you're beefin' someone . . .' I frown again. 'Man, if your crew has a problem, then this crew kills that crew . . . yeah?' I nod, to show understanding and he continues, 'Some people are mad, and to test their gun they shoot themself in the foot.'

'Yes, but you boys have never seen a *real* gun, have you?' Fifty looks away. He's not admitting anything. Cent is more excitable, and leans forward.

'Yeah, Miss, I was at a party once and some boys were chattin' rubbish at us, and so one of this crew went to his car, got his gun and shot into the air to scare 'em.'

Fifty joins in. 'Yeah, man, you gotta watch the quiet ones. If they've got a lot of mouth, you're OK, they just shout, but if they go away and say they're comin' back in a minute, that's when you know you gotta run, cause they're gonna get their gun.' Munchkin is sitting quietly, listening. Adorable and Polish are sat in silence, entirely out of the loop. Fifty cocks his head. 'My friend got stabbed last week in the chest and then my other friend in the arm. 'Cause he tried to rob someone.'

I must look shocked. 'Well, you boys shouldn't be robbing people.'

'Yeah, Miss, they shouldn't. Sometimes they just pop old people 'cause it's easier,' says Munchkin.

I persevere. 'But boys, you mustn't get yourselves involved with these people.'

They remind me that one of their friends in another class at our school is a cousin of one of the headline boys who was shot at the beginning of the year. Fifty informs me that his own cousin has just been 'done' for another one of those murdered boys. Then he explains to me that his cousin has killed 'plenty' but this is the first time he's been caught.

'So how do we stop this?' I ask.

'You can't stop 'em, Miss . . . You can seize as much guns as you want but they'll always find more,' says Fifty.

Cent, who is *twelve years old*, jumps up. 'That's why you have to live every day like it's your last, 'cause you can't be promised tomorrow.'

I'm beginning to wonder whether I'm in a film rather than a

classroom or whether Cent has just been watching too many of them. So I object, but the group starts to yell.

'You can get shot just for looking at someone the wrong way, you know. Or for being in the wrong place at the wrong time.'

Suddenly my speeches about ensuring they get good qualifications, go to university and get a decent job seem silly and naive. Some of these kids don't think they'll live that long. If you genuinely believe you won't make it to twenty-one, what's the point of working for your GCSEs?

The bell goes. Munchkin smiles. I stand at the door as the boys pile out. I smile too. 'See you tomorrow.' They look over their shoulders at me.

'Yeah, Miss. See you tomorrow,' says Munchkin.

'Yes, boys. See you tomorrow . . .'

I just hope I do.

Friday 17 January

Mr Sporty is talking to Wholesome just outside the gym. As I approach, Wholesome heads in to get changed for a basketball match.

'Hey, Sir, great kid, eh?' I say.

'Oh yeah. You're looking at the next Michael Jordan there.'

'Yeah, yeah, I know. But you'll have to wait till he goes to Oxford and gets that degree in English.'

'A degree in English?' The head of PE furrows his brow.

'Well, I think that's what he wants to do. I'm trying to get him to consider applying to Oxford or Cambridge. He stands a good chance.'

Mr Sporty doesn't seem impressed. 'Yeah, well, Oxford isn't the be all and end all.'

I pause. 'Well, no, but it is the *best*. And we want Wholesome to have the best, don't we?'

'True, Ms Snuffleupagus, but then Wholesome might not want to go to Oxford or Cambridge. He could go to Loughborough

University and study sports science – you need three "A"s at A level for that – and that would be just as good.'

Now it's me that's knitting my brow. 'Hmm, yes, I see what you mean. But Oxford is Oxford . . .'

Mr Sporty is getting irritated. 'No, I don't agree with that. As I say, he'd need three "A"s to get to do sports science at Loughborough. It's the same thing.' He starts to bounce his basketball.

'But Oxbridge houses the people who not only read the books but write them too. Wouldn't it be incredible for Wholesome to be taught by those people? Not to mention the doors it would open for him in terms of contacts when he gets out . . .'

Mr Sporty puts on a plastic grin. 'Anyway, Miss, I have to get the boys ready for the match now.'

'Yes, let's hope it goes well!' I hurry off towards my office. What kind of madness –? Argghh! When I reach my office I slam my papers on to my desk. I'm so angry I could cry. Wholesome already has it hard enough. Then he has idiots like us for teachers who can't see the wood for the trees. I want to burst into tears.

Saturday 18 January

Let Down is seventeen years old, white, tall, with longish brown hair. He's in Year 12 doing his A levels. I taught him when he was twelve, in Year 7, when he'd just arrived at secondary school. He was tiny then, bright and interested, and a pleasure to teach. Having now escaped the madness of Years 7 through to 11, Let Down is able to breathe again. Children in our other 'top set' got lucky and, by chance, their class was calm and orderly. Their thinking skills were able to grow. Let Down, however, sat for five years in classes where paper aeroplanes flew across the room and the teachers struggled to teach, which encouraged Let Down to become lazy and lose his interest in thinking.

Now, out of that environment, Let Down's old ambitions and desires have returned. He gets up early on a Saturday morning and drags himself into school for the extra Oxbridge prep class which prepares prospective candidates for the various entrance tests in October. As I'm in school working, as usual, I take a break and decide to sit in on the class. Ms Joyful is teaching an Oxbridge prep class in maths. I notice Stoic is also there. When the lesson is over, I say hello to him.

'Stoic, what are you doing here? I didn't know you did maths. History and *maths*?'

Ms Joyful beams, stepping forward. 'But that's Stoic for you, Miss, always full of surprises.'

Stoic blushes. 'Yes, Miss. I love maths! I like history even more, and that's what I'll do at university, but it doesn't mean I don't want to do well at maths.'

'That's incredible, Stoic,' I say. 'Really impressive.' I look at Ms Joyful and raise my eyebrows.

'Of course, he's leaps ahead of everyone else here. I kind of use him as my teaching assistant. He's just so good.'

With all the other kids now gone, Stoic starts to back out, a little embarrassed. 'Anyway, Miss, I have to go – my dad wants me home to help make lunch.'

We wave goodbye to him and sit down at the kids' desks for a chat. 'So how is it all going?' I ask. 'How is Let Down doing?'

'I have huge respect for him, coming into school on a Saturday' – she shakes her head – 'but he has no chance.'

'Really?' I can't hide my disappointment. 'Can't he catch up?'

'No, sadly. He's a perfect example of what happens if a student's thinking isn't allowed to develop in those crucial first years. The difference between him and the others – well, there's no comparison.'

I wince. 'Yeah, but can't he just do some extra work at home to make up for the lost years?'

Ms Joyful couldn't look more doubtful. 'Look, take Stoic for instance. He's up here' – she holds her hand way up – 'and Let Down is down here.' She holds her other hand down to the floor. 'His thinking skills simply aren't where they need to be for Oxbridge entrance. He can't make up for five years of brain stagnation in a matter of months.'

I have to agree. 'Yeah, you're right. In fact, I'm not sure you can make up those vital teenage years over a lifetime.' I pause. 'People always think that intelligence is something you're born with, and that you hold on to it for a lifetime and can be judged by it later. But, in fact, being intelligent is like being tall.'

Ms Joyful nods furiously. 'Exactly. You can't become tall if you have short genes. But if you're born with the capacity for height, you have to eat to grow. Don't eat, and you won't grow tall.'

'And if you don't force your brain to do somersaults by analysing why the sky is blue and learning how to conjugate French verbs, you stunt your intelligence.'

Ms Joyful winks. 'Yeah, exactly.'

Let Down could have been somebody. As it is, he'll go to some middle-of-the-road university. He won't end up a criminal, so it isn't a complete disaster. He'll be OK. He'll be, as Liberal always says of our future kids, *fine*. But I know the thing that bothers me is that he'll never be what he could have been. Had he been in another classroom, he could have been a contender.

Tuesday 21 January

It's my father's birthday today. When we were kids, my sister and I would often spend the weekend helping our father with chores in the garden, gathering leaves off the driveway and so on. One day, when I was about eight or nine, as he swept by the side of the house, he managed to scrape his knuckles against the rough edge of the stucco.

As I looked on in horror at the blood oozing from his hand, my father explained that I needn't worry as I had someone to tell me what to do and what not to do, so I would always be safe. He said I was lucky to have someone who could advise me on the right paths to take in life. His words must have had some impact. After all, I still remember them now.

I remember how my sister and I loved certain television programmes. I especially liked *Diff'rent Strokes*. Why? Because my dad loved it. And whenever it came on, my sister and I would shout for my dad to come downstairs and watch it with us. He always did. I wonder what my kids do for fun with their families? Can they play on their PSPs with their dads? Do they ever spend family time together? My guess is no.

The state can force dads to pay for their kids, but it can't force them to love their kids or spend quality time with them. And that's what some of my kids are missing: someone to advise them, to gather leaves with, to work hard for. They're missing a father like mine.

Wednesday 22 January

I rush towards what we call the 'spy room'. It's a room attached to a classroom from which one can see right inside the class and do an observation without being seen. I'm about to observe our trainee teacher Bushytail, as I promised last term. I let myself into the spy room, turn on the system so that I can hear what's going on in the classroom and look through the mirrored glass.

I cannot believe what I'm seeing. It looks like my Year 8 class, but it's as if their bodies have been possessed by demons. Bushytail is standing at the front of the class talking. I look around the room. Munchkin, Fifty, Cent and several others are behaving as if Bushytail isn't there. They're chatting away, laughing, pushing each other, banging the desks. Only Polish and Adorable are quietly waiting at their desks, looking in earnest at Mr Bushytail, waiting for him to take control of the class. They wait. I wait. We all wait. But the control never comes.

There is so much noise in the room, I wonder how he can hear himself think. Bushytail keeps stopping, trying to get silence, but he can't ever quite get it, and as soon as he starts talking, the noise increases rapidly. Eventually, Bushytail sets them off on a task. They're meant to be working in pairs. But this just gives them the opportunity to chat about everything and anything but the work they're meant to be doing. Then Bushytail puts them in teams and representatives come to the board to get points for their team. It's chaos; the kids are screaming. I have to wonder whether any learning is taking place at all.

After thirty minutes, I leave the room, knowing that I already have so much to feed back to Bushytail there is no point in gathering even more to beat him over the head with. Poor guy. How do people keep doing this job when that is what they experience, in some cases, for much of the day, *every day*?

What's worse, we all believe it's Bushytail's fault. Just because it's *possible* for a few teachers to control the students it doesn't mean it's *reasonable* to expect the nearly impossible from everyone.

Thursday 23 January

We've invited an organization that deals with 'young fathers' into school to give the kids some advice. They're handing out free calendars.

'Beautiful, let me see that calendar.' She hands it to me, and I flip through. 'What are you doing with this anyway?'

Beautiful hunches her shoulders. 'They was handing them out for free, Miss. What do you expect?'

I take the calendar straight to the head's office. 'Mr Goodheart, a moment?'

'Yes, of course, Ms Snuffleupagus.' He looks up from his desk and I put the calendar in front of him.

'Perhaps I'm too conservative. I don't know. But this thing that I just took off Beautiful . . . it's disgusting.' I begin to thumb through the pages, pointing out various photos. 'How can we be handing things like this out?'

He takes his time looking through. To his credit, he doesn't need me to point out that most of the pictures are of young black men. He doesn't need me to point out that there are hardly any women featured in this calendar. This calendar has twelve photos, all featuring a young man and his child. Some of these 'men' are so young they look like children themselves. Two of the photos feature white men and, of these two photos, one of them features a white woman.

'Where are the women?' I demand. 'I mean, where are the families? Where are the thirty-year-old mums and dads holding hands in the park, pushing the pram?'

The head begins to read some of the quotes on the photos, meant to be from the fathers: 'This is what life is all about'; 'It's changed my life'; 'He's given me joy'; 'Being a dad is like a blessing.'

At eighteen?

'It's outrageous! What are we saying to our students if we're giving them this nonsense? What makes this organization think that such a calendar will make young fathers stick around? There aren't many eighteen-year-old boys who'll want to give up clubbing and their independence to raise a child. We need to discourage them from having children in the first place.'

'Yes, yes, I quite agree. Had we known about this, we wouldn't have had them in.'

I storm down the corridor and run into Munchkin, who's sitting outside his maths lesson. 'Munchkin! Sent out *again*?' He's silent. 'Munchkin, what's going on with you?' But he just looks at the ground and says nothing.

Friday 24 January

Two weeks in, and Furious has already lost his PSP report. Mr Inevitable eventually calmed down after the chicken-shop incident and Furious returned to school the following day. So he turns up at my office for detention, saying goodbye to Dopey and Dreamer as he walks in. His usual sulky, sullen face is now at my door. I greet him with a smile. He drags a chair from outside my office and sits opposite my desk. How very strange, I think. 'It's OK, Furious, you don't have to sit here. I'll put you in one of the classrooms, over there.'

He shakes his head and mutters something about wanting to sit there. So I sit at my desk, not sure what I should do. Do I get on with my work while he sits watching me? Furious rarely talks, especially when he's on his own, so I can't really have a conversation with him. Or so I thought. 'So how come Cavalier has been permanently excluded?' he ventures.

'Well, you know what happened. He brought a weapon into school. That's pretty bad.' Furious nods. He looks almost guilty. 'The thing is, Furious, we don't want to permanently exclude him, or any of you for that matter. But Cavalier made the wrong decision that day and he had to be punished for it, if only to show the rest of you that weapons at school are unacceptable. I know that all of you think that we want you out, but it isn't true.'

Furious's eyes flare wide. 'No, Miss, I don' think that. I always wonder why I'm *not* permanently excluded. I've been in tons of trouble and I've only ever been sent home a day at a time, once for three days. And then twenty days for the fight with Cavalier.'

Ah, so even the kids can't understand why we're so soft with them. Furious goes on to explain that he's shocked by the behaviour of his class, especially now, as they're coming close to their exams, and that he knows he is partly responsible. He seems to be begging me to help them all behave. I look him straight in the eye.

'But Furious, can't you see how what you did to Cavalier has got him kicked out of school? Don't you see what you've done?' He looks down, but I can see his head move in acknowledgement that what I say is true. 'The things we do have an impact on other people, you know.' My head is in my hands. 'Cavalier . . . Jesus, Furious, why didn't you *think*?'

Furious shakes his head, his gaze still focusing on the floor. 'I dunno, Miss,' he mutters. 'I dunno.'

Saturday 25 January

The concept of judging schools by their results is now so deeply rooted in our society that ordinary people no longer question it. Choice is the name of the game, and league tables inform this choice. But what exactly do league tables tell the parent?

The higher the percentage of 'A*'–'C' grades at GCSE, the more selective a school is. It's a mistake to believe that only grammar schools and private schools are selective. Most state schools are selective in some way. Only very few are not, and those are the 'dump schools', which no child or parent would actively choose – schools right at the bottom of the league tables. Laws are bent and broken ad infinitum. Any school that wants to do well in the league tables *must* select if they are to stand a chance. The overarching reason results go up or down is because of a change in the school's intake.

So what is the number-one thing league tables tell parents? That 'better' schools have 'better' children. And in the same way that parents who choose the private sector protect their children from the bad influence of the wayward working class so do the parents who choose the 'better' comprehensives for their children. They make a sacrifice, yes (not to mention saving some 10–15 grand a year), but, unlike Ms Alternative, who chooses to send her child to a failing school, thereby making a *true* sacrifice and holding on to her principles, these parents send their child to a 'good' comprehensive and retain some of that same protection which the private-school children enjoy. Hypocrites they may be. Stupid they are not.

When parents search for a *good* school for their child, what they want is a school which will keep their child away from as many challenging children as possible. They just never say so. So they move out of London when their children hit secondary-school age. They want a school where their child will never be bullied and will never feel scared. Clearly they don't believe that the teachers who live in the Cotswolds are better teachers than those who live in London. Neither do they believe that the teachers in the private sector are better than those in the state sector. They choose a school not in search of better *teaching*. They choose it in search of better *students*.

We like to pretend that 'better' means better teaching, better teachers, better management, better resources, better discipline, better care. Nonsense. If parents actually cared about such things, they would only ever consider the Value-Added score given to schools, which is virtually ignored by everyone.

And what about the kids? What about their learning? What of any semblance of standards? What of the meaning of true success? Our understanding of learning for the sake of learning is long gone, lost in a sea of tables and corruption. Sure, schools should be judged, but league tables are not the way to do it.

Monday 27 January

Mr Goodheart stands up in the staff room. 'Ofsted . . .' There's a hush in the room. People who were daydreaming, gazing out of the window at the snow, stop and turn to look at the head. People who were drinking their coffees stop and stare. We wait to hear the dreaded words . . . Mr Goodheart smiles. 'Ofsted, you'll all be happy to know, will be at Basic School down the road as of tomorrow. They got the call on Friday.' A murmur of relief ripples through the room. 'But that doesn't mean we're off the hook of course. Please remember, people, we are "on alert" at *all times*. We could get the call any day now.'

Hadenough nudges me. 'I wish they'd just get here. Then it would be over soon. We'd be finished with it.'

'Yeah, I know what you mean,' I whisper. 'The wait is just excruciating.'

Tuesday 28 January

Black kids aren't doing as well as their white counterparts. The reasons are complex. And to do something to redress the balance, I organize a trip to the cinema to see the film *Coach Carter*, starring Samuel Jackson. It is perfect. It should explain to the kids why we teachers insist on having high standards, that we do it because we care, not because we hate them. I am hoping to inspire them, to make them want to work that little bit harder and make a success of themselves.

It's the first time the school has ever done anything like this before, open to all kids, but it's an event with a 'black theme' and so sixty kids sign up. The plan is to take the tube. Kids without travel cards are to buy their tickets at the station. We are leaving too early in the morning to qualify for free school-journey group travel on the way there. In the station, I gather together the sixty students and five staff and explain that students should buy their tickets at the machines and meet with their group leader before going down to the designated platform. They all nod, and move off in different directions.

Next thing I know, my kids are leaping over the turnstiles in droves. Dopey, Cent . . . I even notice Munchkin allowing Fifty to push in behind him as he goes through the gate. Ms Alternative looks at me and gulps. 'Let's just pretend they aren't with us, Snuffy.'

Mr Hadenough starts to laugh in horror. I don't know what to do. I can't stop them. There is so much noise and chaos I can't possibly get their attention. Not that they would ever listen to me in this frenzied state. They're clearly doing what they do all the time.

I agree with Ms Alternative and we move slowly towards the turnstiles, our heads lowered, trying not to attract attention amongst the chaos. The kids continue to run and jump. London Transport staff are stunned, watching the scene aghast. They're too scared to do anything. I put my ticket through the barrier. The gates open. I walk through.

'Excuse me, Miss,' shouts one of the guards.

Gulp. 'Yes?' I look up, expecting the worst.

'Are these children with you?'

I look around. By now half the kids have disappeared down the escalators. Some have paid, some haven't, and there's no way of distinguishing. 'No. No, they're not,' I lie. Now I'm a criminal too. The other teachers and I rush down to the platform, bundle them on to a tube, and off we go.

Once at the cinema, we teachers try hard to keep them in their seats. We have to stop them from hitting each other, throwing popcorn, yelling, and the rest of it. Suddenly, Seething appears. Because of her deteriorating behaviour at school, she isn't allowed on school trips. So she's come to the cinema on her own, without permission. She hands me £2. 'Sorry I'm late, Miss,' she mutters.

I hesitate. If I throw her out, she'll cause a scene. If I let her stay, she's bound to cause trouble. What do I do? 'OK, Seething. You can stay. But I'm warning you. One false move, and you're out.' She nods and sits down.

Within minutes, a fight has broken out between Seething and Deranged. What the hell is wrong with these two? One minute they're friends, next minute they're arch-enemies. I run over to them and, with the help of Ms Alternative, we separate them. I march Seething outside and the film starts without us.

'That's it, Seething. I warned you. You're out.' I point to some chairs in the foyer. She reluctantly takes a seat. I breathe a sigh of relief and return inside, into the darkness, and stand in the aisle, arms folded over, surveying the kids in an attempt to terrify them into silence.

I've been standing there for about five minutes when Seething pushes open the door and marches back into the room. I turn around. She's heading right for me. My heart beats faster. What's she going to do?

Stand firm, Snuffy. You're in charge here. Don't let her intimidate you.

Seething growls as she strides towards me with intent.

Don't give way, Snuffy. You're the teacher. Remember that.

On reaching me, Seething twists her body to the side and, with her shoulder, she shoves me out of her way. 'You're a fucking crackhead!' she shouts. As I stumble, trying to find my balance in the dark, she takes a seat next to Psycho.

Now what do I do? Call the police? Would they come? Can she even be arrested? I decide to hold fire, count my lucky stars that I'm still alive and decide I will write up all the day's various incidents and hand them over to Mr Cajole.

Later, back at school, having spent an hour writing it, I hand my incident report to Mr Cajole. He reads about the jumping of barriers, the various fights, the unruly behaviour in the streets, the shoving of a teacher, the swearing, the abominable mess in which they left the cinema, and the absolute lack of respect that some of them have displayed for the law and authority. He pats me on the back. 'Sometimes they can be so *irritating*, can't they?' he says.

Wednesday 29 January

Deranged is wearing the wrong shoes for school today. She's in school because Mr Cajole has decided not to punish anyone for their behaviour on the cinema trip. He says it is best to draw a line under it and move on. When I tell Deranged about her shoes, she's angry.

'OK, Deranged, we need to get you into a pair of shoes. If you don't want to wear the pair of shoes you have at home, you can always buy a pair of shoes from the school.'

Management buy in shoes to ensure that those parents who refuse to buy their children shoes have no excuse for sending their children to school in inappropriate footwear.

Deranged shakes her head. 'Nah. I don't want those shoes. My mum says I don't have to wear them.'

'Well, no, your mum is wrong. You do have to wear shoes, Deranged. The office can lend you a pair for the day if you like and you can bring the money in tomorrow.'

She puts her hands on her hips. 'I'm not paying no money for no shoes.'

'Deranged, it's £4. Come on.'

I ring her mother. 'Hello, Ms Loopy, I'm just ringing about Deranged's shoes.'

There's a huge sigh, and then a voice *à la EastEnders* starts to shout. 'You people never give up, do ya? You people! Why don't you just leave her alone? You just pick pick pick!'

'I'm not sure what you mean, Ms Loopy. I am trying to get

Deranged into a pair of shoes which would be suitable for school. We have some shoes here which she could –'

'You keep your shoes, I tell you. Who do you think you are, telling my daughter what she should wear? What kind of a teacher are you?' She's shouting, very loudly. She's highly unpleasant and, if she were standing in front of me, I'd be frightened of her. 'Ms Loopy, I don't want to get into the details of the matter. I just want to get Deranged –'

'Yeah, yeah. Always the same, you lot, always you don't wanna talk about it. Why can't she wear what she wants? Oh yeah, it's the school rules! That's always your answer. What you do to these children! I tell ya, I tell ya, you're crap. You're just crap you are. How can you treat children like this?'

I'm somewhat bemused, confused and disappointed. But I continue. 'Ms Loopy, I assure you I have Deranged's best interests at heart. I want her to understand how to follow rules. In any case, I cannot make an exception for her when all the other children are forced to wear shoes.'

But Ms Loopy isn't listening. 'You know how I feel?' She's still yelling. 'I'm gonna go to a public forum! I'm gonna tell them about your school! I'm gonna *expose* you! I'm gonna tell the newspapers! I'm gonna let them know what you do to these children!'

You're going to tell the newspapers that we insist that children not wear trainers to school?

'Ms Loopy, if Deranged cannot wear shoes to school, I will have to get the deputy, who will most likely send her home. And then she won't be allowed to return until she is wearing a pair of shoes.'

'You do that then, you send her home. And save what you have to say about it all, 'cause I tell you one thing, she ain't ever coming back!'

Click. Down goes the phone. And so the conversation ends. I wish this type of conversation were exceptional. I wish I could say that Ms Loopy is the only parent who I have known to be like that. I wish.

As I send Deranged off home and watch her meandering down

the street, I wonder what her life is going to be like in the future, what kind of life she could possibly ever have with a mother like that. Parents are everything. And poor little Deranged has drawn the short straw.

Thursday 30 January

I'm rushing down the corridor when the head catches up with me and pulls me aside. 'Ms Snuffleupagus, just a moment. It's about Dopey. He's the only child in Year 11 to have been predicted not to get a single pass at GCSE.'

'Yes, well, I mean, he's a lovely boy, but . . .'

'Yes, I know, he isn't very academic. Nevertheless . . .'

My eyebrows shoot up in apprehension and I step back, as if that would help me to read his thoughts. Of the several different statistics used to judge a school, one of them is the percentage of children who manage to get one GCSE. Like every other head in Britain, mine wants 100 per cent.

As I draw back, the head taps my forearm. 'Get me a "C",' he says.

My heart sinks. I don't like to say no to a challenge and neither do I want to let the head down.

Then I see the look on Mr Goodheart's face and capitulate. 'OK, Sir, I'll try.'

Bloody hell. What on earth have I just agreed to?

Friday 31 January

We're looking at persuasive writing techniques, so I put up one of Churchill's speeches on the interactive whiteboard. 'OK,' I say, 'so you can see here how Churchill was trying to persuade his audience that –'

Fifty screws up his face. 'Huh? Whaya say? What's that?'

'What's what? Churchill?' The class looks blankly at me. I put my hands on my hips. 'Come on now, we do know who Churchill was, don't we?' They shake their heads. But this isn't possible. I

137

know they do Hitler to death in history. I know they've been taught this stuff. How do they not know? I reach to the ceiling. 'OK, everyone: Churchill. Think carefully, you've all heard of him, I know you have. He's someone really important. Think.'

Suddenly, a look of comprehension crosses Cent's face. 'I know, Miss. I know.'

'Yes, Cent? Why don't you tell the class?'

Cent smiles proudly as if he's just won a prize. He puffs out his chest. 'He's that dog.'

'*Dog?*'

'Yeah, yeah!' Munchkin claps his hands. 'He's that dog from TV!' The class is a mass of bobbing heads; they've all remembered now. The penny drops in my head. They mean that insurance advert . . .

'No, Churchill wasn't a *dog*. Come on now, I want you to think! I know you know this. Remember what I said: Churchill was a very important man.'

'I know, I know,' Munchkin shouts. 'He's a football manager!'

I groan. 'No. I know I said "important", but I mean "important" in a different way.'

No one has a clue. In the end I tell them. And when I do, no one says, 'Oh yeah'; no one expresses any recognition. It was as if this was the first time in their lives anyone had ever told them about Churchill's existence.

Perhaps it shouldn't matter that they don't know who Churchill is. Perhaps it shouldn't matter that they know nothing at all. But when other children know, when other children understand the world in which they live and mine do not, I have to wonder how fair that is. Does it really matter if they know little black history when they hardly know any history at all?

Sunday 2 February

Liberal, Marx and I are on our way to the cinema. Marx is an old friend of ours from Cambridge. He's white with spiked black hair. I tell them about Seething and her usual defiance. I took her out of her lesson because, when Ms Joyful told her to put her uniform blazer on properly, she did so with extreme annoyance and said, 'For fuck's sake!' in the process. In the end I handed her over to Mr Cajole, the deputy, to be sent home.

Liberal is horrified. 'Snuffy! You think this girl should be sent home for swearing?'

'Yes. Of course I do.'

'Was this the first time she'd done it?' Liberal's jaw hits the ground. Marx, too, is shocked.

'No. But that's not the point. It wouldn't matter if it were. One has to be consistent. She swore. She needs to be punished in a way that shows that this kind of behaviour is totally unacceptable.'

Marx starts to laugh. 'Bloody hell, Snuffy! What's happened to you? Since when did you become this right-wing nut?' He nudges Liberal. 'Hey man! Since when did your girl go over to the other side?'

'Right wing? What are you talking about? The girl swore in front of her teacher!' Marx and Liberal laugh.

I want to go on with the story, in which Mr Cajole tells me that there's a difference between Seething swearing *at* a teacher and her swearing *in front of* him, so he won't be sending her home. But Marx and Liberal are still laughing at me, so instead I pull my coat in around my neck. 'OK, OK,' I say. 'We just have to drop this, because you two are going to make me really angry. What I'm saying is so basic. But you're telling me I'm a right-wing nut because I have standards!' Liberal and Marx keep laughing and I get more and more furious.

'Snuffy, what's happened to you? Where's the lovely leftie girl who used to read theory and talk about bringing down the system? Where's the Snuffy I used to know and love?' teases Marx.

'I'm right here! I'm still that same person. I want that girl punished not for my sake, but for *hers*. Why can't you see that?' By now, I'm shouting. I'm so angry I want to hit both of them. 'What you two don't get is that *you* are the problem. *You* are the people I'm fighting. *You* are the people who keep my kids poor!'

Marx and Liberal look at me, flabbergasted. 'Don't you remember how we used to sit by the river and eat picnics, Snuffy? Remember the photos I showed you? What's happened to you?' says Liberal.

I look at them both. I can feel the tears building up in my eyes. 'Forget it,' I manage.

Liberal puts his arm around me. 'Hey, come on, Snuffs, we still love you.' He steps back, seeing how upset I am. 'OK. Tell us what you're saying.'

'Seething is a mess. She has chaos at home. She needs to find order and structure at school if she's going to survive.'

'And sending her home for a day is giving her structure?'

'I only wish we could do more. But you're right. The problem is that kids like her, well, she gets excluded for a day or two all the time, keeps coming back, just like Furious does, and they keep misbehaving.'

'Isn't there a final punishment?' asks Marx.

I let out a harsh little laugh. 'No, that's just it – no! And they know it.' I look at them both. 'Anyway, forget it. Let's go and enjoy the film.'

Liberal squeezes me, looking at Marx. 'Hey, man, I was showing Snuffy these photos the other day, and *man*! Do you remember those shorts she used to wear? Man! She looked so *hot*!'

Monday 3 February

Dopey, Dreamer and Daring are in detention. We are using this time to do our coursework 'together' because, frankly, if I don't stand over them, they just won't do it. Daring is new to our bottom-set class. He isn't stupid, but he won't behave anywhere else, so now I have the joy of teaching him. He's white, tall and slim and always looks a little scruffy. As they are packing their stuff to go, he smiles. 'You ever straightened your hair, Miss?'

Dreamer and Dopey start yelling. 'Yeah! When we was in Year 8! Don't ya remember?'

Daring shakes his head. 'Nah Miss, man, you should straighten your hair, man.'

'Yes, yes, OK, I'll think about it. Now, the important thing this weekend is that you get that coursework written – '

Daring cuts me off. 'So, Miss, do you straighten your hair for dates?' Dreamer and Dopey exchange a glance, shocked that he'd ask.

I shake my head. 'What a silly thing to ask.'

'I swear, Miss is married, you know,' Dopey leaps about. 'Look at her finger. There's the wedding ring.'

The boys look at my hand and grin. They become shy and all three start dancing around the room. 'Yeah! Yeah! But, like, Miss, yeah, 'cause like school is your life, innit?' says Dreamer.

Dopey pipes up from behind. 'Yeah, 'cause Miss, like, she works all the time.'

They're all muttering in agreement.

'Exactly,' I say pointedly. 'I work all the time for you boys and I expect you to do the same for me.'

Dreamer hangs his head slightly. 'Awwhh, Miss! You know what?'

'What?'

'My life is better than yours.'

'Yes, maybe it is . . . Come on, boys, now get out of here. You have work to do when you get home, you understand?' As they run down the stairs, I notice that the piece of work Daring has given me isn't very long. I chase after them.

'Boys! Boys! Stop!' I wave the sheet of paper in Daring's face. 'You need to add something to this. It isn't long enough.'

'Awwh, Miss! Nah, man, I don't wanna!'

'Well, you have to.'

'OK, Miss, but only if you straighten your hair.'

'Hahahahaha!' Dreamer and Dopey burst into laughter.

I roll up the sheet of paper and bop Daring on the head. 'I am *not* bargaining with you. This is *your* coursework. Get home and do as I said.' I smile. Daring grabs the sheet.

As they run out the school doors, they yell, 'But Miss, man, we have games to play! What you making us do all this work for?'

As I wander back up to my office, knowing that, on this particular evening, work will stop for me at about nine thirty, I figure Dreamer is right in thinking his life is better than mine. But how lovely is it that he knows it, and that somewhere inside him, he is grateful.

Tuesday 4 February

'Miss! Miss!' It is after school and Beautiful comes rushing into my office, with Deranged right behind her.

'What's wrong, girls?' I ask.

They don't say a word, just look at each other. I keep asking, and they keep looking not at me but at each other. 'Anyway, girls, I'm glad you've come to see me, because I've been meaning to talk to you.' I take a deep breath. 'Look, you've only got a few months left with us. You're both really bright girls. I want you to make an effort with your work. Just for these next few months. Then you can do what you like.' They giggle. 'I'm being serious, girls. Look, you've got' – I start counting on my fingers – 'February, March, April and half of May: three months left. You still have time to get those "C" grades.'

'Yeah, yeah, you is right, Miss,' says Deranged.

'Think about what you girls want to do later. Think of a goal. And then find out what qualifications you need to get there.'

'Yeah, yeah, OK.' Deranged moves closer. 'But Beautiful has something else she wants to talk to you about.'

Beautiful sits more upright in her chair. 'My dad says he's gonna ring the school to talk to you.'

'Why would he want to speak to me?'

''Cause he knows . . . like . . . Furious is on report to you. And he thinks maybe something is going on between me and Furious.' Beautiful throws her hands together as if she's begging. 'Please, Miss, please don't tell him! He'll kill him, I swear. He'll kill him!'

'OK, OK, Beautiful. Calm down. Your father, if he phones, is no doubt a reasonable man –'

'No he ain't,' she breaks in, Deranged now standing by her side. 'He'll kill him!'

'Why would he kill Furious?' I ask, naively.

''Cause he knows someone is giving me a hard time.' Deranged strokes Beautiful's arm.

'What's Furious doing to you exactly?'

'Nuffin', Miss. Really, nuffin'. He was angry, that's all.'

'Look, Beautiful, you know that I think this relationship of yours with Furious . . . well, it isn't very healthy.'

Deranged jumps up and down. 'You tell her, Miss. She won't listen to none of us. I keep telling her but she ain't listening.'

Beautiful tucks her hair behind her ear. 'Yeah, yeah, Miss. Look, just sort me out, will ya – when my dad rings?' She starts to back out of my office.

'OK, but just a sec, maybe we should have a chat about Furious –'

'Gotta go, Miss, Furious is waiting outside.' Beautiful's phone starts to ring. 'That's him now,' she says.

Deranged and Beautiful run off down the corridor and I am left wondering what on earth I say to her father if he ever rings. I never signed up for this! When I became a teacher, I didn't think I would be lying to dads about their daughters being beaten up by their boyfriends. Was I just being naive?

Wednesday 5 February

I open the door to my office and Ms Expert walks in, clocking the Kit-Kats on my desk. She's back in school for two days. 'Oh?' She arches an eyebrow and points over at them. 'You gave in to the idea of chocolate for prizes then?'

'No, no. They're for the teachers in my department. For the first ones who get all their coursework in.'

'Oh really, Snuffy? So let me get this straight. You believe in rewarding staff with chocolate, but not the kids?'

I burst out laughing. She's got me. She's really got me. And we haven't even started the meeting! 'Yes, but . . . it's different with them. I don't have a responsibility to the staff to make them into well-functioning human beings. But I do to the kids.'

'You're not very consistent, are you, Snuffy?' she says, but there is a smile on her lips. I return it.

'Well, you'll be glad to know that I've been giving out some Haribo sweets as prizes since we last spoke, and I've been using more games.'

'And? Did it work?'

'Yes. The kids like it. They're more interested in the lesson as a result. They love those Haribos.'

'Oh good, I'm glad. That's what we wanted.'

'Yes,' I say, and thank her. Yes, I guess that's what we wanted.

Thursday 6 February

Parents' evening is, at last, over. Phew! I'm tired, having been working non-stop for nearly thirteen hours (it's after 8 p.m.), and I'm packing my stuff away when a parent approaches my table. Ms Vamp is about thirty years old, a Jamaican light-skinned woman with one of those weaves tied on to her scalp that makes her look as if she has long, blond, streaky hair. She is wearing a ton of make-up and her painted fake nails are at least an inch long. I take off my coat and gloves and sit back down.

Ms Vamp begins aggressively, staring at me as if she's going to thump me. 'So what's the problem with Munchkin, then?'

I'm thrown off balance by her obvious fury, but I launch into an explanation nevertheless. 'Oh, hello there, hmm yes, well, Munchkin is a very nice boy, of course. He isn't disruptive – at least, he isn't with *me*. It's just that he doesn't do much work these days, which is odd. He used to. I'm wondering whether anything might be wrong?'

You might have thought I'd told her that I hated her son. She grimaces and her face becomes the picture of anger. 'Yeah, but you said that he was a *major concern* here on his report.'

As teachers, we have to choose whether the child is 'Excellent', 'Good', 'Some Concern', or 'Major Concern'. And then we write a little note about their progress in the subject. 'Yes, that's right,' I explain. 'He's a nice boy, as I said. But he has not done any homework for me all term. You will have received the letter I sent home recently, yes?' She acknowledges she has. 'Yes, so you see, he doesn't do his homework and, in the last couple of weeks or so, he hasn't been doing any work in lessons either. Sometimes he puts his head down on the desk and goes to sleep.'

Her eyes shoot heavenwards and she grabs his report, rips it open and points one very long and ornate fingernail at one of the lines. Munchkin, who is sitting next to her, hangs his head and rests it in his hands, as if to suggest he is embarrassed by his mother's behaviour. I look at the report, wondering if maybe I've written something inaccurate.

'Yeah, yeah, but you said here that sometimes you can't even get him to pick up his pen in lessons. Why you saying he's a *major concern*?'

I pause. Is that a trick question? 'Yes, exactly. I can't get him to pick up his pen. That's why he's a major concern.' She bats her long eyelashes at me. 'Don't you think that would make him a major concern?' I ask tentatively. Clearly not. 'It's that Munchkin is a major concern *academically*,' I finally say. 'He has great potential to do really well, and he isn't achieving that potential. He isn't doing well *academically*.'

'Oh, *academics*! Oh, I see what you mean.' Her face relaxes. 'Yeah, yeah, I suppose that makes sense. He isn't doing well with the *academics*.' She pronounces the word 'academics' as if it is something precious and new.

Thank goodness for that. She isn't going to hit me. I sink back in my chair with relief. No wonder teachers often avoid giving children bad reports. Sometimes you have to consider whether giving them a 'Major Concern' is worth the 'Major Headache' that necessarily comes with the bravery of telling a parent the truth.

Later, as Ms Vamp is leaving, I happen to be standing by the front door. I hold my hand out. 'Goodnight,' I say.

She takes my hand and shakes it. 'Thanks for your help with Munchkin.' She looks down at him. 'One good thing, though, is that he's not being picked on any more . . . no one's stealing his stuff any more.'

'That's great,' I squeak.

My eyes follow them as they wander out through the car park. Munchkin turns around to look at me. I wave. I whisper under my breath, 'Goodbye, Munchkin.'

Friday 7 February

I'm standing in front of staff from various schools at a training event talking about diversity and black underachievement. I talk about Stoic, who is in Year 13, and Wholesome, who is in Year 10, both Oxbridge candidates, hard-working, polite and proud young black men. I even interviewed them beforehand and play a recording of them explaining why and how they have made themselves into successes.

A black woman in her forties, a mentor in one of the local schools, puts up her hand. 'It's because black history isn't taught in schools,' she says. There's a chorus of agreement from the rest of the audience.

I can't help but think that knowing lots of black history isn't something that either Wholesome or Stoic ever mentioned as a reason for their success. 'Yes, but of course that isn't exactly the case. You'll find that there is some black history taught in most schools.'

'Yes, but it's hardly anything. I mean, there's black history month, but what's that?'

It's one whole month out of ten school months, actually. That's a hell of a lot. And schools don't just teach black history in October. But I don't want to anger her or the crowd so I smile and say I'll come back to this.

Later in my talk, I say that it's important that we think about the real reasons for black underachievement and not pretend that it's something that it's not. I motion to the woman who spoke earlier. 'While the point about black history is an interesting one and may have some truth to it, we should consider the fact that we don't teach any Indian or Chinese history whatsoever in schools. There is no Chinese month, nor is there an Indian month and yet both of these communities out-perform their white counterparts.' As the words come out of my mouth, a number of the black staff (most of whom are mentors, not teachers, so have no idea how difficult it is to control a class) look at each other and grimace, annoyed and dissatisfied with what I've just said.

Some time later, while we're talking about something entirely different, the same woman shouts out: 'I still say the lack of black-history teaching is the cause.'

Sometimes it feels as if some people are simply not interested in the truth.

Saturday 8 February

Heading down St Martin's Lane to see a play, gloves and scarves on, Liberal and I run into an old friend from university, Typical. He tells us that he's a solicitor for a corporate firm in the City. Typical is white, tall and good-looking. Liberal and Typical used to be great friends. Liberal grins. 'It's great to see you, man!' They grab each other by the hand and hug.

'Yeah, yeah, you too. Cambridge was so long ago. So what are you two doing these days? I see you're married now.'

'Yeah, well, I'm working at the Tate – you know me and my art . . .'

'The Tate? Really? Wow, that's impressive, man. Really fantastic.' He takes back Liberal's hand and squeezes it. 'Gotta hand it to you, bro': you said you'd do it and you did it!'

Liberal blushes slightly. 'Oh, it isn't such a big deal.'

'You kiddin', mate? The Tate?!' Typical looks over at me. 'And what about you, Snuffy? What are you up to?'

'I'm a teacher.' Typical looks blank. I think he's wondering whether or not I'm joking and whether it would therefore be appropriate to laugh at this moment. I try to fill the awkward silence. 'Yes, yes, I know, seems kind of crazy, but that's what I do. I teach.'

Typical takes a step backwards. 'Wow. That's uh, well, that's um . . . very interesting . . .'

He looks shell-shocked. Snuffy is a failure and Typical is so embarrassed he doesn't know what to say. Liberal knows it and pulls me towards him. 'Snuffy works all the hours God sends, you know. You wouldn't believe how difficult her job is . . .'

'Yeah, yeah, sure. But if you wanna know about long hours, you should try my job.' He laughs. ''Course, for what they're paying me, I should bloody well hope I work hard!'

Liberal looks at his watch. 'Mate, we gotta go . . . theatre tickets, you know?'

'Yeah man, 'course.' He shakes Liberal's hand. 'Great to see you both.'

'Yes, Typical,' I answer. 'It was good to see you too.' I kiss him on both cheeks and hope we never run into him again.

Monday 10 February

'I'm sorry, Stoic. I'm sorry about the Oxford thing.'

Stoic smiles. 'That's all right, Miss. I'm OK about it now. I mean, at the time, I was really upset, because I worked so hard for it, but it's OK. I'll be fine.'

Now it's my turn to smile. 'Yes, of course you'll be fine. That's the kind of person you are. But have you thought about taking a gap year and applying again?'

'Well, yes, but I don't want to. I don't want to take a gap year. I want to go to university. And what if they were to reject me again? I don't think I'd like that.'

'Well, yes, they could reject you of course. It's all such a lottery. No one can possibly predict. But often people get in that way. If you'd applied to a different college, if it had been a different year, you could very well have got in.'

Stoic makes a face. 'Hmmm . . . yes, but if they reject me, then I'll have taken a year for nothing and, well, I'm not sure I really want to be there anyway. When I went for interview, it felt so alien, and I'm not sure I would be happy there.'

Stoic and I talk for some time. I keep looking at my watch, aware of how much work awaits me on my desk, but I'm stuck on the chair, unable to abandon the conversation. As we talk, it becomes increasingly clear that Stoic believes without question that he will be rejected again. He explains how he 'knew' he would be rejected this time, so why would it be any different next year?

'But I promise you, Stoic, people do it all the time.' I pause. 'I haven't had this conversation with anyone else, you know. I haven't spoken to any of the other students who applied and were rejected. I'm speaking to you because I think if you apply again you have a real chance of getting a place.'

'But why would they take *me*? Who am I?'

'Who are you?' He nods. 'I have been teaching for years. So have all of your teachers. And in all of our years, with all of our experience, you are one of the best students we have ever known.' Stoic looks at me, incredulous. 'We all talk about you. Even the teachers who don't know you. You're our head boy. You're amazing. If the name Stoic is mentioned, the teachers always say, "Oh yes, that Stoic, isn't he superb?" And it's true. I'm talking to you about this because, if you want to go for it again, you should – because I think you stand a real chance.'

Stoic bows his head, blushing. 'Well, thank you, Miss. That's very kind of you. I mean, it was really nice . . . when I was rejected, the teachers emailing me saying how upset they were for me.'

'That's because we know you should have got in. You're incredible. You just don't know it.' Stoic shakes his head, and my back stiffens. 'Look . . . do you know what private schools are really good at doing? They're really good at building confidence in their students. And we haven't done that with you. The thing that strikes me in talking to you is that it's rejection that scares you the most, because you think it means there is something wrong with you. And you're wrong. But somehow you don't realize that. And you know what? That's our fault. We haven't taught you to believe in yourself. If anyone is to blame for this, we are.'

'Oh no, Miss –'

I tap the table. 'No! Listen to me.' My voice begins to rise. 'I'm telling you, *we* are at fault . . . not because we're bad at our jobs, but because we have so much else to do . . .'

'Hmm, yes, maybe . . . and of course, state schools are filled with teachers who themselves were educated in the state sector, so perhaps they too lack confidence.'

Ouch. OK, go easy: let's not get too carried away. But he kind of has a point.

We talk on, and on, and in the end I leave, not really sure I have achieved much at all. And what chance do I have? Here I am, a state-educated kid myself, trying to persuade another state-educated kid that he is worth something. And how long have I got? About thirty minutes. Those private-school kids have been told they are owed, a hundred different ways, by a hundred different people, over a lifetime. The world owes them a life full of wonderful surprises. What does the world owe Stoic? Or, indeed, what does the world owe me? If I'm perfectly honest, the question has never even crossed my mind.

Tuesday 11 February

I'm making my way to the loo during one of my non-contact periods, when Ms Alternative rushes up to me. 'Snuffy, I need your help,' she gasps. 'My phone, it was stolen earlier today.'

'Oh dear.'

'No, that's not the problem. It's miraculously reappeared at the office.'

'Oh. So who took it?'

'That's just it, I don't know. Can you help me investigate? Apparently Dopey was the one who found it and handed it in.'

'OK, I'll go and find Dopey now and ask him.' I go to Dopey's classroom and ask the teacher, Ms Joyful, if I can talk to him briefly. When he appears at the door, I say, 'Tell me about the phone.'

Dopey starts to back up. 'Nah, Miss, nah, I didn't do nuffin'. I just handed it in. I was with Furious and Dreamer and dat, and me and dem, we found the phone.'

'Yes, but –'

'Miss, man, I tell you! It wasn't us!' Dopey is shaking his head.

'OK, OK . . . go back into your lesson.' It's impossible to get anything out of kids when things get stolen. Some teachers have a real knack for this kind of thing. I don't. I find Ms Alternative and explain that I haven't managed to find out anything. She doesn't seem to care that much. The phone has been returned, and that's all that matters. She smiles at me. 'Thanks for your help, Snuffy. I hate these phones. They're such a disruption in school. You know, my boy's phone got stolen the other day at school.'

'Really? I'm sorry to hear that.' Inside, I'm thinking, of course his phone got stolen – just look at the school you've decided to send him to!

Ms Alternative nods. 'Yeah. He was in tears. It was awful. I've had to get him a more expensive phone to make up for it.' She laughs. 'He's so spoilt!'

As I head off down the corridor, I begin to wonder about that. Is that what some parents do? Do they make bad decisions for their children and then buy them material things to make everyone feel better? Is that why so many kids have wide-screen televisions in their bedrooms, trainers which cost over £100 and several different mobiles? Hmm. I wonder . . .

Thursday 13 February

It's 7 p.m. and I'm outside in the school car park carrying a bunch of work to do when I get home. Hadenough approaches, wheeling his bicycle towards the main gates.

'You're looking pretty beat,' I say.

'Yeah, I'm exhausted. I can barely keep my eyes open.'

I try to cheer him up a bit. 'Don't worry, tomorrow it's over. We'll have a whole week to recover.'

But Hadenough seems genuinely worried. 'It isn't enough. I won't be ready after a week. I won't be able to get through to Easter. I'm dead on my feet.'

'Come on – spend the whole week sleeping. Don't do any work. Just sleep. You'll feel better in a week.'

Hadenough just looks at me. 'I had two weeks off before this half-term, and look at me now. How the hell is one week going to be enough for me to survive until Easter?' He has a point. I don't know what to say. 'Snuffy, every fucking day I have to give detentions. Every fucking day! Every day I have to shout, over and over. They won't listen. They won't fucking do what we say!' I keep quiet, listening. 'It isn't meant to be the norm, it's meant to be the exception. We aren't meant to hand out several detentions every day. All we do is fight these kids. I can't take it any more.'

'I know, I know. It's hard. But you'll feel better once you've slept a little. One more day. You can do this. Think about next week. Think about sleeping in on Saturday. You'll feel human again, you'll see. You'll be OK. Go home. Sleep.'

'Yeah, yeah. Fucking hell.' Hadenough manages a smile. 'Oh yeah, you're off to Jamaica, aren't you? Bloody lucky. Get out of this cold weather. See you tomorrow, then.'

As he cycles off, I wave. Do the people in government know that this is how their teachers feel? Do they know that teachers talk only of survival?

Friday 14 February

My Year 8s are misbehaving, so I pause, as I often do, and explain to them that we are wasting learning time. 'You misbehave, and we fall behind. Don't you get it?' I raise my voice, exasperated. 'You all think that our school is the world or, in fact, that this classroom is the world. But you have no idea what others are learning and achieving in other schools.' They're all quiet, listening to what I say. The competition is fierce out there, I explain.

Adorable agrees. 'Miss is right. My cousin is five years old and, 'cause she goes to a private school, she gets to learn Mandarin.' The class is outraged.

'That's not fair!' shouts Cent. 'Why don't we get to learn Mandarin?'

I twist my mouth to show disapproval. 'But we do have Mandarin lessons at this school.'

Munchkin scrunches up his nose. 'Really? When's that?'

'Mondays after school in room –'

The class cuts me off with lots of laughter and jeering. Munchkin doubles over, almost in pain from it. 'But that's after school!'

Adorable is giggling uncontrollably. Even Polish is shaking her head in wonder at my naivety in thinking they might want to attend an after-school class. Fifty splashes himself across his desk.

I stand up straighter, annoyed. 'But you know that at private schools and perhaps at the one where Adorable's cousin goes, they have lessons at all hours, till 6 p.m. sometimes, and on Saturdays too.' But they aren't interested in this small, forgotten fact. Life is unfair. They are disadvantaged because they go to a state school and so they cannot learn Mandarin.

I look at Fifty and Munchkin, who are sat together. 'Munchkin, Fifty – what about the two of you? Why not try it out tomorrow after school? Chinese . . . you could come back to our lessons and teach the rest of us how to count to ten in Chinese.'

Fifty cocks his head back. 'What's the point of that? The only time I see Chinese people is when I go to buy Chinese food.'

'Innit,' Munchkin says, backing Fifty's point. Fifty and Cent laugh, and I look at Munchkin in wonder at how fast he is changing.

Of course, we have several Chinese children at our school, and two in this class, so I'm slightly confused by the comment, but I continue. 'Yes, but boys, one day you'll do something with your lives, and you don't know what that is.' I look to the whole class.

'That goes for all of you! You might run a business which will require travel to China.' Once again, the whole class explodes into laughter, Munchkin, Fifty and Cent laughing the loudest. 'What? I don't get it. What's so funny?'

'I ain't goin' China. I is goin' *Jamaica*!' Fifty exclaims.

Jamaica, China . . . Why is it that in their worlds, one necessarily cancels out the other?

'Innit!' Munchkin yells, looking towards me. 'You is going to Jamaica for half-term, innit, Miss?'

'Yes, that's right, Munchkin. I leave on Saturday. I'm going to be visiting a couple of schools out there. It'll be very interesting.'

'Where ya goin', Miss?' Fifty asks.

'To Kingston. I'm going to visit my aunts, cousins and my mum and dad.'

The black kids in the class are grinning at me as if to show that they are really proud of me. Fifty leans across his desk. 'Oh yeah, I forgot you is Jamaican, Miss.'

Munchkin is nodding. 'Cool, Miss, cool.'

Cent winks. 'You gonna bring us back something, eh, Miss?'

I laugh. 'Yeah, right! Come on everyone, back to work!'

Half-term

Sweet. Liberal gave me a dozen gold pencils for Valentine's Day so that I could use them as prizes for the kids. Just lovely. Jamaica tomorrow. I can't wait . . .

Tuesday 18 February

It's hot and sunny, and the light suit I've put on seems too heavy on my shoulders. Liberal has gone to the beach and my father has arranged for me to visit one of Jamaica's private schools. I'm trying to look as demure as possible. It is, after all, a girls' boarding school.

The school is out in the countryside, a long drive from the city, surrounded by fields and flowers. The girls wear dresses as their uniform, and straw hats. As I wander about the campus, I realize that I'm the only teacher not wearing a skirt. All the teachers and girls are black. There are four male teachers at the school, and all the teachers live on site. As I move about, the passing girls often call out, 'Good morning!' to me.

The school is not fully staffed. Neither are there many resources. Old blackboards and chalk are what they use. At home, we have interactive whiteboards in every classroom, our computer rooms have flatscreen computers and, if kids ask nicely, they can use the colour printer. We have cameras, video recorders, televisions, laptops even, which we loan out to the kids. In this school, one of the top private schools in the country, there is one room with a few computers. They look like the kind of thing we threw out many years ago.

As I walk about on the tour, I notice that in some classes there is no teacher. The girls explain to me that this sometimes happens, because they are understaffed. In the classes where there is no teacher, one of the brighter girls has been designated 'teacher' for the lesson and stands reading to the rest of the class, who sit quietly.

At some point I sit alone with some of the girls for a chat. I am on a chair and they sit around me on the ground. Some have short hair, some long. Some are lighter skinned, some darker. Some are pretty and some less so. But essentially, the girls all look the same: same perfect uniform; no jewellery or make-up; same boring school shoes.

The place is like a prison, they say. They want to meet boys. They want access to the internet. (It is banned at the school.) They want to see their families. They want more than just fifteen minutes of television a night. They want the lights to go out later than 9 p.m. They want more free time. They think three hours of forced silent private study every day after school is too much. They want fewer punishments. They want the right not to eat dinner if they don't want it. And they hate their headmistress. She's an old Irishwoman whose husband died some time ago. They hate her with a kind of polite venom. Even the good girls in the group cannot stop their feelings from showing on their faces. All they want is to be like everyone else. They want to be like the kids who are at my school. They want to be free.

'What do you think, Mam? What do you think?' they chorus.

Someone from the land of the free has come to tell them how justified they are in their sense of injustice, and they want to bathe in it. I think of Deranged, Seething, Psycho and Beautiful. 'The thing is, girls, while I know things seem tough at the moment, and it is true that, in one sense, my kids have far more freedom than any of you, I actually believe that you are the ones who have the advantage. You are the ones who are truly *free*. You're free to learn, free to grow up into sophisticated, well-spoken young ladies, free to develop critical thinking tools which will serve you well for the rest of your lives. What restricts you now is the very thing that will free you later.'

The girls squirm about, sitting on the floor, listening carefully to what I'm saying, though I worry that it is falling on deaf ears. After all, I'm rejecting everything they've been feeling for years.

'Girls, I know it sounds odd to say, but while you might feel as if you're in prison, actually, you're in paradise.'

The girls stay still. And like nothing I have ever seen before, for the first time in my life, I realize that a bunch of children have listened to me and properly understood what I was saying.

Wednesday 19 February

Having seen the best Jamaica has to offer, I decide I need to see the worst. I too have heard talk of the gang-infested, chaotic schools here. And I cannot wait to see one first hand. Despite protestations from his friends, my father arranges for me to spend a day in Kingston's drug-filled, crime-ridden deep inner city, which houses one of its most troubled schools. I could be killed, they say. Anything could happen to me in this school, they tell Liberal. How irresponsible of both my father and him to allow me to go to such a place. The road where one can find this school is somewhere most of them would never go, not even in the daytime, and if they ever do, their car doors are locked at all times for fear of those who live in the area.

'You will be careful, won't you, babe?' Liberal kisses me on the cheek as I get into a taxi. It's so hot the seat is already burning.

'Don't worry, I'll be fine. You know me.' I wave to him and my father as the beaten-up taxi tears off down the road.

'Be careful, soldier girl,' Liberal calls after me.

I try to wind down the window, but it's broken. Inside, I'm a little afraid. What if this place *is* as bad as they say?

I go round all the classrooms chatting to the children. Everyone is black: children, teachers, workmen. The classrooms have broken blackboards, broken tables and broken chairs. Nothing seems to work. There is dust everywhere and the old stone buildings have not been painted in decades. Not a single computer in sight here, except for the ones in the main office.

Noise comes from the classes in the way that I'm used to when not everyone is on task, and there are pockets of chaos here and there. All of a sudden, I see a child run around the corner into a door, clearly rushing because he doesn't want to get into trouble. It's all very familiar to me.

The children aren't bright like they are at the girls' boarding school. Jamaica has a stringent testing system which streams the children from school to school. Children aim to be in the best school they can be. These children are at the bottom of the ladder. So I cannot have conversations about freedom with them. Instead, we chat about their favourite subjects, and they smile with embarrassment.

When I walk into a classroom, the children stand immediately. 'Good morning, visitor,' they chant, some of them waving with delight. I remember my own children in London, who often laugh at visitors, mocking them as soon as they turn to leave.

I chat to one of the teachers, Ms Jambo, who is in charge of the SEN (Special Educational Needs) children. I ask her what it's like to work at the school. She explains that she has been there for over ten years but that, at first, it took her a while to get used to the difficulties of the inner city. I ask her what she means.

'Well, 80 per cent of the children come from single-parent homes. About 50 per cent rarely see their fathers. Some fifty children have no parents at all, and as the state doesn't look after them as we do here at our school, well . . .'

The stats are far worse than those of any school I have ever worked in, or indeed even *exists* in England. I'm blown away. The school doesn't feel like a madhouse. In fact, the children generally seem well behaved.

Ms Jambo explains that the children's family situation has a negative effect on their behaviour and that sometimes they can be very rude.

So I ask her to tell me about a time when a child did something really bad. She takes a deep breath, and I pull my chair closer to her desk, waiting to hear the delectable details. 'Well,' she starts, pausing as if to catch her breath, 'once I told a boy to sit down, and –'

I lean in closer. 'And what?' I ask, waiting for the gore. She whispers, 'He said he didn't want to sit down.' Her eyes are enormous as she sits back, satisfied that she has shocked me to the core.

'What's it like at your school in inner-city London?' Ms Jambo asks.

'Much the same,' I lie, smiling.

Spring Term Part Two

I'm standing in the canteen at break today, all refreshed from my week away on the beach in Jamaica but hiding from the cold outside, when Seething and Deranged start arguing. The rest of the kids gather round, egging them on, shouting, laughing, licking their lips at the thought of the girls scratching each other's eyes out.

'Who the fuck you think you are?'

'Tramp!'

'Are you fucking *mad*?'

'Yeah, yeah, yeah!' screams the mob. Beautiful and Psycho are in the midst of the madness, also yelling. Children are dashing in from the cold and the frost, charging towards the free entertainment, jumping up and down, trying to see above the crowd.

I move to the centre of the fuss and ask everyone, and Seething and Deranged in particular, to disperse. Suddenly, another mini-fight breaks out in the surrounding crowd, someone pushes someone else, and *bam*! Seething and Deranged are at each other's throats with me somehow wedged in between.

I try to separate them, try pulling them apart, pushing them apart, but nothing works. They're ripping at each other's hair, grabbing each other's throats, whacking each other and me too as they flap their arms about.

Deranged growls, 'I'm gonna get you, you skank. You wanna fuck with Beautiful? You wanna fuck with me?'

'*Bitch!*'

I fly around the room with them, and eventually I'm thrown to the floor. The other children are yelling like jackals, Furious the loudest. As I'm falling to the ground, Ms Magical rushes over and tries to separate the girls. But she's a fifty-year-old woman who has a bad leg, so she can't do much.

I stumble back up, blurry-eyed and aching from the fall. I lurch towards the girls and grab hold of Seething. Ms Magical takes hold of Deranged. I look past the girls, staring Ms Magical in the eye. We yank as hard as we can and their hold on each other gives way. Success.

Ms Joyful runs up to me. 'How can I help?'

I blink. 'Can you take Seething to the office?' By now, Seething has stopped struggling to get out of my grasp. Ms Magical has already marched Deranged away.

Ms Joyful takes Seething by the arm. 'Of course, Ms Snuffle-upagus. Is that your bag on the floor?'

Oh my goodness. My bag. I drop to the floor and begin to pick up the various bits that have fallen out: pencils, red pens, paraceta-mol, wallet, Visa card . . . but my phone? Where's my phone?

Dopey and Dreamer leap around me. 'You all right, Miss? You found everything?'

'No, boys. My phone. I can't find my phone.'

They scuttle about looking for it. Eventually, they have to admit defeat. The phone cannot be found. It was my favourite phone ever. And now it's gone.

Tuesday 25 February

The Black Police Association is a good thing. It does a lot of work on race with the police as a whole and helps to recruit black and Asian officers. There is so much distrust of the police within ethnic-minority communities that such an organization is crucial to establishing a working relationship between the police and black London. I am 100 per cent supportive of the existence of the BPA, and I admire the people who work within it.

The BPA also does work with schools. They run leadership programmes with young black people, helping them to become upstanding, thoughtful and committed adults who can lead black people on to the right path. The programme is not paid for by the children or their parents. It is entirely free and lasts for one year. It includes a week-long residential over the summer, where the chil-dren get to make friends with other black children across London.

Over the year, they attend Saturday sessions, write essays, give presentations and go to various extra classes. At the end of the year, if they meet the requirements of the programme, they get a GCSE.

For the second year running, I have chosen a handful of children to put forward for the programme. In a couple of months, this year's group will 'graduate' and there will be a Saturday-evening ceremony. So I find the children in question and ask them how things have been going. I tell them that I'm going to be at their celebration event in a few weeks' time, and that I'm looking forward to it.

Psycho, Seething and Beautiful practically fall over themselves laughing. '*You're* gonna go, Miss?' they ask.

'Yes. It's your graduation. I'm excited about going,' I say. 'I want to see all the hard work you've put in this year, and share in the celebration.' They kiss their teeth and turn their heads.

'Yeah, well, Miss, you'll be the only one there. I mean, we ain't going.' Psycho twists her head round and they all laugh some more, until Seething pokes the others.

'Nah, man. Yuh haf to go. Otherwise that woman's gonna come drag ya out of ya house, innit.'

They're in hysterics. I'm feeling rather awkward and uncomfortable and beginning to wonder why I am so keen to go to this thing. 'So, girls, you'll be going then? It should be a nice evening. There'll be a proper sit-down dinner. You should be looking forward to it.'

This makes them angry. Seething contorts her face into a scowl. 'Look forward to it? Nah, man. It's a waste of time, man. What's the point? They is taking up our time to do crap when we could be at home.'

'Yeah, it's my shopping time that they take,' screeches Psycho.

Beautiful tilts her head. 'Man, that woman who forces us to go . . . man, she is so *extra*.'

They're talking about this lovely black woman in her twenties who works so very hard at helping to run this programme, so much so that she will go to their houses and demand to know why they have missed a session. She believes in helping them so much that she works day and night to make this programme a success.

'But this programme is about making you all into leaders, remember?' I say cautiously.

'But they make us do all this work. They're so *extra*!' Psycho and Seething are now doubled up with laughter.

'Well, of course you have to do work, girls, you get a GCSE at the end of it.'

Beautiful pauses, looking pensive. 'Yeah, man, that GCSE. That's the only reason I've stayed the course.'

Their heads bob in agreement. I ask them how many of the other children across London have made it to the end. They tell me that most have dropped out, that less than 50 per cent of those who began the course last year are going to graduate. Sometimes I forget that my school isn't so bad in comparison to others. As awful as they are, my kids are some of the best that London has to offer.

I'm reminded of a black doctor friend of mine who sent his eldest son to Harrow. His son is now at Cambridge, speaks Japanese and spent last summer living and working in Japan. My friend visited my school last year to speak to my kids, at my request, and was so horrified by his experience that I have been unable to persuade him to return. 'It's just too depressing, Snuffy,' he explained.

'What is?'

'Our black kids. Even the good ones are crap.'

Clearly he isn't talking about his own children, who understand what it means to work for something, but he's a criminal barrister, so he knows what he's talking about. Surely, in essence, my kids are no different to his kids? They weren't born this way.

Giving up, I start to walk away from the girls. As I do, Beautiful runs after me. 'Yo, Miss!' I turn around. 'Maybe I'll go to this celebration graduation thing.'

'Really?' I say. Beautiful nods. 'That's great, Beautiful.' I want to ask her about Seething and Deranged and why they're always fighting, but think better of it as Seething is in earshot. 'See you there then.'

Maybe the good ones aren't so crap after all.

I'm with my Year 8s again and I somehow get to talking about how I was annoyed yesterday evening because my husband is away for work, I have lost my mobile and, coincidentally, there was a problem with our phone line. No phone, no internet, no TV. The class lets out a gasp of horror.

'No internet?'

'No telly?'

'But Miss, what did you do?' asks Adorable.

I try to answer, but alarm has frazzled their little brains, leaving their eyes on stilts and their mouths propped open. 'No internet? Can you imagine? What do you do? What *can* you do?' The room is buzzing out of control.

'Just go to sleep,' yells Munchkin.

'Yeah, sleep: that's all there is left,' adds Fifty. I'm left in no doubt that this is the only answer.

'Is that what you did, Miss? Did you sleep?' Fifty asks curiously.

'Oh my God, Miss, what *did* you do?' shouts Cent. 'Did you go for a walk out in the cold, all by yourself?' He's hugging himself, pretending to cry as he speaks. He leaps out of his chair. 'Oh my God, Miss,' he says again, 'how did you cope? You should have just *died*!'

I bang my board pen on the table. 'Right! I want everyone's attention! Everyone looking this way now, please. 3 – 2 – 1.' They turn dutifully, silent now. 'Come on, everyone. OK, now, let's think: no phone, no internet, no TV . . . what can you do instead?'

'Bake a cake.'

'Go shopping.'

'Have a bath.'

'Get drunk.'

Get drunk? I smile. 'Good, good. What else could you do?'

'Go Nando's.'

'Yes.' I grin.

'Or the cinema.'

'Or a friend's house.'

'OK, is there anything else you could do at home? Apart from sleeping of course.'

Eventually, Polish pipes up. 'You could *read*, Miss.'

The others take little notice of this idea. No one mentions chores. Certainly no one mentions homework. And why would they?

Thursday 27 February

Carphone Warehouse, much to my disappointment, informs me that my old phone is out of stock and is about to be discontinued. Hrumph. So now I've got some free upgrade which I can't for the life of me figure out how to use and I'm missing my old, clunky, out-of-date phone. I can't stop complaining. Luckily for me, Dopey is listening.

'Miss, man, you really don't like your new phone?' We're standing in the playground surrounded by other children kicking a ball around on the asphalt.

'No. I hate it. Can't use it. My old phone may not be trendy but it was easy to use.'

Dopey sidles up to me. 'Miss, man, look, I can get you your old phone if you want . . .'

'You mean you know who stole it?'

Dopey steps back. 'Nah, man! 'Course I don't know that. I mean I can get you a phone which is the same as your old phone and then we can swap and you give me your new phone.'

Dopey is no fool. He knows the phone I have is worth three or four times the phone that I actually want. I insist it is a lost cause. It has been discontinued.

'Nah, Miss, I promise you. I'll get you your phone. I have my *people*.'

'Your *people*?' I look at him suspiciously. 'I want it in a box, you know. You can't go round stealing other people's phones to make a deal with me.'

'Nah, Miss, don't worry. I won't steal it. I have this friend, Miss, and he is a real neek and it's his phone. I'll buy it off him.'

'Yeah, Miss,' Dreamer butts in. 'Dopey won't steal it. I know his friend. He is so neekie. Yeah. He does so much better in school than us.'

'OK, boys, I'm going to trust you with this one.'

The bell goes. 'Come on, boys, we gotta go.'

Am I crazy to trust them? Maybe.

Friday 28 February

This morning, Dopey shows up at my office at 8 a.m. The sky is grey outside and the sun has not quite woken up properly yet. I have never known Dopey to be so early to school. He holds in his hand a version of my old phone, charger and all. We swap SIM cards. He works his magic with the digits, copying numbers from phones to SIM cards, and – shazam! – I'm back in business.

'You know, if I'd been in the canteen earlier, I mean, when you fell, Miss, I would have helped you,' he says, sheepishly.

'I know, Dopey, I know.' And I place my shiny, flash new phone in his grubby little hands. 'Nice doing business with you, Dopey.'

'Yeah, Miss. You too.'

As he leaves, I shout after him. 'And if you can get into school this early for a business deal, then you can do the same to do your English coursework.'

He laughs as he heads out to the playground. I can't help but love that boy. I only hope he didn't steal this phone.

Five minutes later, Mr Hadenough pops his head in. 'Hey, Snuffy, did Dopey get you that phone then?'

I hold it up, laughing. 'That Dopey is gooood!' He takes the phone and studies it. 'Snuffy, I've been wondering about Ms Alternative. Do you have any idea when she's coming back? I mean, she hasn't been in school since before half-term. What's going on?'

I shrug. 'I don't know. She said she's at home with her kid. I think he's been having some trouble at school. Who knows?'

Mr Hadenough sighs. 'Yeah, but the kids, her classes – what the hell? How can she stay away for that long?'

'She's off sick. There's nothing Mr Goodheart can do about it.'

Mr Hadenough isn't having any of it. 'But what about the kids? She's teaching some of the top classes at A level, and they're depending on her for their results to get university offers. Don't they matter too?'

I laugh to myself hearing Hadenough defending the kids. 'You know, I doubt she'll be back for a while, if at all.'

Hadenough shuffles uneasily. 'As a matter of fact, Mr Goodheart may have to be looking for a replacement for me too. I really have had enough.'

'What? Don't be crazy. You're a great teacher. Teaching is brilliant. Come on, you wouldn't want to leave all this!'

'Nah . . . I mean, I like working with all the teachers here, but the stress is too much, and this Ofsted business . . . I just don't want to be here.'

Suddenly I realize Hadenough is serious. 'Wait a minute . . . you're not really thinking of leaving, are you? Think of the difference we make to these kids. Think of how rewarding the job is.'

'But I don't want to turn the school system around like you, Snuffy. I don't want to work all hours. I just want to teach, see my girlfriend, have a life . . . you know? And then look, these other teachers who laze around, take time off sick, do whatever, and it doesn't matter. Why should I work so hard?'

'Yeah, I know, but . . .'

'No. You may want to sacrifice your whole life to this goddamn education system but I don't. I'm sick of it. I need to do something else with my life.'

'Wait a minute. You're just having a bad day.'

Hadenough jerks his head up. 'No, it's not that. My girlfriend said to me the other night that she thought I might have a nervous breakdown. She said I had to change my life or she'd finish with me.'

'Oh, don't be silly, she's just saying that. It'll be fine. Look, Easter holidays are around the corner. Two weeks, right?' I smile. 'Come on.'

The bell goes. Hadenough leaps up. 'Shit. Gotta go. See ya.'

Oh God. Poor Hadenough. Am I really sacrificing my whole life? Poor Liberal . . .

I'm late too. I grab my books and run.

Saturday 1 March

I'm standing in Tesco doing the week's shopping with my friend Inspirational, looking over the choice of veggies as he tells me about how awful a recent trip at his school has been. They went away for three days to some place a couple of hours out of London which offered a bunch of fun activities like archery and go-karting. Some two hundred children went. It was meant to be a bonding experience. As it was, some of the children were so badly behaved they had to be sent home.

'They were *that* bad?' I ask.

Inspirational nods. He hasn't slept for three days and two nights and he looks like it. He has turned a ghostly white and the circles under his eyes have deepened. 'They were awful, Snuffy, just awful. We had to send twenty of them home.'

'Twenty?' I can't believe what I'm hearing. I mean, I've heard of sending home a kid or two, but *twenty*? Inspirational tells me various tales of chaos and disobedience and I stand there by the tomatoes and cucumbers, listening in horror. 'Well, that was the right thing to do, Inspirational. Teaches them a lesson.'

'Yeah, I know, but the thing is, it cost the school £1,000. It was £500 to hire a coach to take them home, and then they had to be back in school for two days, which was unplanned, so we had to hire supply teachers for them, and that's another £500. But then, that's nothing when you consider how much the school spent on the whole expedition.'

'You mean the kids didn't pay?'

'No. We managed to get some money from somewhere and, as we wanted everyone to go, so that we could bond, well, we paid for it.'

'So how much did it cost?' My heart's in my mouth as I ask.

'£22,000. Oh, and another ten kids never even bothered showing up, even though their places had been paid for.' I stand
absolutely still. 'Come on, Snuffy. What're you doing? What're
you getting? Let's go!' But I can't hear him. I'm standing there by
the tomatoes and cucumbers, and all I can hear is: '£22,000.'
'*Snuffy!* Come on! Where is Liberal anyway?'

'We hardly see much of each other these days, with me working
all the time. He's at some art event today.' I shrug. 'Maybe we can
join him there later if you like.'

'Yeah, maybe,' Inspirational says. 'Got a lot of work to do . . .'

'Yeah,' I say. 'I know exactly what you mean. Need something
to get us through.'

And off we go in search of the ice-cream section.

Monday 3 March

Sitting at a table with a bunch of other teachers in Manchester, I
listen to the Guru. The Guru has everyone laughing and hanging
on to his every word. The Guru is clever, charming, funny and
charges so much money to speak to a crowd it boggles the mind.

But I get a little irritated when he insists that it's a teacher's job
to close the achievement gap and help working-class children to
achieve more. I think it's our job to help all children, whatever
their class or colour, to achieve their potential. He regularly makes
quips about the Tories and the *Telegraph*, and I begin to feel even
more uncomfortable, especially when he starts laughing at everyone for marking the children's work. He shows us studies which
prove that giving marks stifles progress. Class A gets a comment
and a mark. Class B gets only a comment. Over time, class B makes
progress and class A does not. Even the children who get high
marks don't make progress, apparently, and it becomes clear that
the only way to encourage children to achieve is never to give
them a grade.

At the break, I want to approach the Guru and say: 'Hi there. I'm
a great fan. But I'm just wondering about the classes in your sur-

veys. You see, I agree with what you say about marks stopping kids from looking at the comments. So instead of just handing out comments and marks without thinking – as they do with class A – I do things like give a target for improvement in one lesson, and give out the grade in the next lesson. Or give a target and then force the kids to discuss their targets and feed back to the class about what their partner's target is. Or I just tell the kids that I spent my whole Sunday writing their comments and if they don't read them and know them by heart by the end of the lesson, then I won't let them leave the classroom. My worry, though, is that if children are never allowed to fail at all in school, then how are we preparing them for life, where one is graded all the time? Surely learning what it is to fail and try again is one of the best lessons in life?'

Frustrated, I start voicing my thoughts at the table I'm sitting on, and I find that my fellow teachers are listening intently. Their instinct is to agree with me. But then I make a fatal error. 'We all get graded in life,' I point out to them. 'We, as teachers, for example, get graded all the time.'

They look at each other, galvanized. 'Yeah,' says one middle-aged blond woman, 'we get *graded*.' She looks as if someone has just kicked her in the face. I know what they're thinking. We get graded and we don't like it. The Guru, it would seem, is speaking to the perfect audience.

Tuesday 4 March

Furious leaves Beautiful at the end of the corridor and saunters towards me, holding out his report. I take it from him. 'What's this?' I ask. 'Where are this morning's lessons? Why is this morning blank?' Furious grins sheepishly but doesn't answer. I step into my office and offer him a chair. 'OK, Furious. What's going on? Where were you this morning?' He remains perfectly silent. If only he could be this way in lessons, I think to myself. 'Look, Furious, come on. You know I'm not going to let you go until you tell me where you were.'

Furious grins and then begins to laugh. I can tell he wants to talk to me. But he's too shy. Something's up. He's come to me to tell me something, but he wants me to get it out of him. I know him too well. He's been on report to me for nearly two years and, frankly, I'm the most consistent thing in his life. 'So?' I give in.

'Yeah, well, you know, I was in town.' He's still smiling.

'In town? Where in town? What were you doing there?'

Furious gives me a nod with his chin, gangster style. 'Yeah, man, you know, I had an appointment.'

'An appointment?'

'Yeah, man.' He grins. 'Yeah, so I gotta get back to my lesson.' He disappears down the corridor, grabbing on to Beautiful as he goes.

I call after them. 'I'll be checking up on you. I've noted the time. Both of you need to get to your lessons now!'

I shut my office door and sit down. Appointments. When kids say 'appointments' it tends to mean they're going to the sexual health clinic. The clinics will see you whenever and they won't say anything to Mum or Dad. These kids go there for all sorts of things. And I guess that's good: this way they don't get STDs and spread them around. Right? These kids have sex all over the place. Sometimes we catch them at it, right here at the school: in the toilets. Yeah, that's right: in the toilets.

Wednesday 5 March

I have speakers who come into school every now and then to talk to the kids about their careers. More often than not, I try to choose black speakers, as most of the children attending this after-school enrichment activity are black. The idea is to try to make them think about careers in fields other than football or MTV. Today I have Bank with me. Compassionate worked her magic and he has agreed to 'give something back'.

'Right, everyone, looking this way, please!' I wait for them to settle. The sea of mainly black faces looks Bank up and down. 'This is Mr Bank. We're very lucky to have him here with us today because he's a very busy man, earning a *lot* of money in the City. He drives a nice Mercedes, which is out in the car park, and he's an investment banker.' Upon hearing that, the kids sit up straight, listening. Some of them strain their necks to see out in the car park, to get a glimpse of his car. I continue. 'Mr Bank is originally from Ghana but he grew up in London, just like you. I know a lot of you say you want to be rich and own fancy houses and so on . . . well, listen to Mr Bank and perhaps you can find out how it's done.' I smile and Bank steps forward.

Bank begins by explaining that he didn't have an easy life growing up. His dad left his mum when he was small and he never saw his father again. He explains that, while his wife comes from a very privileged background, he had to fight for everything he has. I listen to him and realize that I've misjudged him. I thought he was just some rich idiot. Turns out he's a little more complex than that.

As Bank speaks, it dawns on me just how posh his voice sounds. He went to a grammar school and then to Oxford. I guess he perfected the accent as he grew up. Funny how I've never noticed before. But here, in my school, his accent dribbles about the room like a pierced football. Here, amongst my kids, in this completely different world to the one of dinner parties and theatre where I normally meet people like Bank, his voice makes me shiver.

A few minutes into his speech, I can see the kids switch off. He may be black, but he isn't one of us. The few white kids here aren't interested either. This man is an outsider simply because of the way he sounds.

After his talk, I thank Bank for his time. 'They didn't seem that keen, did they?' he says.

'No, no, that's just what they're like,' I lie. 'Our kids are hard to control, unless you're showing them a PSP game or a Jackie Chan movie. And the younger ones – Munchkin, Fifty, Cent – I saw them listening. I think they got some of what you were saying. And Deranged and Beautiful were completely with you. In fact, I was pretty impressed by how interested they were.' I thank Bank and send him on his way. To finish up, I ask the kids what they think. Hip, Wholesome's best friend, one of the cool white boys, puts his hand up.

'Miss, why do you want us to be lawyers and doctors anyway? I mean, what's wrong with being a footballer?'

'Yeah, footballers earn a lot more money than doctors,' Seething says.

'Well, first of all, it isn't about being as rich as possible, it's about living a worthwhile life. But putting that aside, the point is that there are hundreds of thousands of lawyers out there. And there are hundreds of thousands of doctors out there. But *footballers*? There are about fifty!' The kids look at each other, considering what I've said. 'Thinking you're going to become a rap artist is like buying a lottery ticket,' I say. 'I'm not saying you should only be doctors and lawyers. You can be plumbers and artists and charity workers. I just want you to have a *choice*. Do you understand?' They stare at me blankly. 'OK, everyone, thanks for coming and listening. Well done. See you tomorrow.'

As they walk out the door, I catch Deranged and Beautiful. 'Girls, can you tell me what's going on with Seething? I mean, why, Deranged, are the two of you always fighting?'

Deranged flicks her ponytail. 'No reason, Miss. I just don't like her. Anyway, Miss, I'm gonna be a beauty therapist. After what you said the other day about having a goal, I went and found out . . . and you need five "C"s at GCSE to get into the college I want.'

I'm amazed. I want to run after Bank and drag him back to hear her speak. 'That's fantastic, Deranged.' I look at Beautiful. 'And what about you, Beautiful? Have you got an idea of what you might like to do?'

'Well, you know that police thing we is been doing?'

'Yes?'

'Well, like . . .' She steps back a little, looking awkward. 'Well, maybe I could be in the police, like . . .'

I grin. 'I think that's a wonderful idea, Beautiful.' The girls turn to go. 'Girls, if you need any help with any of this, you'll let me know, right?'

"Course, Miss!' And out they go. I feel happy. I only need to get one. Just one of them makes it all worthwhile.

Friday 7 March

Today I'm speaking to Mr Sporty, and he's explaining what he does when children turn up late to his lessons. He simply doesn't allow them to participate and sends them away. They're so disappointed they're never late again. How hilarious! If teachers of academic subjects tried that, no one would ever turn up to our lessons on time.

Later, I'm talking to Mr Truthful, who teaches PE this year but, for most of his career, has been a language teacher. 'Snuffy, you know,' he says, 'it's great being a PE teacher. The kids do everything I say. They love me.'

'Really? What do you mean?'

'I mean the kids really, really like me. Now that I teach PE, they'll do anything for me. I'm able to discipline them like never before. Because I'm in charge of something they love, they want me to like them so that I'll never take it away from them.'

He moves his head closer to mine. 'You know what, Snuffy? I don't think I can go back to being a language teacher. PE teachers don't have to do any marking, we're loved by the kids . . . Life as a PE teacher is something else.'

If only children could love history like that, or languages, or English, or science, but no, those are 'difficult' subjects, subjects we have to force down their throats, or trick them into learning through games. And why do we play games in lessons? Well, I suppose it helps the academic subjects look . . . well, all the more like PE.

Saturday 8 March

I'm a teacher governor, and this means I sit on the school's governing body. This also means that, twice a year, I spend a Saturday morning helping governors plan the future of the school.

A school is run by its head, its senior team and its governors. The governing body at most schools is usually made up of a couple of teacher governors (who are voted on by teaching staff), a few parent governors (voted on by parents in the know) and random members of the public. Who hires the head of a school? The governing body.

Imagine the reaction if I went to Deutsche Bank and asked to be on their board of directors. I should think they would first ask about my background in banking. Schools? Anyone will do.

The question on the agenda today is: how do we get the children to be Independent Learners? Ugh. Here I am at school, on a Saturday, and I have to talk about this for the forty-fifth time? And it's a nice day too: the sun, for the first time this year, has decided to show its face.

Mr Well-Meaning is one of our governors. His son Smartie was in Year 11 last year – the one who got a string of 'A*' and 'A' grades. He is white, middle class and I'm guessing he reads the *Guardian*. He wears trendy jeans and T-shirts, and is kind, well spoken, and I am fond of him. Today, he is chairing one of the groups of governors. Not for the first time, I listen to him with dismay.

'Well, you know what I think,' he ventures. 'We want exciting teaching which makes the kids into interesting, happy people. We don't want our young people to be like those poncey kids at private school who are just dull. The problem with the school,' he continues, 'is that it doesn't appreciate the wide variety of talents we have in our kids. Why don't we get the students to teach the teachers? We could get them to give the teachers lessons in texting, for example. These kids are so skilled, you know. I remember, once, my son Smartie walked home with one of the boys here who lives on an estate, and he taught him street sense. He showed him that someone moving slowly on a bicycle is probably selling drugs.'

I look at Mr Goodheart, who has just walked in, and he looks back at me. He knows what I'm thinking. I know what he's thinking. No doubt he's worried that I have reached boiling point, as he garbles some kind of gently critical response, and Mr Well-Meaning laughs.

'Oh no!' He chuckles. 'I'm not saying that we should teach the kids how to recognize drug dealers!'

Then what *is* he saying, I wonder? My guess is that he isn't quite sure. He simply believes deep down that the world and this country are unfair. And to redress the balance, he is making wild and ludicrous suggestions that will form the basis for our school's strategic action plans. If he were alone in this, then perhaps it wouldn't matter. But most state-school governors are similar in their liberalism. Lefties become governors. Right-wingers do not.

What then of the children whose texting skills will be rewarded? Who are they? For the most part, they are black, or working class or from single-parent families. What does this 'appreciation of such skills' do for them? It tells them that skills such as algebra aren't so important. And so it encourages them to give up on the skills that would make them into successes.

What we desperately need, it seems to me, are experts in education running schools, not laymen. Good teaching takes years of training. It's not something you do when you cannot do anything else in life. The real enemy is well meaning, friendly and kind, but their amateurism makes them deadly.

Monday 10 March

I'm on duty outside the school when I notice Excluded hanging about. Excluded is Mishap and Seething's little brother. He has dark-brown skin and a short haircut. Excluded was asked to leave the school permanently a year ago because of a terrible track record of constant disruption, bullying and aggression towards teachers and students, so he is not allowed to be by the premises. Had he managed to stay the course, he would now be in Year 10, doing his GCSEs. I catch sight of him as he is walking away.

'Excluded,' I call.

He steps back, throwing his hands out to the side, gangster style. 'What? What you doing, man? I ain't done nothing!'

'OK, Excluded, I just want to talk to you.'

'Yeah?' His manner is aggressive. He snarls like a fox cornered by dogs. 'What you doing coming up to me like you're some kind of policeman?' he shouts.

'Policeman?' I force a laugh. 'Am I carrying a truncheon? Am I in uniform? Maybe I should have become a policeman. The uniform would have probably suited me, don't you think?'

A smile nearly breaks out across Excluded's face, and for a moment I think I see the boy I taught in Year 7, cute and full of energy. I remember how he used to have his hand up all the time: 'I know, Miss, I know! Pick me, Miss!' I used to love teaching him.

I ask Excluded what he's up to these days, and I remind him that he isn't meant to be around the school. 'So what, man?' he responds. 'You all don't own the road, you know. I can walk up and down here as much as I want. Anyway, my niece, she tells me that someone took her phone and stole her SIM card, but she won't tell me who it is so, like, I come down to sort it out.'

As Excluded totters from side to side as if he has ants in his pants, I make the usual speech about how violence isn't the solution, that he should leave his niece's business to her, that it is best for him not to be by the school gates. Then, 'So how is Mishap?' I ask.

'Yeah, man, she's good, she's good.'

'Wasn't it great that she got her "C"?'

'Oh yeah?'

'Yes, she did. I tell everyone about her "C". What is she doing now?'

Excluded shrugs. 'College,' he says.

It feels like we're almost friends again. I remember him, staring out the window of my classroom: 'Excluded! On with your work!' 'Sorry, Miss, it's just that it's hard.' 'I know, Excluded, I didn't explain it properly, let's have a go at this together . . .' I only taught Excluded for a year. He had a growth spurt overnight between Years 7 and 8. Before me now, he is large, and his face is no longer that of a boy. He even has facial hair.

Mishap was a naughty girl but not excessively so. But she was friends with some real criminals in her own year so, at a very young age, Excluded was introduced to a world of miscreants who were much older than him, a world which, given his fast-developing physique and his lack of academic sophistication, was the only world in which he would find success. 'And what is Mishap studying at college?' I ask eagerly.

'Media, I think.'

'And you, Excluded? Where are you, now?'

'Nowhere, man.' Excluded spits on the side of the road.

'Nowhere? You must be somewhere.'

'Yeah, well, you know, I go centre.' Excluded means he is at the local Pupil Referral Unit. And yes, I guess that kind of means he doesn't go anywhere at all.

'It was nice to see you, Excluded.' I wave, and move away.

'Yeah, you too.'

No 'Miss' in that goodbye. Excluded doesn't use such sissy words any more. His sister, two years older, who has left school, still does. As he struts down the street, kicking the pavement with anger, I feel like running after him. I want to grab him by the hand, turn him around and skip towards the school gates. Let's turn the clock back two years, Excluded. Let's do it all again. Come back inside the gates with me, let's find that baby-face of yours . . .

As I daydream, Excluded is moving further and further away.

Wednesday 12 March

Stoic is eating alone in the canteen, as he always does. I sit at the table by his side. He's surprised. 'Oh, hello, Miss,' he says, smiling.

'Hi, Stoic. You know, I've been thinking about you . . . about how extraordinary you are, so hard-working, so focused.' His smile grows broader. 'So what is it that's made you like this?'

'Thank you, Miss. That's kind of you.' He pauses. 'Well, there are my parents, of course.' He talks a bit about how his parents have always had high expectations of him, how he has tried to make them proud of him.

'Is that it then, Stoic? Are your parents the only reason you are so different to some of the other students?'

Stoic shakes his head. 'No.' He turns to face me properly. 'Miss, when I was in Year 8, I turned and looked at the others in my year group and I noticed that the black kids were always misbehaving and getting into trouble.'

'Only the black ones?'

'No, obviously lots of children misbehave. But I noticed that, to have friends, to be considered "cool" ' – he makes quotation marks with his fingers – 'if you were black, you had to be bad.' He shakes his head. 'So I made the decision there and then to go without friends and to work hard instead.'

'Go without friends?'

Stoic nods. 'Yes, and I attend this after-school organization which supports inner-city kids who are trying to do well.'

'Oh really? I'd love to see this organization. Could I go with you to one of your meetings?'

'I'd like that very much, Miss. As you know, I don't have many friends, so, yes, please come, if you like.' He looks pleased.

I look around the canteen and note how the other students are taking no notice of Stoic sitting next to a member of staff eating his lunch. He doesn't even appear on their radar.

I take my tray to the metal plate and tray stacker and, as I scrape the remains of my food into the bin, I think of the kind of resolve and strength of character it must take for a thirteen-year-old to make a decision to go without friends in favour of a future career and success. If this is required for black children in the inner city to truly succeed, is it any wonder that so many of them don't?

Thursday 13 March

Knock. Knock.

Deranged and Beautiful are standing at my door. 'Miss, we need to speak with you.' Deranged takes Beautiful's arm and pulls her into my office.

'Of course, girls. Have a seat. What's happened?'

'Well, Miss, Beautiful ran out of history. She couldn't take it any more. So she ran out, and I ran after her to make sure she was OK. It's like you said, Miss. We're trying to make an effort.'

Beautiful starts to cry. 'I just can't stand it any more, Miss. It isn't fair. They shout and scream at the teacher all the time and I can't hear myself think!'

'Who shouts? Whose lesson have you come out of?'

As Beautiful sobs quietly, Deranged explains that, in their history lessons, Psycho and Seething cause havoc. She explains that they're so loud poor Beautiful cannot learn.

'Psycho and Seething? Girls, I've asked you before. What's going on with Seething?'

Deranged tosses her head. 'I keep telling Beautiful but she won't believe me.'

Beautiful folds her arms over. 'Well, I do now! They're skanks. I want nuffin' to do with them since what they did on Facebook.'

'Facebook?' I echo.

Deranged pulls her chair closer. 'Look, Miss, the reason we is fighting all the time, yeah . . .' She glances over at Beautiful, who is wiping her eyes. 'Is 'cause I know that Seething slept with Furious yeah . . .'

Beautiful starts to sob loudly and Deranged rubs her arm. 'But I never told Beautiful, yeah, but that skank Seething, she ain't got no shame, man, and then dem on Facebook, they writ up on their profiles, Psycho too, that Beautiful is Furious's bitch.' Deranged leaps up as if she's ready for a fight.

'OK, let's calm down. So do I have to be worried? Is there going to be another fight today?'

Beautiful looks up. 'No. I think they is lying. Furious wouldn't touch Seething if she was the last girl left. I don't care no more. I ain't interested. We comes to you 'cause we're worried 'cause exams are coming. We're really trying, Miss. And Deranged, she manages to block out the noise. But I can't. Psycho and Seething are always laughing, shouting at Ms Useless, and they take the piss out of the rest of us.'

'What does Ms Useless do when they shout?' I ask.

Deranged jumps in. 'Ms Useless waits until they stop. But that takes for ever. Sometimes she shouts back at them and then they get into big arguments. And we aren't learning anything!' Deranged lets out a deep breath. 'Beautiful's really upset. She doesn't think it's fair. And it's true, Miss, I'm being really good these days. I wanna get my GCSEs. I wanna be a beauty therapist. I wanna have *choice*, like you said.'

'Have you spoken to Ms Useless about it?'

'Yes,' Deranged shouts. 'I've asked if I can work in the library but she says it ain't allowed. We're not going back there, Miss. We have our GCSE exams, like, in a minute, and they act like we was in primary school! They don't care what they get, yeah? But we do.'

What am I meant to do? We can't exclude them. Even detentions are made difficult to administer, and staying for an hour after school is no big deal for a lot of these kids.

Beautiful looks up at me, her weary, tear-filled eyes blinking with hope. Hope that I might bring her relief, hope that I might give her the opportunity to learn at this crucial point in her school career. How can I tell these girls to make an effort, do all this stuff to inspire them, and then, when they come to me for help, say there is nothing I can do?

Tuesday 18 March

'Seething, you and I have spoken before about this. You are getting into trouble all over school.' We're standing in the corridor, on the way to afternoon lessons.

She chomps on her chewing gum and I hold out a bin in front of her. She spits it out. 'Yeah, I know, Miss. I can't help it. That's just the way I am.'

'How's your boyfriend? Is he still being nice to you?'

'Yeah, yeah, he's good.'

'And you're still using condoms? How old is he again?'

'Twenty-three. Yeah Miss, man, ever since you told me, we use dem, yeah.'

'Good. Well, Seething, you have your exams coming up. And

you know Ms Sensible is going to pull you out of lessons if you are disrupting the learning for everyone else.'

Seething shrugs. 'Don't care.'

'What?'

She jerks her shoulders. 'It don't matter. I'm leaving this place when I'm done. And my boyfriend says he's got my back. What do I need exams for?'

I try to explain to Seething that her boyfriend may not stick around, that qualifications are important, that she should have a goal in life, but this sixteen-year-old girl with her sharp short hair-cut and glass earring isn't listening. I try a different tack. 'So is everything OK now with Deranged? Are you two getting along?'

She breathes in through her teeth. 'Nah, man. Dem bitches can just keep demselves to demselves.'

'OK, well, what's important right now is that you try to make an effort with your schoolwork, yes?' I look at her for some acknowledgement that what I'm saying makes sense. 'You only have a couple of months left you know.'

Dring.

Damn. The bell. Is it that time already?

Seething starts to back off. 'I'm gonna be fine, Miss. You'll see.'

And we both rush to our respective lessons.

Wednesday 19 March

Today, the office tells me to go out to the front of the school and find Ms Sensible, the deputy. 'She needs your help,' they say.

Out I skip, down the road, and find her. 'Hello, Snuffy,' she says. 'You going to the shop?'

'No. I've come to help you out,' I say. 'I was told to find you.'

She looks at me in disbelief. 'You mean *you* are my back-up?'

'Erm, well, yes.' I'm slightly embarrassed because I immediately understand why she seems so taken aback. I try to make light of it. 'Yeah, sure I'm your back-up!' I twist my fists into the air as if I am Muhammad Ali. 'What's happened?'

Ms Sensible explains. 'On Monday, Let Down was out here smoking. Do you know him? He's been coming in on Saturdays to attend Ms Joyful's Aim Higher maths classes.'

I nod. 'Yes, I know him well.' Suddenly a vision of his cute Year 7 self flashes in front of me. Small, with brown shaggy hair, a face spotted with freckles, an oversized uniform. He was so cute.

Ms Sensible points down the alley in front of us. 'On Monday, he was attacked by a gang of boys. They took his iPod and his money.'

'Really? I didn't know.'

'And they had hammers. He's been in hospital. He's had several stitches in his head.'

I'm horrified. 'But who attacked him?'

'Well, that's just it. Seems it was some of our Year 11s. The attack was a reprisal, so Let Down must have done something. But Let Down won't name anyone, so we're stuck.'

'Do we have any idea who did it?'

'Not really. Dopey was spotted down here, as were Dreamer and Furious, but who knows? We haven't got any evidence.'

'Dopey? Bloody hell. These *kids*!'

'I know. Anyway, doesn't look like there's anything to worry about here for the moment.' Ms Sensible turns to return to school. 'Let's head back.'

As we're walking along, that image of Let Down in Year 7 keeps running through my mind. Why couldn't he have just stayed like that, cute and cuddly, for ever?

Thursday 20 March

'Here you are.' I hand Dreamer, who has walked in late, a past GCSE exam paper.

He flings himself across the desk dramatically. 'Aarggh! I don' wannit. It's hard, man!'

'Dreamer, pick yourself up now. Come on, we have work to do.'

Dreamer pushes the paper away. 'Nah, man. It's a 1996 paper – I'm not doin' dat!'

The others around him look a little distraught. They know what he's saying. And they kind of agree. But they're too scared to say so. They know I'm going to hit the roof if they dare to say that they don't want to work hard, that they want me to go into the filing cabinet and bring out a paper from 2005 onwards, that we all know that a 1996 paper is going to be bloody hard and, frankly, what on earth is the point? I mean, let's face it, we're in 2009, and the paper this year isn't going to look anything like the papers did in 1996.

'Dreamer, come on, I need you to make an effort. There isn't any point in you coming into our early-morning revision session if you're not going to do anything.' The irony is that, here he is, at 7.45 a.m., having dragged himself into school for a voluntary revision class. 'Open up the paper,' I demand.

'Just listen to Miss, man,' says Beautiful impatiently. 'What's wrong with you lot?'

Dreamer gives me dagger eyes and groans. 'But I don' like doing stuff that's hard. I wanna do easy stuff. I don' wanna think.'

Dopey is sitting behind, and decides to back Dreamer in what he's saying. 'Yeah, 'cause you never know what's gonna happen on the day.'

'No,' I reply. 'I *do* know. I can already predict who is going to fail and who is going to pass. As I keep on saying, do what I say and you will get this GCSE; don't, and you won't. You all keep telling me you don't want to fail. So do what I say.' I look at Dreamer. 'Open up the paper.'

'Yeah, but maybe on the day,' says Dreamer, 'I'll just end up with an "A★". You never know. You can't tell us, you know. You dunno who is gonna get what.'

I visibly grit my teeth, squeezing my hands into fists. 'No! That isn't going to happen. You aren't going to wake up one day and know everything just like that. You have to *work*. Just believe me when I say it's all about *work*.' I slam my fist down on the table.

The bunch of misfits all look at me as if I've told them that rain falls upwards, even though I've had this conversation with them a dozen times. Dopey puts his hand up and pats the air. 'OK, Miss, calm down,' he says, trying to pacify me. 'Hallelujah!'

Dopey regularly responds with 'Hallelujah!' after one of my speeches. The others laugh. Dreamer's eyes sparkle. 'Don't worry, Miss,' Dopey continues. 'We'll do what you is saying. Don't worry.' He taps Dreamer on the back and says in a low voice, 'Open up the paper, man.' And Dreamer does as he is told. But I know he isn't doing the work because he understands its importance. He's only doing it because he doesn't want to let me down.

Saturday 22 March

Liberal rings me while I'm in my office at school. 'When are you coming home?' he asks.

'Soon, soon. I'll be back for lunch,' I say. 'Sorry.'

I can sense his frustration down the phone. 'I haven't seen you properly in two weeks. Last weekend was governors, then there was that parents' evening, and that drama production and, well, you're in that bloody school all the time!'

'Sorry, sorry. I just need to get this marking done, and sort out my emails. End of term will soon be here and then there'll be loads of time.'

'But you're going on that India teachers' trip thing during the Easter holidays, so I won't see you then either.' He's getting angry.

'Well, that's only a week. We can hang out in the second week. Look, I'll be home soon, OK?'

'Well, Marx and I are going out. I'll see you when I see you.' And with that, he hangs up. Am I being unreasonable? Maybe I need to stop working like this. But I can't.

Monday 24 March

I turn up at Ms Useless's history class to remove Munchkin, who is being so badly behaved that she has asked for another teacher to get him out. He storms down the corridor in front of me.

'Slow down, Munchkin,' I call after him. 'What just happened in there?' He stops and turns around in a huff, arms folded across his chest.

'It wasn't me, it was Fifty. She's always blaming *me*, man.'

'That isn't what I want to hear, Munchkin. I'm very worried about you. What is going on with you these days? You used to be so well behaved and nowadays you're behaving badly across the school. You think we don't see what's going on? Fifty and Cent are not boys you should be hanging around with.'

'It wasn't me, man. She just hates me, yuh know.'

'Look, can we forget about Ms Useless and what happened in history for a moment? I'm talking about the bigger picture. You do know they're a bad influence on you, yes? And you do know that you come to school to learn? So what do we need to do to help you learn better?'

Munchkin seems to have been listening but still comes out with: 'Ah nah, Miss, I just can't be bothered. Anyway, it's too late now. Schools should bring back that whipping thing, Miss.'

'Whipping thing?'

'Yuh know. Like when they'd send you to the principal to get whipped, innit. Yeah. Then we'd do some work. Even Fifty and Cent.'

'Oh really?'

'Yeah. 'Cause then they'd be scared, innit. They'd be scared, and they'd work. I'd work. And then I wouldn't be so dumb.'

'You're not dumb, Munchkin.'

'Yeah, I am. It's 'cause, yeah, none of us work, like yuh said. 'Cause none of us is scared. And 'cause, you see, Miss, what's happening is that dem Polish people is getting all the money.'

'What money?'

'Yuh see, 'cause they like to work, and we people in London, well, we don't like to work, so they is sending back all their money to Poland to build houses.'

'Where do you get these ideas?'

'Yuh know, houses in Poland,' he whispers, as if he is telling me something top secret. 'And they is clever, see. But we in London, we don't wanna work. We need to bring back that whipping thing. 'Cause we is just g'ttin' more dumber and dumber.'

'Well, Munchkin, maybe we need to have you as prime minister. You have some interesting ideas.'

'What? Me, Miss? Nah. I wanna be a footballer.'

Tuesday 25 March

This morning, at break, I rush into the library to book it for a lesson in the afternoon. I'm in luck. It's still available. As I'm scribbling my name down, I notice Beautiful and Deranged at the corner table, studying some revision guides. I walk over to them. 'Girls, I'm impressed! You weren't lying . . . You really have changed.'

Deranged looks up and smiles. 'Yeah, told ya, Miss. Told ya! You never hear nuttin' these days about me, do ya?'

'No . . . it's true. Your name rarely comes up these days for getting into trouble. So I take it that everything's been sorted with Seething then?'

Beautiful sits up in her chair, her face relaxed. 'We ain't interested in dem no more, Miss. We is just working.'

Deranged lifts a fist in salute. 'I'm gonna be a beauty therapist!' The girls giggle together. For a moment, I see the lovely girls they both were in Year 7.

I head back towards the library doors and wave. 'Keep up the good work, girls. Only a couple of months left – you can do it!'

They call after me, 'Yes, we *can*.'

Wednesday 26 March

I look at my watch: 6 p.m. I really need to get out of here soon. I promised Liberal I'd be home early tonight. At least with the clocks having gone forward, it isn't pitch dark outside. As I'm about to shut down my computer, another email pops into my inbox.

I remember the days before email, when we had to write memos and notes to each other. Mr Cajole was telling me the other day how he gets over a hundred emails a day from staff. So I shouldn't really complain with my forty or so per day. But then, unlike him, I spend most of the day teaching. And when you think of the amount of follow-up some of those emails require (usually the ones about bad behaviour), it's no wonder we're working round the clock.

Oh! The email is from Hadenough. I click to open it.

I WANNA STICK MY SEXY STICK AND SEX IT WITH LOTS
OF SEX

What? I read the email again. What the hell? I stare at the screen. Stick my sexy stick? Has the madness of school finally got to him?

Suddenly Hadenough comes screeching around the corner and appears at my door looking horror-stricken. I look up from my desk, laughing. 'OK, so who did it?'

He growls. 'I dunno.' He shakes his head. 'I'm gonna get the little bastard, though.'

I can't stop laughing. 'But you have to admit, it's pretty funny.' I look back at the email and read it out. 'I wanna stick my sexy stick and sex it with lots of sex.' I shriek with laughter. 'I mean, what the hell does that mean anyway?'

Hadenough plops himself down on a chair and starts to snigger. 'Yeah, I guess it's kind of funny. But Snuffy, he's sent it to the whole of the staff!'

'You mean everyone's got this?'

'Yeah. I guess even Mr Goodheart's got it.'

I put my hand over my mouth. 'Oh no, that's *bad*. He's gonna flip . . . How'd the kid get your password? Oh my God, you're gonna have a lot of explaining to do.'

'I dunno,' he says. 'I guess they watch us type them in all the time in class. It's pretty easy.'

Just then, I hear Ms Joyful down the hall. 'Snuffy, is Hadenough with you?'

'Yeah,' I shout out.

'Ms Sensible says Mr Goodheart wants to see him. He'd better get down there.'

Hadenough makes a face, and then grins. 'Why is my life so *shit*?' And then he gets up and disappears out my door. And I head home, feeling happy because, for once, I'm leaving school before him, and because that email has put a smile on my face.

Thursday 27 March

We are having a 'Community Evening', where parents and members of the community are invited to have drinks and canapés with the staff. As I can schmooze with the best of them, I'm in charge of Mrs Important for evening drinks. Mrs Important is a solicitor, well spoken, well dressed and utterly middle class. She is Adorable's very English mother.

I smile, shake her hand and move towards the drinks table. Mrs Important must be kept happy. Not only is she one of our prized middle-class parents, but she also provides work experience for one lucky Year 10 student every year. As I hand her a glass of wine, I wonder whether I should be bowing too.

I chit-chat well, but clearly not well enough. 'Tell me about the school,' she says, 'as you've been here for a while.' I give her the standard acceptable response.

She winces slightly. 'Well, what I mean is, what is your opinion of the discipline in the school? To be truthful, I'm a little worried about Adorable, who, as you know, is in Year 8. I mean, I know this is a very good school, but she tells me stories of some terrible behaviour, and of children sticking their heads into her classroom, interrupting the learning, and running off. What do you think about this?'

Gulp. Do I tell her what I truly believe? Do I tell her that, if Adorable were my daughter, I would sooner move to Mars than send her to a state school in London? Do I tell the truth? Do I compromise my school? She is our prize, our delight, our only route to survival. Tell her my true thoughts, and I not only betray my school, my profession, and my honour, but I also take the food out my colleagues' mouths.

I keep smiling, pause, thinking, stalling for time. 'But Adorable's class is such a delight to teach. Adorable is getting an A-class education in there.' The expression on her face says she wants to believe me, so I continue. 'You see, Mrs Important, if we want to have schools which are truly comprehensive, this necessarily means that children from a variety of backgrounds will be educated together.' I take a deep breath. I take a sip of my orange juice, awaiting either approval or execution.

'Yes, Ms Snuffleupagus, I think that's right.' I breathe a sigh of relief. 'Adorable does find their behaviour odd, but she's very happy at the school.'

'I'm so pleased to hear that.' I motion to some teachers across the room. 'Do let me introduce you to some of the other teaching staff . . .'

Friday 28 March

With Beautiful and Deranged in mind, I set up a meeting with the history teacher, Ms Useless. After I've talked to her she admits, 'I know, Ms Snuffleupagus. Seething and Psycho are out of control. They're like this with everyone.'

Ms Useless is clearly annoyed. The trend in schools these days is not for children to feel shame for their behaviour. The teacher is so used to being blamed for their bad behaviour, now, it's Ms Useless who feels responsible.

'I understand, Ms Useless. I'm not saying it's your fault. I'm just trying to find a way to support you. I could remove them from your lessons for the next few weeks. It so happens that I'm free when you're teaching them.'

But Ms Useless is reluctant to agree for some reason. 'I have called their homes. I have set detentions. It doesn't make any difference.'

'What about Beautiful? It isn't fair that she is unable to learn because of these girls. Wouldn't it make sense if you left Seething and Psycho with me for that lesson?'

'No, it isn't fair. But Beautiful is never going to get a "C" grade. She's always hated history. Psycho and Seething *will* get "C"s though, if I can keep them in the class.'

Ah. Now I understand. Teachers are judged by how many 'A★'–'C' grades they get. Results are not the children's successes. They're ours. If I help Beautiful, I necessarily hurt Ms Useless.

It makes you wonder what would happen if we judged the kids rather than the teachers.

Saturday 29 March

Inspirational settles himself down on our living-room sofa. The birds are chirping outside and the sun is shining. Liberal stands up. 'Can I get you a drink?' he offers.

'Yeah, a triple vodka.' Inspirational chuckles. 'Nah, you know, some juice or something.'

I sit next to Inspirational and pat him on the knee. 'So how's it going then, at Basic? How's the mixed-ability situation?'

Inspirational groans. 'Snuffy, oh my God! More like mixed-ability *madness*. What on earth were we all thinking?'

I pull myself up on the sofa. 'Why? What's happened?'

'Jesus, you wouldn't believe it. I have Year 7 children in the same class ranging from level 2 to level 6 – it's bloody impossible! Who can teach that?'

'Well, if *you* can't, then nobody can. Funny, isn't it, that we would never put seven-year-olds in a class with fourteen-year-olds, but that's essentially what we're doing with mixed ability.'

'Well, actually, what you describe is preferable to what I have. At least the seven-year-olds with level 2s might be very able and could develop conceptually with speed and attempt to keep up with the older ones. As it is, my level 2s are soft cabbages!'

'Well, at least there's no bottom set, right? That's one advantage.'

'Yeah, but you know, the cabbage kids are very much aware that they aren't very clever. It's bloody obvious! They see it every time they can't understand the questions that the bright ones *can* understand. Mixed ability highlights their inadequacies all the more for them.'

Liberal hands Inspirational his drink. 'Sorry to hear you're having it so hard, man.'

'Thanks, Liberal. Oh, you know, it isn't so bad, all of the time, but I'm so exhausted. I can't keep this up, you know. I'm thinking about leaving teaching.'

'Leave teaching? Are you mad? You're the best teacher in London, you can't leave!'

'Yeah, well, mixed-ability madness will make you do any number of things.'

'But you're the one who decided to leave in search of this intellectual challenge to teach mixed ability!'

Inspirational seems to slump in his seat. 'I know, I know. How wrong I was. I should have stayed at Ordinary. I have to work all hours with my planning to keep them all engaged. And while I'm willing to spend my life on this, the other teachers aren't, so we have chaos everywhere.'

'Oh, I'm sorry, Inspirational. It sounds terrible. At least you have calm in your classroom, though.'

'You know, Inspirational,' adds Liberal, 'I always wonder how you guys do your jobs. Really. My job is so easy in comparison.' I look at him, feeling really proud. He gets it. He really gets it. If only the rest of the world did too.

Inspirational slumps even further; he looks like he might cry. 'I tell you, I'm not sure I can take any more.'

About half of the schools in Britain are mixed ability and have no intention of ever changing. I feel for those poor children, both bright and not so bright, who are being taught, or indeed *not* taught, in a system of political fantasy which only serves to satisfy the liberal ideals of the adults, who, for the most part, never had any personal experience as a child of mixed-ability teaching, and never will

We gather in the staff room for a briefing. The notice boards have thousands of papers pinned to them. I stand next to Mr Hadenough by the door. We're two of the last to arrive.

Mr Goodheart stands at the front. 'Still no phone call, everyone. But it's going to come soon, so keep on your toes, please.'

Flippin' Ofsted.

Mr Goodheart straightens his tie. 'Some news that I think we were all expecting: Ms Alternative will not be returning to Ordinary. As some of you know, she was having increasing difficulty with her son at school. She has decided to move out of London and seek employment at another school. This isn't ideal, but we wish her all the best.'

Rumour has it that her son, in Year 7, was caught with drugs on him. They say he was a dealer, but I'm not sure I believe it. Mind you, anything can happen at Infamous School.

Mr Hadenough leans over. 'Yeah, she's out of London so she can feel satisfied about sending her kid to a state school without him being surrounded by any real state kids.'

I laugh, nodding. 'Yeah, exactly . . .'

Mr Goodheart coughs. 'We are of course very concerned about her classes, and Mr Replacement is going to be taking over her lessons until the end of the year.' He points to a small white man in the corner, who waves to everyone.

Mr Replacement looks as if a strong wind might blow him over and take his toupee with it. I nudge Mr Hadenough in the ribs: 'I give him two weeks.'

'Where do they get some of these people?'

And what of her exam classes? Her kids are all going to fail, and they have university applications to make. I guess beggars can't be choosers. I remember once speaking to the head of Basic School, and he said that when they advertise for science teachers, they don't get a single application. By that, he didn't mean they don't get a single *good* application. He meant they don't get anyone applying at all. Some science departments in London are made up entirely of supply teachers.

Poor Mr Goodheart. I look at him as he continues talking about the week ahead. Sometimes I wonder how he does his job, how impossible it must be for heads trying to run their schools with their hands tied behind their backs with all the control freakery coming from above. He clears his throat. 'Lastly, I understand that a certain email did the rounds last week.' We all start to snigger. I nudge Hadenough again. 'You can be certain that we are looking for the culprit; and I think we have him, actually. But can I remind all of you to be extra careful with your passwords, and make sure you change them regularly – at least once every half-term.'

As we pour out of the staff room I say to Hadenough, 'Do you know who did it then?'

'No. But I'm gonna speak to Mr Goodheart right now to find out.'

Tuesday 1 April

Politicians like to show they are 'bridging the gap' and making a difference. Sitting in town with some of our Year 11s, in some fancy company filled with lots of public-school-educated white adults, I listen intently to the speakers, who are trying to persuade my kids that their world is not only desirable but accessible too. 'Desirable' is easy. These people are clearly well off. The offices are pristine and trendy. Life on this side of the sea is pretty sweet.

The speaker is telling us that, in this business, it's all about knowing the right people, going to the right events, remembering everyone you meet. Seething, who is curled up on the sofa-type chair at the back, cuts in. 'Yeah, so like, I turn sixteen next week. Would ya give me a job?'

The man is trying to answer when he is interrupted by Psycho. 'Yeah, well, I'm sixteen *now*, so can I have an application form?'

An application form? Poor kid thinks she can fill out an application form as if this were McDonald's, and get a job at the snap of her fingers. Poor kid thinks that interrupting the man who might give her the job is a clever thing to do. Never before has that gulf between the haves and the have-nots been so clear to me.

Why do I persist in being 'had' by events like these? The day would have been far better spent teaching my kids some manners, thereby moving them closer to getting the kind of job that is had without an application form. But I can't teach them that, can I?

As we walk out of the building, Seething runs up to me. 'What's wrong, Miss?' she asks.

'Nothing,' I answer.

'It's a load of *crap*, innit?' She laughs.

'Yeah, Seething, yeah. I guess it is.' And I laugh with her.

Wednesday 2 April

I'm in the canteen, sitting at a student table because there isn't any more room on the staff table, and Hadenough comes to sit beside me. 'Hey, so I hear it was Fifty who stole your password,' I say.

'Yeah. Little bastard. He was out of school for two days 'cause of that stunt. What about these new controlled assessments, eh?'

'Load of bollocks.' I smirk. 'Just more changes, as usual, so we can keep busy trying to manage the bureaucracy instead of thinking about teaching and learning.'

Hadenough pulls his chair in. 'Yeah, but don't you think marks are going to go down?'

'No. If anything, they'll go up. We're in charge of administering them and we're the ones who are being judged by the results. It's just like coursework. For God's sake, they send us on courses which teach us how to bend the rules with coursework so that we can "raise our results"! At least with exams, you can't cheat. You can't let the kids rewrite their work a dozen times until they get it right.'

'But our kids could never make it if it were all about end-of-year exams.'

'Well, we might be raising results, but we're only doing so by lowering standards.'

'What are you gonna do, then? Exclude them all?'

I pause and look up at the ceiling. 'Yeah. If necessary. Do what Giuliani did with New York. Hit them with the small things. That's how you turn around any failing school. It's how Giuliani turned around New York.' Hadenough groans. 'I'm being serious! To begin with, we'd have a lot of temporary exclusions, but the children, in the end, would rise to the standards we set for them. Any good head knows he has to do that, it is just that the system frowns on him if he does. And any child is capable of doing what we expect of them. The problem is very simply that we expect too *little*.'

'So that's it? What about the ultimate sanction?' Hadenough smirks.

I nod. 'Yeah, well exactly, we need to be allowed to permanently exclude. And you'll say but where will they go?' I shake my head. 'We need more Pupil Referral Units. We need to involve the police. Maybe parents could be fined. Maybe the kid could get community service.'

Hadenough burst out loud into laughter. 'What? You mean misbehave too much in school and you'll have to work Saturdays cleaning up rubbish off the street?'

'Yeah, that's exactly what I mean. We have to hold these kids to account for their behaviour! It can't just be a free for all! We have to face the problems instead of pretending there is nothing wrong and fix the system for the better.'

He laughs. 'I know. Snuffy to the rescue! You'll save us all, right?'

I look at my watch. 'No way, mate. I have too much work to do.'

Thursday 3 April

Lovely Beautiful walks into my office with her long black hair swishing behind her and sits down. Her father follows behind. He's a small Pakistani man with receding hair. Funny how today Beautiful is wearing her skirt long, in a frumpy sort of style. Her father shakes my hand. I am dreading what this man might say and trying to figure out what my response might be.

'Morning, Sir, good to see you again. Please have a seat. So what is it that you wish to discuss this morning?'

Beautiful's father, Mr Serious, lets out a sigh. 'Well, Ms Snuffle-upagus, this situation with Furious. I am very worried. Beautiful tells me that they are just friends. And I hope that this is the case. What is this boy Furious like in school?'

Beautiful looks at me sheepishly, wondering what I will say. 'Hmm, yes, Sir, I can understand your concern. Furious is a boy who has various issues at school. He isn't very well behaved.' I look at Beautiful. 'It might be best for Beautiful to stay away from him.'

Mr Serious nods his head vigorously. 'Yes, exactly. This is what I have been saying.' He taps his daughter's arm. 'You must no longer speak to this boy, you hear?'

'Yes, Dad.' She casts her eyes down. 'But we're also here to talk about history, yeah?'

I sit up straighter. 'OK, yes, what's the problem?'

'Miss, it's like I said. I can't learn in history. And my dad wants to know what we can do about it.'

'I know, and Sir, it is very good of you to come in. You know that we're trying our best to support Beautiful's class.'

'I know, Miss, but our class is so bad. Only Mr Ogre can control us. And Ms Useless is just . . .' She blinks, embarrassed. She doesn't want to criticize her teachers in front of her father and me.

'I know, Beautiful, I know.' I want to make sure she knows I'm listening.

Her father looks at me, his eyes filled with hope. 'As her form tutor, is there something you can do to help?'

'Now, look, Beautiful, you can't let this beat you. In life, some-times you hit obstacles. But you don't let them get you down. You set out a plan of attack, and you figure out a way to beat them.' I look at her father in his check shirt. He looks back at me, his eyes twinkling.

'But Miss, I try to get on and do my own thing. I sit at the front of the class. I ask the teacher for extra work. I get it marked out-side of class. But I have to teach myself this stuff at home 'cause the teacher can't teach. And it's so hard.' Tears start to fall down Beau-tiful's face.

Her father mumbles, 'It wasn't like this in my day.'

I put my hand on Beautiful's knee. 'Now, now, Beautiful, no crying now . . . that means you've given up. And we never give up in the face of an obstacle, now do we? We don't let them beat us!' Beautiful blinks through her tears and smiles. 'What did Martin Luther King do, huh? He had a big obstacle to overcome, didn't he? What did he do?'

Beautiful wipes her face. 'He didn't give up, Miss.'

'That's right. And when you go for college interviews, and job interviews later, they'll always ask you that magic question: "What are you like when faced with a difficult situation?", and you, Beau-tiful, will be able to talk of this time in your life, when you didn't let this obstacle get you down.'

Beautiful grins. 'Yes, Miss. Yes, Miss. You're right, Miss. I'll just work harder.'

I talk through with her and her father various ways in which her teachers and even he, her dedicated father, can help, using revision books and the like. Eventually they stand to go. Her father takes my hand. 'Thank you, Ms Snuffleupagus, thank you,' he says.

As they walk away, I wonder how it is that Mr Serious hasn't shouted at me. He sends his daughter to school to learn, not to meet unfortunate boyfriends and survive classroom chaos. I won-der how it is he hasn't got angry at my incompetence, at my inability to defend and protect his child, and at my impotence to simply provide a school where the teachers can teach and the chil-dren can learn.

Easter Holidays

Friday 4 April

School is out for the holidays. Children are tearing down the street. But Dreamer and Dopey are standing in my office. Daring is sitting behind them, slumped in a chair, as if an alien had sucked all the life out of him. At least Dreamer and Dopey have some energy about them.

'Tell me why I am the one having to chase you? Why am I having to ring your parents? Why are they promising me that you'll be here at 8 a.m. today and you are nowhere to be seen? Why am I still nagging you to write a piece of coursework?'

They can see I'm annoyed. They smile, nodding, knowing that they're in the wrong.

'Yeah, Miss, we know.'

'OK, have a seat, get your pens out, you can write it out now.' Dreamer and Dopey exchange glances, then look at me. 'What's the problem, boys?'

'Well, yuh see, the thing is, Miss, that we ain't got the work with us. We didn't learn it, see. We don't know it. We can't write it today.'

My eyes nearly pop out of my head. 'What do you mean, you *don't know it*?' I'm ready to explode. I've been talking about nothing else for weeks. They've missed every deadline going. I gave them the opportunity to do it after school several times over. But they didn't come. Then I finally rang their parents and asked for them to come in early today. Were they there? No. Of course not.

The boys start shifting about, hands in their pockets. 'It's OK, Miss, we'll just come in in the holidays,' offers Dreamer.

'But I'm not going to be here.'

Dreamer pulls a face. 'What? What you mean you isn't gonna be here for the whole holiday, Miss?'

'Yes, that's right.'

'What? You mean you isn't gonna come in at all during the holiday?' He looks at Dopey in confusion.

'No. I'm going to India.'

'But what do you mean, Miss? You is always here.'

'Yeah? Well, I've decided to get a life, like you told me to. So there. I'm not coming in.'

Dopey is clearly dismayed. 'You can't do that, Miss. Please, Miss, what about tomorrow, Miss? Can we do it tomorrow?'

'No.' I fold my arms across my chest. The boys are howling like lost wolves.

Dreamer jumps up and down. 'Please, Miss, we don't know it now. We can't do it now. Please, Miss, tomorrow, Miss.'

Saturday bloody morning. First bloody day of the holidays and I'm flying out Sunday. Not to mention I'm so exhausted I feel like I'm living in a fog. But then I start thinking I could get some of those books marked tonight and then maybe I could drop them off tomorrow morning when I come in. And I could phone some of the other parents in the class, and get some other kids in too . . . Hmm.

'OK. 10.15,' I say. They've won. 'But I'm only coming in for the two of you, you understand?'

'Yeah, Miss, we'll be here.' Dreamer gives me a reassuring nod of the chin.

I stand up, wagging my finger in their faces. 'Because I swear, if you don't show up, I'll . . . I'll . . .'

'Yeah, Miss, don't worry. We said we'd be here. We'll be here.' Dreamer slaps Dopey's hand, turns around and struts through the door. 'See you tomorrow, Miss.'

With them out of the way, I turn to Daring, who has sunk down low into his chair. 'Right, guess where you're going to be at 10.15 tomorrow?'

'Aarrgh!' Daring throws his head on to the table and nearly falls off his chair.

Well, at least I got him to move. And if God takes pity on me, maybe he'll even write me a piece of coursework tomorrow morning.

Saturday 5 April

I'm off tomorrow to India with some other English teachers to go and visit some schools. I can't wait. Liberal is annoyed that I won't be around for the holidays, but how could I pass up this opportunity?

The kids came in this morning to write their coursework during the revision session, and they got quite a lot done. Dopey seems to be revising round the clock. Even Beautiful and Deranged seem to be turning over a new leaf. They're really trying. Let's hope they pick up a book or two this Easter.

Note to self: spend more time with Liberal when you're back from India.

Tuesday 8 April

I am with my white English colleagues and some Indians in a small, stuffy room with only an old fan making the heat bearable. The Indians are describing their schools and the expectations of the students. These are slum schools, where children come from families who exist on less than a dollar a day. One of the issues is getting these children to remain in school. But the reasons couldn't be more different than in the UK. It's not because the children don't want to attend. On the contrary, detentions are useless here – the kids love them, because school for them is such a precious resource and opportunity. But with their families being so poor, often they are needed to go out to work and bring home an extra 20 rupees for a day's work. Given that the father might earn some 50 rupees a day if he's lucky, a child's income can be very useful.

Various NGOs work with these families, trying to support them with government schemes, trying to enable the children to attend school. Unfortunately, some 100 million children are forced into work, sometimes from the age of three or four.

Thursday 10 April

In India, the number of children who live in abject poverty and who cannot attend school outweighs the entire population of Great Britain. But there are moments of sunlight in the darkness. Rich Indian men and women sometimes use their savings to set up charities to help where they can. Westerners also volunteer their time or their money to change people's lives.

I'm sitting in a school set up by a white American woman which was established to educate the poorest of the poor from the slums. To be eligible for a place, the family must earn under £50 a month. Every year, hundreds of children apply and, every year, they take only seventy.

I chat with some of the three-year-olds at the school. They look up from their tables, pencils still in hand. They are delightful.

'How did I get here from England?' I ask. After several guesses, finally they come up with 'By aeroplane.'

'What else flies?' I ask.

'Helicopters!'; 'Rockets!'; 'And birds, Ma'am, birds' come the responses. Yes, I say, so could I have come to India on a bird instead? 'No,' they shout. 'No.'

Really, I say, but why? One boy puts his hand up.

'Because a bird is too small, Ma'am.'

Talking with the sixteen-year-olds, I ask them what they want to do later in life. Lots say some kind of engineer, others accountants, businessmen; one wants to be a cricketer; another a magician. 'And what do you think about Michael Jackson?' I ask. 'King of Pop!' they yell. He was definitely murdered. They are certain of it. When I ask them what their friends in the slums think of them coming to this school, they tell me that their friends believe them to be very lucky indeed.

Back in the principal's office, my colleagues express their

amazement at the children's commitment to learning, the silence in the classrooms, the order, the motivation, the inspiration. The principal is a very forward-thinking woman who believes in good teaching and working hard. Some of my colleagues are very confused. How can it be that poor kids in India are so well behaved and our kids in Britain are terrors?

As an Indian man told me today, when the rich man looks at the poor man and presumes he is unhappy in his poverty and cries for him, all he is doing is revealing his own unhappiness; he is in fact crying for himself.

Summer Term Part One

Tuesday 22 April

The sun is shining brilliantly outside. Six weeks until Year 11 go on study leave. I've taught this class for five years, since they were eleven years old. The final climb begins. Mr Goodheart's demand that I get Dopey a 'C' echoes in my head. Every early-morning revision class, Dopey is there. 'I think I can, I think I can' is our motto. Beautiful and Deranged, too, are now attending regularly; they, too, seem determined to win this thing.

Ms Joyful bursts into the staff room and runs up to me. 'Snuffy, you have to look at this,' she says. She hands me a past maths exam paper. 'You have to look at these answers.'

'I don't know any maths. I'm not going to understand the mistakes.'

'Trust me, Snuffy, you'll get it.' So I look at the paper.

Impossible	Likely	Unlikely	Certain	Even

Which word from the box best describes the likelihood of each of these events?

    a. You throw an ordinary dice and get an even number.
    b. You throw a coin and get tails.
    c. Wednesday is the day after Tuesday.

At first, I take no notice of the student's answers. I'm stuck on the word 'dice', thinking, but I'm sure the singular of 'dice' is 'die'. But then this is the exam board. What do I know? I reread the question to be sure I've understood it, and then I look at the student's answers:

    a. Unlikely
    b. Likely
    c. Impossible

I laugh out loud. 'Wait a minute, this is a GCSE paper?'

'Yeah, it's one of the "G" questions.'

What she means is that this is from a set of questions designed for those students who are aiming just to get a 'G'. They're a lot easier, but even with full marks they won't be awarded anything higher than the lowest grade. Clearly, this student isn't even in the running for this.

I throw the paper in the air. 'This is ridiculous! This student isn't even able to answer the "G" questions.'

Ms Joyful sniggers. 'Well, you never know, if the right paper comes out on the day, and if the world is on my side . . .'

Yeah, maybe in that possible world not only will Wednesday follow Tuesday, but this student will know that it does.

Wednesday 23 April

Dreamer plops himself down in my office. I've asked for his brother to come in, as he just isn't putting in the required effort for that elusive 'C'. His brother, who is about twenty-seven, is well groomed, in a suit, and oozes dignity, sits down beside him. They're from Afghanistan. I've never had the nerve to ask about their parents. All I know is that Afghan is Dreamer's only family. They've been in this country for a few years and Dreamer has become increasingly badly behaved as each year goes by.

'It's a pleasure to meet you, Afghan. Dreamer has been working in my lessons, but he can also be silly and, well, at this stage in the game, he doesn't have time to play with. Not to mention that hat.' I point to Dreamer's head. 'He wears it all the time, which he knows is against the rules.'

Afghan gives me a deferential nod. 'I know, I know. I just told him to take it off. I am so embarrassed. It makes me feel shame, all of you teachers ringing me to complain about him.'

I look at Dreamer. 'Do you hear that, Dreamer? Do you hear how you have humiliated your brother? Do you know who works to put the clothes on your back? Do you stop to think that all your brother wants is for you to behave yourself, and yet you continue to make a fool out of him?'

Dreamer avoids both our eyes. His brother talks directly to me. 'I keep telling him and telling him. And I try to spend time with him too, even though I work twelve hours a day. And I have my own family too. I have my little ones to look after. And one of them is disabled. I can't take this stress.'

I look at Dreamer. 'Do you hear what your brother is saying?' Dreamer looks at the floor. 'Answer me, Dreamer, do you hear what he is saying?' I've raised my voice.

'Yes, Miss, I hear him, I hear him.' Dreamer is still avoiding eye contact.

'And how does it make you feel?' Dreamer is silent. 'Answer me, Dreamer! How does it make you feel?'

'It makes me feel bad, Miss. I feel sorry.'

'Hmm, yes, that's right. You have no idea what your brother went through to get you that coat.' I point to his shiny jacket. 'You don't know how hard it is to work for a living. But he does it, and all he asks is that you should behave yourself.'

Afghan becomes animated. 'Yes. Yes, Dreamer. Look at me. Just look at me. What am I? I am nothing. Am I a teacher, a doctor, a lawyer? No. I'm nothing. I never went to college. I never got an education. Why? Because I gave it up to look after you and your brothers. I gave up my life for you.'

'You hear that, Dreamer? Your brother gave up his education so that you could have one, and you throw it away as if it means nothing.'

'Yes, Miss, I'm sorry, Miss.'

His brother grabs his arm. 'I don't want you to be like me. I want you to be better than me. I want you to make something of your life, so that you don't have to work twelve hours a day for nothing.'

Dreamer nods, understanding. We finish our meeting with a sense of hope and purpose, with Dreamer promising to turn himself around in the short time left. We'll see. I shake his brother's hand. As he walks away, I think about how lucky Dreamer is to have him. And I wish he could see himself through my eyes. Afghan wants Dreamer to be better than him? I'm not sure that is even possible. He may not be a teacher, a lawyer or a doctor, but he's more of a man than most will ever be.

Friday 25 April

'Come on, we have to get this right. Deranged is going to be back any minute.' I look out the door into the corridor.

Hadenough is running out of patience. 'This is impossible! Why are we doing this anyway?'

''Cause it's good for our kudos with the kids. And it's fun. They'll love it!'

Hadenough faces the wall of mirrors. We're in the drama studio. 'OK then, get over here.'

I move over to the stereo and hit play. Out booms some loud hip hop. I run over and stand next to Hadenough. 'OK then: 1 . . . 2 . . . 3 . . . 4 . . .' We throw our arms out in front of us, wiggle our hips and move as if we're in a music video. After a while, Hadenough makes a wrong move. 'Dammit,' he yelps. 'I can't do this!'

Deranged comes running through the door. 'Sir! Sir! Look, it's like this . . .' She faces the mirror and does all of our moves with such speed and agility I look on in wonder. 'You get it? See, move your hips like this? Yeah?'

I put my hand on my forehead. 'This is so difficult.' I touch her on the shoulder. 'It's really good of you to help us out.'

Beautiful leaps in through the door. 'You kidding, Miss, this is gonna be *brilliant*. You and Mr Hadenough – imagine! You and Sir dancing at the dance show in front of everyone: it's gonna be hilarious!'

Mr Hadenough looks at me. 'You sure we aren't going to make fools of ourselves?'

'No. We're gonna be fine. Come on.' I face back to the mirror and motion for Hadenough to do the same. 'OK then, Deranged, where were we?'

Saturday 26 April

'Do you think this thing will be good?' Inspirational asks. 'We're trying so hard to redress the balance at Basic, especially with the Caribbean boys. I'd love to go in on Monday with some workable ideas for everyone.'

What can I say? 'Well, don't hold your breath. There'll probably be some known leader or politician talking. And what do they know? But maybe the workshops will be good.'

As I've done lots of specific work in this area with the kids, I'm hoping to hear some exciting ideas on raising black achievement. It is Saturday morning after all. Any teacher who is here must be super-dedicated. The hall is packed.

As I suspected, one of Britain's prominent black leaders stands to speak. When Prominent stands on stage, the mostly black audience, filled with teachers and parents, applauds loudly. She speaks of a time when she was at primary school, when she always got 'A' grades. At some point, Prominent was given a new teacher, and handed in her first essay expecting more of the same. To her surprise, the teacher refused to grade the essay because it was so good she was convinced the girl had cheated. The teacher looked at this little black girl – the only one in her class – and could not believe that a black girl could produce something of academic worth.

Prominent throws her fist into the air. 'This is why I am so committed to education. This is why I've dedicated myself to stamping out racism in the teaching profession.' She holds her head high. 'The media is always talking about black boys being *aggressive*, being *rude*, being *frightening*. We need to stop this kind of racist talk *now*!'

The room erupts in applause. I start to twist uncomfortably in my chair and, out of the corner of my eye, catch Inspirational wincing. Sorry, Inspirational. Sorry for bringing you here, giving up your Saturday morning because you're so keen, only to be told you're a racist by a woman who has no idea what you sacrifice for these kids. I want the ground to swallow me up.

A young black teacher who I know from another school leans back on her chair and whispers to me, 'But they *are* aggressive. What's she talking about?'

I grin and look at Inspirational, who smiles back, looking somewhat relieved. This young black woman is confirming that he isn't mad. Yes, your reality is mine too, she's saying. No, you're not a racist for thinking this. No, the true racists are the people standing up on stage.

Clearly, whatever caused black underachievement in the seventies is the same as what causes black underachievement now, thirty years later. Clearly, Britain is not more open-minded and tolerant as a society than it was thirty years ago. Clearly, black underachievement can have nothing to do with the increased chaos that one sees in Britain's black communities.

And what of all Prominent's other teachers? A child must have anywhere from twenty to fifty teachers in the course of their school career. What about all the other teachers who taught her? Were they all racist too? What about the excellent teachers who helped her prepare to get to the top university in the land?

Somehow, Prominent doesn't remember her many successes at school, the inevitable motivating and inspiring conversations she will have had and the support she will have been given during the times when she thought she wasn't good enough. She only remembers her one racist primary-school teacher. And all her influence on educational policy, all her passion in making a stand, in trying to 'change the system', is a direct result of this one solitary experience that happened a lifetime ago.

I suppose it's human nature to remember what hurts the most. When our black leaders ask us to stand next to them in the fight against racism, who would say no to that? What *black person* would say no to that? But I have known hundreds of teachers who teach in London. I don't know about the schools in Bradford or Bristol and cannot comment on them. Neither can I comment on the schools where there are few children of a minority ethnic background. But I do know London multicultural schools. And I know that the kind of racism Prominent experienced in the seventies is extremely rare.

As we are leaving, Inspirational turns to me. 'What would Ms Magical think of this event?'

I laugh. 'She'd think it was a load of bollocks. She'd think that what black boys need is some good old-fashioned discipline!'

Inspirational scratches his head. 'So why don't we just give it to them?'

I put my arm through his. 'What the hell, Inspirational! What am I? A fountain of knowledge?' I rush us along the road. 'I have no bloody idea.'

Monday 28 April

Ms Desperate, Furious's foster mother, marches into my office and sits down with him. I pick up my files and papers from the table and push them to one side. 'Sorry, this place is always in such a mess,' I mutter.

'That's all right, Ms Snuffleupagus. My only concern is Furious. What are we going to do?'

Ms Desperate looks as if she might cry. I've asked her to come in because of another incident. Furious and Beautiful had a shouting match at lunch on Friday last week and then he went to the nearest door and kicked in the window.

I address Furious first. 'Well, there's the cost of the window, Furious. Ms Desperate is going to have to pay for it.' No response. My tone becomes less even. 'Furious! Are you listening to me? Did you hear what I said? Ms Desperate is now going to have to spend her hard-earned money on a window which you broke deliberately!' A reluctant apology. 'You're always sorry, after the event. You're on a PSP! Do you know what that means? You're hanging on to your place here by a thread.'

Ms Desperate clasps her hands together. 'Please, Ms Snuffleupagus, I don't know what to do. He's so rude to me at home, he's so bad at school, he's completely out of control.'

'You're originally from Nigeria, right?'

'Yes, my parents returned to live in Nigeria last year. I came to London when I was five years old.'

'So could Furious go to live there? With your parents, I mean? Once, your husband suggested sending him to live with your mother.'

Ms Desperate nods slowly. 'He did? Yes, I suppose Furious could go to Nigeria. They don't really think of him as their grandson, but yes, I suppose they would help out.'

'Well, that's my advice to you then. Send him to Nigeria.' I feel as if I'm betraying Furious, but I have to remember to do what's best for him. I lean forward. 'I've seen it happen dozens of times, children who are out of control get sent back to the Caribbean or to Africa, and they transform. The discipline that exists in those countries gets them back on the straight and narrow.' I fix Furious with a look. 'The same could happen to him.'

Furious raises his head for the first time. 'I ain't going no Nigeria!'

Ms Desperate stands up. 'Yes, well, we'll see about that.' She grabs him by the arm and yanks him up. 'We're leaving.'

She holds out her hand and takes mine. 'Thank you very much, Ms Snuffleupagus. It's been very interesting talking to you.'

As she disappears out my door I wonder whether she has enough backbone to send Furious to Nigeria. I wonder whether she has the strength and the courage to give up on the dream of the mother country saving her son and saving us all. And then I wonder whether I do.

Wednesday 30 April

I rush towards the office. I have a funny feeling that today is going to be a hard one. It is one of my non-contacts, when I'm used to support other teachers who are teaching, taking students out of their lessons if need be.

'Yo, Miss,' shouts Munchkin from one of the chairs outside the office. 'I've been kicked out of geography.' He doesn't seem too put out by it.

'Oh no, Munchkin . . . what have you done?'

'Ms Snuffleupagus!' One of the office staff, Miss Reliable, is calling me.

'I'm coming back, keep going with that work.' I point at the books in front of him.

Miss Reliable points at Fifty, sitting on a chair around the corner. 'Fifty has trainers on. Can you go and speak to his father in the premises office?'

'Premises office?'

'His father is one of the premises staff.'

Bloody hell. How do I not know that his father works at the school? I head towards Fifty. 'Why are you wearing trainers, Fifty?'

'Dunno, I just am, innit?'

'OK, Fifty.' I motion with my hand. 'You'd better come with me.' We begin to walk down the corridor.

'Ms Snuffleupagus!' Psycho suddenly sprawls herself in front of me. 'What about me?' she shouts. 'You said Ms Sensible was going to send me home!' Fifty slithers back down on his chair.

'Psycho, I've asked you to sit down. Can you sit down, please?'

'Not till you phone my mum.'

'Psycho! You are to sit down, please. Miss Reliable is ringing your mum.' As Psycho trundles off back to her seat, I look at Fifty, who stands up. So does Munchkin.

'But what about me, Miss?' shouts Munchkin. Fifty sits back down.

I look at Munchkin, gesturing with my hand that he should sit. 'I'll be back in a minute, Munchkin, have a seat.' I look at Fifty. 'Come along then.' Fifty stands, sighing, and follows me to find his father.

His father, a short black man, hard-working and kind, is astonished when I point to Fifty's trainers. 'His shoes have a hole in them is all,' he says. I explain that a new pair must be bought, that Fifty cannot stay in school in incorrect uniform. He tells me that he cannot afford it, and does not know when he will be able to afford it. 'Send him home, if that's what you must do,' he says angrily.

So back to the office I go, Fifty in tow, with me trying to think what my next move will be. Fifty is sitting down for what seems like the hundredth time when Dopey comes bounding towards me. 'Miss! Miss! Oh my God, Miss! Miss!'

'Yes, Dopey, calm down. Now, what's the problem?'

'I need to go home, Miss. I need to go home. I just live five minutes away.'

'But we're in the middle of a lesson, Dopey. Why do you need to go home?'

'I forgot my PE kit, Miss. Please, Miss! I have PE this afternoon.'

Munchkin jumps up. 'Yeah, me too, Miss. I forgot my PE kit too, Miss.'

'Sit down, Munchkin!' I shout across the foyer, and turn back to Dopey. 'You can't go home now, Dopey. At lunch, OK?'

As Dopey nods gleefully, Miss Reliable from inside the office tells me that she has Psycho's mother on the phone. Ms Sensible has given the OK for Psycho to go home, but her mother won't agree. She wants to talk to me. Psycho leaps up from her chair. 'Aha! My mum is gonna tell you what's what now!'

'Sit down please, Psycho.' I ask several times, but she pretends not to hear me, and instead is skating across the floor. I take the phone.

'What's this I hear about you wanting to send my daughter home for bad behaviour? She hasn't done nothin' wrong.'

'Hello, Mrs Crackpot. Unfortunately, as Miss Reliable was explaining, Psycho has not been behaving well today. She refused to do as two teachers asked, she had to be sent out of science for swearing and now she is disrupting the office foyer by refusing to sit down.'

Mrs Crackpot is furious. She is convinced I'm lying. 'How am

I meant to know you're telling the truth, huh? You gonna put it in writing?'

'In writing? Well, I can do that if you want, but I'm not sure that will make much difference. Right now, for instance, Psycho is refusing to sit in a chair as I asked her to a moment ago.'

'You gonna write that down?' she demands.

I look at the office staff, who are all listening to the conversation, and roll my eyes. 'Write it down? But I'm telling you that she is standing right here in front of me, at this very moment, skating on the floor.'

Mrs Crackpot demands to speak to Psycho, who, when asked if she is indeed skating, confirms (by some truth-inducing miracle) that she is. Psycho hands the phone back to me, saying, 'My mum isn't finished with you.' She places the phone carefully in my hand, cackling.

Mrs Crackpot promptly launches into a tirade about how all her daughter is doing is exercising her right to stand. And on she goes, refusing to give me permission to send Psycho home. As I'm talking, a blondish woman in her fifties walks into the foyer from outside, clearly distressed. I tell Mrs Crackpot I will ring her back and head towards this woman.

'You remember me, yes?'

I frown. 'Oh, yes, of course . . .' I'm sure I've never seen this woman before in my life.

She laughs. 'I need you to get Ali for me.' She explains that Ali is in his lesson and that this is of the utmost urgency.

As we are talking, Fifty interrupts. 'Miss! What about my shoes?'

'Yes, Fifty, I'm coming, just give me a minute, I need to deal with this first.'

I look back at the woman, trying to figure out whose mother she is, but I'm drawing a blank. 'I'm sorry. I don't know Ali. What year is he in?'

'NO! NO! Not a child! Ali! Ali! You know! I've been talking to Ali and he said he is here at the school. Ali. You know, the boxer.' Munchkin, Fifty and Furious (who has just appeared, having also been kicked out of his lesson) stare at the woman, who keeps on repeating: 'You know, the boxer.'

I sit down opposite her. 'You mean Ali is . . . er . . . Muhammad Ali?'

'Yes, yes! The boxer! I saw his car drive away from my house, you see, this morning, when he came to visit, but he told me he is here at the school, so you must get him for me, from his lesson.'

I swallow hard. 'But Madam, I don't think that Muhammad Ali is on the premises.'

'Yes, I tell you! He told me himself that he is here! You do know who I mean, don't you? Ali? The boxer?'

'Yes,' I nod, 'I know who he is.' That's why I am pretty damn certain he ain't on the premises, but I look back at her and smile, trying hard to explain that Ali is unlikely to be at school.

The kids are all silent, listening to this maddening conversation. I am unable to persuade this woman that Ali is not in the school and so I go in search of someone sane. Jesus, what did I do to deserve a day like this one?

I march into the head's office, breaking into his meeting with Ms Sensible. They both look up, startled. 'I'm sorry to interrupt, Sir, but I need some help. I have a woman in the foyer, looking for Muhammad Ali. And then there's Psycho, whose mum won't give us permission to send her home. And then there is Fifty, who needs new shoes.' I explain the situations in detail.

Both Mr Goodheart and Ms Sensible look at me and, as if rehearsed, respond in unison: 'Muhammad Ali?'

'Yes,' I say, exasperated.

'You mean, Muhammad Ali, as in the boxer?'

'Yes,' I say, at the end of my tether. Both Ms Sensible and Mr Goodheart spontaneously burst into laughter. And I laugh too, stunned by the craziness of my job. When I decided to become a teacher, I had no idea it was going to be like *this*. I look at the head, whimpering, 'What should I do?'

'Persuade the woman to go home. You get some money from the safe and send Fifty to the high street to get some shoes.'

OK. I march back out into the battlefield to face the madness once more. 'Madam, now where were we . . .' I sit next to her and smile.

God takes pity on me and, somehow, I manage to persuade this woman to head home. 'You never know,' I say, 'perhaps he could turn up at the house, and then you'd miss him.'

I reassure her that I will contact her immediately if Ali appears at the school. That done, I grab Fifty. 'Come on, let's go and see your father about you buying a new pair of shoes.'

Fifty and I go around the school grounds until we run into his father. I explain that the plan is for the school to lend the money for shoes and that Fifty can go and buy a pair right now. I have rung the shop, I have the address, I know his size is there and the salesman is waiting for him.

Fifty's father looks at me in disgust. 'What? Pay for my son's shoes? You tell Mr Goodheart he can keep his deeam money! I'll pay for my own son's shoes. You send him home today, I'll get the shoes later on tonight and he'll be in tomorrow, in the correct uniform.' He is livid.

Poor man. I feel so sorry for him. 'OK then, that's fine. You know, we can't keep him in school like this because the other students will all start doing the same thing. That's why. We have to keep to the standards.' He looks at me as if I'd just insulted him. I smile at him. 'Come along, Fifty, off you go home then.'

I run away as fast as I can and head back to the office, only to find that the woman has returned. Miss Reliable sticks her head out of the office. 'This woman is here to see you, Miss Snuffleupagus.' She winks at me and closes the door.

The woman leaps up from her chair. This time, she's aggressive. 'I know what you're doing. You're keeping me from Ali! You're keeping me from seeing him.' She's screaming. And everyone is looking at us: Furious, Munchkin, Psycho (who is still skating) and another set of parents who have come in to see Mr Goodheart about their son, who is on the brink of permanent exclusion.

'Madam, please, I'm just trying to sort out this situation. Please, let's talk in the room across the foyer.' Suddenly she gets up and runs down the corridor, trying to escape, trying to get to wherever it is that I'm hiding Muhammad Ali.

'Please, Madam. Please have a seat,' I call, running after her. What if she goes into lessons? I have to stop her.

As I'm running down the corridor, up gets Munchkin, running after me, and then Fifty – where did he come from? – and up get Furious, Psycho: 'Miss, what about me? What about *me*?' They all charge down the corridor after me, me charging after a madwoman.

'Go and sit down, all of you!' I wave my arm in the air. 'Madam! Madam!' I manage to overtake her. 'Please, Madam, please have a seat in the foyer.'

She looks at me suspiciously, reluctantly turns around and returns to the foyer to sit down. And so it goes on, for some time I might add, the kids leaping and dancing, this woman descending further and further into pure psychosis, and me thinking I'm soon about to join her. In the end, our local PC comes to help. And, quite literally, he drags her away.

At this moment, I'm utterly convinced that I'm on some kind of comedy TV programme. This can't possibly be real. But then I remember . . . lunch. Oh yes, I haven't yet had lunch. I look at my watch. Damn! I charge back into the office and grab my things. As I do, a gaggle of boys is coming down the corridor. Looks like the aftermath of a fight. I look at Ms Reliable.

'Get someone else. Get someone else to sort this one!' I shout.

Ms Reliable looks at me pleadingly. 'But where are you going?'

'I'm going to *teach*.'

Thursday 1 May

'Miss, can I speak to you a sec?' Sure. I pull out a chair, and Beautiful sits down in my office. It's after school, about five o'clock, so I'm wondering what she's still doing here.

'I wanna break up with Furious,' she says. 'He's too much. He won't let me do nuffin'. He says I'm not a proper Muslim.'

'OK. That sounds like a good idea to me.'

'But how do I do it, Miss? What if he goes mad? And my dad, Miss, what if he finds out?'

'I thought your dad was going to come back to speak to us about the whole history situation?'

'Nah . . . it's too late, innit?'

I nod, reluctantly, knowing that she's right. 'Look, school is out soon, and then you have study leave for exams. Maybe that would be the best time to do it? Here, with both of you at school, I guess it makes it difficult?'

'Yeah, yeah, that's what Deranged said. Wait till we is gone.' Tears start to run down her cheeks. 'But I don't know when that is.'

We don't tell the kids when we are letting them out on study leave because, if they know, then they bring in eggs and flour and sometimes worse. We just let them go suddenly one day without warning. I hand her a box of tissues. 'It's soon, Beautiful, it's soon.' I pat her knee. It'll get easier, Beautiful. I promise. With time, you'll soon learn to forget him.'

'I know, Miss, I know.'

'And you're going to join the police force, aren't you? Who needs Furious to protect you when you're the one who is going to be protecting the rest of us?'

Beautiful smiles, blinking through her tears. 'Yeah, Miss.' She gets up. 'Thanks.'

As she walks out the door, I shout out after her. 'Come see me any time, you know.'

'Yeah, Miss, I know.'

Friday 2 May

'Have you boys paid your money for the trip tomorrow?'

'Yeah Miss, man, 'course we 'ave!' Dreamer bops about in front of my office with Dopey by his side. 'We left it in the office.'

Dopey jumps up and down. 'Five pounds, innit, Miss? I left my £5 at the office.'

'OK, come on, boys, we need to go check. Why do you always do everything so last minute?' I walk through the playground towards the office, with Dopey and Dreamer on either side of me, slightly behind, strutting as if they're my bodyguards. I see Beautiful and Deranged. 'Hey, girls! Have you paid your money for the Oxford trip tomorrow?'

'Yeah, 'course we have,' shouts Beautiful. 'We wanna be successes.'

As I walk through the playground with Dreamer and Dopey by my side, I see Fifty deliberately knock Polish over. 'Hey, Fifty! What are you doing? Could you give me your diary, please?' I want to note down in his diary what I've just seen.

Fifty is distressed. All the kids have diaries to write their homework in and for teachers to write notes to parents. I suppose his mother must regularly check his diary. He holds his hands up as if I'm holding a gun to his head. He moves towards me. 'Nah, Miss, please, Miss, I didn't do nuffin'. Please, Miss. Please, Miss.'

As he approaches, Dopey and Dreamer step forward and stand in front of him before he reaches me. 'Hey!' yells Dreamer. 'What'cha think ya doing?'

'Yeah!' Dopey makes a couple of fists and shows off his muscles. 'Don't you put your grubby hands on her!'

I look at my new bodyguards and laugh. 'Come on, boys! We need to get to the office!' Ah . . . sometimes these kids just make my day.

Saturday 3 May

I have organized a trip to Oxford University. I manage to get some money from school to pay for the coach and the kids make up the difference with a £5 contribution. The most extraordinary thing about it all is that we are going on a Saturday, so they aren't missing school, and yet they still want to go.

I can't wait to show them the different colleges, explore some history together and open up their eyes. We're on the coach, gliding through the beautiful countryside with the sun beating down, when Dopey leaps up, his face pressed against the window. 'Look, man. Look!' he shouts out. Dreamer, Beautiful, Seething, Furious and the others all look round, out of the window. Dopey bangs on the window. 'It's a cow, man.'

Dreamer squashes his face against the window too. 'Yeah, man, it's a cow!'

'Yes, boys, it's a cow. What's the big deal?'

'But it's real, Miss!' Dopey laughs hysterically. 'It's a real *cow*, man!' I put my hands on Dopey's head and shake them, as if there were something rattling inside. The others laugh. Seething is annoyed and folds her arms across her chest.

'What's wrong, Seething?' I say.

'Miss, how long is this trip? And what's so special about Oxford Circus anyway?'

Suddenly it strikes me. They have no idea where we're going. 'We're going to Oxford *University*. It's in a town called Oxford, which is about an hour and a half out of London. David Cameron went to Oxford. Lots of people in government went there. I want you to see things you've only ever seen on TV.'

Dopey and Dreamer burst into laughter. 'Rah, man! That's happened already, Miss. Didn't you see that cow?'

Sunday 4 May

'Liberal, you're making dinner tonight, right? I have to sort out Furious's reports. I'm meant to be updating Ms Sensible first thing tomorrow morning on his progress.'

Liberal looks up from his book. 'Yeah, sure. Don't I always? What's happened to that kid anyway? He's the one who was in that fight, right?'

'Yeah. But he's doing really well these days. I'm so proud of him. I think he might make it.'

Liberal kisses me on the forehead. 'I'll never understand you, babe. I'll never understand your job.'

'Why do you stick it out with me, eh?' I wink at him.

''Cause you've got so much energy, 'cause you've never sold out, 'cause you give everything you've got to these kids of yours.'

I wince. 'But that means there isn't much left for you, doesn't it?'

Liberal shrugs. 'Yeah, maybe . . . ah. . . who knows? Maybe I need to see a therapist. I always liked strong women – you know that. All I know is there's no one else in the world like you.'

'Awhhh.' I throw my arms around him. 'That's so sweet. I love you,' I say.

Monday 5 May

'Snuffy, you really think Ofsted will come this year?' Hadenough stands by my office window, staring out into the distance.

'I dunno. Maybe. I hate this bloody wait, though. I hate it.'

Hadenough jerks round. 'I can't stand it much longer either. Everyone is on edge. I tell you, if this is what teaching is about, then I'm going. I'm sick of this. All we ever do is try to be "outstanding". What bollocks! Only in teaching is "satisfactory" *un*satisfactory.'

Ofsted's verdict comes in the form of a single digit: 1 is outstanding, 2 is good, 3 is satisfactory and 4 is inadequate. 1s and 2s are acceptable. Anything else is to be branded a failure.

'Yeah. And it's so impossible to get a damn 1 on a lesson. Even 2s are getting more and more difficult to get. And all "outstanding" means is having the ability to perform like a seal, doing things which aren't even necessarily best for the children, when an inspector is in the room.'

Hadenough agrees. 'Yeah. And I can't do it. I'm a good teacher. I know I am. But I can't do what these idiots want. And I don't want to feel like I'm shit any more. I want to be happy.'

I shake my head. 'It's crazy. How can a whole school be filled with outstanding teachers?'

'I hate it, I tell you. I've had enough.'

'OK, OK. Calm down. What's got into you?' The bell rings. 'Shit. I'm on duty.' I get up and rush to the door. Hadenough gets up too. 'Sorry. We'll talk later, OK?'

'Yeah, yeah.' Hadenough heads off down the corridor, head down, kicking the floor with every step.

Tuesday 6 May

'Miss! You straightened your hair, you straightened your hair!' Dopey jumps up and down, clapping. 'Look, Dreamer, man. Look!' He points at my head. 'Dreamer! Just like we asked! She straightened her hair!'

Dreamer almost blushes. He nods in my direction. 'Yeah, Miss, looks good. Yeah. You should wear your hair like that all the time.'

The other boys nod. The classroom is buzzing with talk of my new hair. Finally we get to work, which they manage relatively well for a while. But Daring at some point complains of a headache, pulls his hood over his head and lies down over the desk. 'I'm not doin' no more,' he mutters.

'Get that hood off and sit up!' I command.

'Nah, I told you' – Daring speaks from under the hood – 'I have a headache.'

I turn to the rest of the class. 'Now, you see this? You see what he's doing? Life isn't easy, you know. Sometimes it gets hard. And what do you do when it gets hard?'

'We persevere,' Dopey calls out.

'Yes, that's right. You all think that Obama got to where he is just like that? Don't you realize what he had to do to get to where he is?'

The boys start to laugh. Dreamer jabs the boys next to him. 'Yeah, yeah, we know, he just went to his crew, man.'

'Yeah, yeah, he just made some threats, man.' They laugh.

'Yeah, he just said, "Gimme the job, bruv,"' chirps Dopey.

Beautiful groans. 'Miss, you're always telling us this. You're always giving us some speech about trying. But they aren't listening.' She points to the boys and sits up straight as if she suddenly realizes what she just said. 'I mean, I listen to you, Miss . . .' – Deranged sits up and nods, mouthing, 'Me too' – '. . . but *they* aren't listening.'

Hearing Beautiful, the boys sit up too. 'We's listening, Miss. We's listening. What does she know?'

Dreamer frowns. 'I is listening! Ever since you spoke to my brother, Miss, I've been good, innit?'

'Yes, you have . . . OK. So how did Obama get to where he is, then?'

Dreamer looks at me blankly. 'I dunno, Miss. We dunno.'

Dopey looks round at Dreamer like he's some kind of idiot. 'Yeah, we know: he *persevered*.' Dopey looks back at me, smiling, waiting for confirmation that he got it right.

'And what did Obama do when he got a headache at school?'

Daring jerks up and throws his hood off, grabbing his book in front of him, as if he's had enough. 'OK, man, I'm listening. I'm up.' He turns to the other boys. 'Now that Miss has got her hair straightened, she thinks she's *special*.' He glances in my direction, knowing he's walking a fine line, wanting to check that what he said will pass.

I point to the textbook. 'OK, now where were we . . . ?'

Wednesday 7 May

Surrounded by our best students, not necessarily the brightest, but the most loyal, the most interested in making something of themselves, the most driven, I ask them what they think is the number-one thing that would make them happier at school. There are about fifteen of them on the school council, boys and girls, some black, some white, Indian, Chinese: a real mixed crew. Adorable, Polish, Hip, Wholesome and Stoic are in the group.

'Would you learn more if you had "better" teachers?' I ask. 'Or what if you had bigger classrooms? Better textbooks? Better food at lunchtime? What about smaller classes, would that help? Perhaps learning would improve if we used computers more? What if we played more games in lessons? Perhaps if we set you more homework?'

Adorable leans forward. 'No, Miss, none of that stuff is important. Well, I mean, it's important, but we'd learn so much more if everyone in the class just listened to the teacher.'

'Ah, so the *behaviour* of other students in your lessons is the thing that stops you the most from learning?' All the children around me nod vehemently. They say nothing at all. 'That's interesting. I'm guessing that you find that pretty irritating, do you? I mean, you must get very annoyed that there are these other students who are preventing the teacher from teaching and you from learning, right?' Again, they nod in unison, as if I had pushed an electronic button that makes their heads suddenly bop up and down. 'So what could we do to make school better for you?'

Let Down pulls his chair up. 'Make them stop talking, Miss, stop them interrupting, make them listen to the teacher.' I guess he's remembering his five years of madness before he got to the sixth form, when his development was so stunted that he is now no longer a possible Oxbridge candidate. The stitches in his head from the hammer incident have more or less disappeared now. We never did find out who did it.

I look around at these keen, eager-to-learn children, who are staring at me, their eyes wide open, wanting me to fix it for them, wanting so badly to simply go to school and learn, and a feeling of depression sweeps over me. All these poor kids want to do is to go to school and learn without disruption. If they went to school in India or Jamaica, they wouldn't have this problem.

Thursday 8 May

The hip hop music is blaring loudly. Hadenough and I move with some ease, shaking our bodies in ways which I never knew possible. We get to the end of our routine without a single hitch.

Deranged and Beautiful clap loudly. 'Woohoo! Yeah! You got it, Sir! You too, Miss!'

Hadenough and I look at each other. 'We are *so* gonna make fools of ourselves at that Dance Show . . .'

Deranged does a few moves in the mirror. 'Nah Sir, man! It's gonna be sick, you'll see, everyone's gonna love it! All we need to do now is get you to grind down on Miss.'

'Grind down? What's that?' Deranged and Beautiful show us what they mean, looking at themselves in the mirror as they do so. Beautiful, who is playing the man, is holding still as if she were sitting on a chair, and Deranged then 'grinds down' on to her, revolving her bottom as she moves closer to nearly sitting on Beautiful's lap.

Mr Hadenough looks aghast. 'No way!' He starts to head to the door. 'We can't do that, Mr Goodheart would have our heads! We can't do it. The routine we have is enough.'

'Oh come on, Sir!' I say. 'Where's your sense of adventure? Let's try it! Who cares what Mr Goodheart says?' I run after Hadenough and pull him back to face the mirrors.

'Yeah! Come on, Sir!' Deranged and Beautiful are yelling so loudly I wonder how people aren't coming in to see what's going on.

We all stand in front of the mirrors. 'OK, girls, do it again so we can copy you.'

Friday 9 May

It's lunchtime and I'm walking outside the gates, looking for kids who are trying to jump the wall to go to the local chicken shop, from which they are banned during school hours. The sun is hiding behind the clouds today and I wrap my coat around me. I see Fifty and Cent trundling along towards the high street. 'Fifty! Cent!' I shout out after them. They turn around. When they see me, they run. From behind me, Munchkin appears. 'Where are you going?' I ask him.

'Nowhere, Miss.'

'You planning on following Fifty and Cent to the high street?'

'Fifty and Cent? Nah . . .'

'I've told you, Munchkin: stop hanging around with those boys.'

Munchkin shrugs and turns to go back into school. 'See ya, Miss.'

After ten minutes of standing there, I decide to go and get some lunch. Hadenough is at the door to the canteen and waves to me. I wave back. As I do, I turn round to look at the gate. Munchkin makes a dash for it, and I see him running down towards the high street.

I approach Hadenough. 'Bloody Munchkin. He's gone down to the high street with Fifty and Cent to that stupid chicken shop. I wish he'd stop hanging around with them.'

'What else is he meant to do? Anyway, those guys are down at that chicken shop nearly every day.'

'They are?'

Hadenough laughs. 'Sure! Who's looking? Who cares?'

It's true.

Monday 12 May

Stoic has invited me to a celebration event tonight for the mentoring scheme for black kids he told me about. He's been part of it for the last five years. I'm looking forward to going and supporting him, and learning from their successes. I take Liberal with me so that he can have a taste of what my life is like.

Various kids stand and speak about all that they have been achieving. All of them are black, most of them are boys. Stoic is inspirational, as usual, but so are the others. Here, he is no longer exceptional but, rather, the norm. I am stunned by how articulate, confident and capable these kids are. They speak of ambitions that are normally reserved for the privileged. They talk of learning how to 'speak', not just publicly, but 'to get rid of our London accents', as one girl says. And it's true, the edge on their voices has magically disappeared. They describe learning how to walk, as if they have been to finishing school. And with it, there is no shame, only pride at bettering themselves. I am truly and profoundly impressed.

After the event, we go next door to get some food, and when we enter the dining area, the tables are all full. One table of kids dutifully gets up and gives us their table, without hesitation. I'm reminded of those rugby boys at Wineaton.

We tuck into the food and Liberal turns to me. 'Yeah, the food is good, but I feel bad.'

'Why?'

''Cause we got our food before the kids had theirs.'

'So? They're kids! We are the adults. We're meant to eat before them.'

As we munch, I think about why these kids have become such successes. One, they are the best the inner city has to offer. Two, they have been inspired by this scheme, which has supported them in small groups outside of school. Some kids simply cannot survive the factory belt. But then, there is also number three: the scheme's back-to-basics approach.

I have seen dozens of schemes like this in my lifetime. And never have I seen such outstanding results. The difference with this one is that the kids have been taught how to walk, how to smile, how to speak. The people who run the scheme don't care whether it is 'un-PC' to try to tone down the kids' London accents. They understand that it matters how you sound. And they don't insist that the world change its standards; they learn to conform and reach that set of standards instead. Suddenly, I understand why Stoic reads the newspaper at school in plain view, and where his confidence comes from.

Liberal and I are heading out the door on our way home when Stoic comes up to me. 'Thanks so much for coming, Miss,' he says.

'No, Stoic. Thank you for inviting me. It was a real eye-opening experience. You're very lucky to have been part of this scheme.'

Stoic nods. 'Yes, I know, Miss, I know.'

'I look forward to seeing you at school tomorrow morning with your newspaper!'

'Miss, I may not see you before the end of the week, and with us going off on study leave for the exams, well, I wanted to say thank you. Thank you for everything you've done for me since Year 7.'

'You're very welcome, Stoic. If only all our students could be like you. It's been a pleasure knowing you. I hope you'll come back and tell us what you get up to. You got into King's in the end, didn't you?'

'Yes, that's right. History.'

I shake Stoic's hand. 'Fantastic. You'll do great. Good luck to you.' As we walk out the door, I put my arm through Liberal's arm. 'I'm gonna bake you a cake this weekend.'

'A cake?' Liberal frowns. 'Why?'

''Cause you're the best guy on the planet. And I need to be someone kids like Stoic can look up to. I can't just disappear into my work all the time.'

Liberal kisses me on the forehead, grinning. 'I can't wait,' he says.

Tuesday 13 May

Today was one of those days which I'll remember for ever. Today we pushed the boundaries, we went out on a limb, we tried to change the world. Today we had the dance show. Hadenough and I were at the very end. The kids went insane. As we jumped around like Beyoncé, they all stood, cheering and screaming at the top of their lungs. They leapt about, throwing their arms in the air, gangster style:

'Go, Sir!'; 'Go, Miss!'; 'Yeah! Yeah! *Yeah!*' And when I grind down on Hadenough, the crowd goes completely wild. It was amazing.

Hadenough charges into my office. 'We did it! It was fantastic!'

'I told you it would be. We were *good*!' I'm grinning from ear to ear.

Hadenough hugs me. 'You were right. It was great. We even got the grind right. Almost makes me want to stay . . .'

'Exactly! Ordinary's brilliant. You don't wanna leave us.'

'Maybe you're right. I'll think about it.'

I look at my watch. 'Look, it's eight thirty. Let's get out of here. Drink?'

'Yeah, Ms Joyful and Mr Sporty said they're going to the bar round the corner. Let's go and find them.'

Wednesday 14 May

I'm walking home. It's about 7 p.m. Inspirational is walking with me because he dropped by to pick me up on his way home from school. I'm pushing my bike, both baskets stuffed with books, making it heavy and difficult to manoeuvre.

Walking along, I see the bus stop in front with its rain shelter and some of our girls, Psycho and Seething now out of uniform, standing by it. They take up the whole pavement. Their garish earrings and questionable choice of clothes catch my eye. They see me. They look at each other as if to suggest the enemy is in their midst.

I don't want a confrontation, which is what normally happens if you ask students to do something they don't want to do, like move to the side so that you can get past. It's after school, and I don't have recourse to detentions, my office, authority. I know what will happen: I'll ask them to move; they will sigh and grunt and then finally shuffle themselves out of the way with a big huff, as if I have asked them to climb Mount Everest. They might say something rude as they do so. I will then have to pick them up on their rudeness. They will then take offence at my refusing to tolerate their disrespect and the rudeness will increase in tempo and magnitude.

So I look to the kerb to see how high it is, judging in my mind the difficulty of lowering my heavy, laden bike into the street, to pass around the bus shelter instead of demanding courtesy from my girls. But, as we approach, a miracle happens: they move. They move to the side of the shelter, to make room for us. We walk through.

I smile at them. 'Thank you, girls. That's very good of you.'

'Hi, Miss.' They lower their heads slightly, like the rugby boys did at Wineaton. 'You was brill, Miss. You grinding down on Sir!' Psycho nudges her chin towards the sky. Seething nods. 'Yeah, Miss! We was there. We saw you.' She grins.

I blush slightly. 'Yes? Were we any good?'

'Yeah, you was good, Miss. You was *good*.' Seething and Psycho laugh. 'Yeah, it was the best bit, Miss!'

'That's good to hear, girls. You have a good evening.'

'You too, Miss.'

As we walk away, Inspirational turns to me, aghast. 'My goodness, Snuffy, that was fantastic. Not only did they move, but they were *nice* to you!'

'Yeah, it was, wasn't it?'

'Yes.' He can't believe it. 'Well done, Ms Snuffleupagus. What have you been doing with them?'

Working miracles I guess.

Thursday 15 May

'Ms Snuffleupagus! Have you been here for some time?'

I look around me. I'm in the doorway of the corridor that leads to the girls' changing rooms in the gym. 'I don't know. A few minutes. I was hoping to catch —'

'Yes, well, there's been a theft.'

'A theft? What of? When? Who?'

'In the girls' changing rooms. This lesson. A phone was taken from one of the girls' bags while she was doing PE. We don't know who took it.'

'What is it with phones going missing?'

'I know. It looks like we have a phone thief. They're probably selling these phones down the high street. Who knows?'

'Whose phone was taken?'

'Adorable's. Poor thing. She's so upset.'

'Hmm, yeah, I know how she feels.'

Ms Sensible smiles. 'So did you see anyone out here? Or coming out of the girls' changing rooms?'

I think. 'Well, when I arrived, Furious and Dreamer were going around that corner.' I point ahead of me down another corridor. 'I don't know where they were coming from, but it could have been from here.'

Ms Sensible's eyes light up. 'Furious? Really? We need to talk to him about it. Can you do it, Snuffy?'

'Me? I can't do it. I'm terrible at that kind of thing. I may be hot in the classroom but a police officer I am not. I'll never be able to break him.'

'OK, I'm no good at it either. I'll ask Mr Cajole to do it.'

'It won't make any difference. This is Furious we're talking about. He won't break for anyone.'

'Well, we have to try. It's the only lead we have.'

Ms Sensible goes to comfort Adorable, who I can see at the entrance to the changing rooms down the corridor, in tears, with Polish stroking her arm. Poor girl. What is it with these phones? Furious and Dreamer were rushing when I saw them. Hmmm, I wonder: could it really have been them?

Friday 16 May

I'm with my Year 11s. It's our last lesson together and the sun is bright outside. All the children have taken off their blazers. It's so hot, they're sprawled across the desks. 'Can we go outside, Miss?' Dreamer asks, looking up at me from under his lashes. As he asks, I wonder whether Mr Cajole has questioned him and Furious yet about the phone theft.

'Are you crazy? This is the last opportunity we have to revise together and you're asking to go outside? Absolutely not.' As I say the words, the teacher and her class next door head out towards the sun.

'See! How comes *they* get to go out?' the kids screech.

'Because they don't have *me* as their teacher.'

Dopey doesn't want to take no for an answer. 'Come on, Miss, you is meant to be *cool* now! I saw you grinding down on Sir.'

The class giggles. 'Yeah, Miss! You was *good*.'

'OK, OK, OK . . . can we get back to work please?' I smile to myself as I hand out some past papers and demand we go through them. They reluctantly obey. Towards the end of the lesson, I get out a little surprise. I tell them how I'll miss them, that I've taught them for five years, how they've done me proud. And then I give them some chocolates. They gobble them down, waiting to hear what more I have to say.

So I put on a DVD. This footage was taken when they were in Year 7. They have forgotten it, of course. We did some speeches and I videoed them. As they watch their little faces, younger by five years, and as they hear their younger voices, still theirs but those of young children, they squeal with delight. I, too, cannot help but laugh as we watch the entertainment of years long past.

We have ten minutes left. 'OK, everyone,' I gesture for silence and they look up at me. 'So remember everything we've learnt together,' I say. 'And remember, you'd better revise: the exam is on *Tuesday* and, remember, we have the revision session at seven forty-five. So you had better be there . . . because if you aren't, I will find you, and I will *kill* you.' They laugh. I even manage to get a smile out of Seething. 'Now go and enjoy the sunshine.'

Off they run through the door, heading toward the rays. 'Bye, Miss,' they call back. 'Promise we'll revise, Miss.'

Dopey looks at me with his big eyes. ' "Choo choo," Miss. "Choo choo!" '

The others around him laugh. Deranged nods in my direction. 'Cool, Miss.'

I point my finger at her. 'Remember: beauty therapists need GCSEs!'

'Yeah, see ya, Miss,' says Beautiful.

I wink at her. 'You still going to do it?'

She nods. 'Yeah, Miss. I think so.'

Seething and Psycho jut their chins towards me. 'See ya, Miss.'

'Bye, girls.'

And then suddenly, the room is empty and silent. It's eerie, almost unnerving. There is no more laughter. They're gone.

Wednesday 21 May

It's early morning on the day of the last English exam, and Dopey is the first to arrive at my revision class. At eight fifty, the children start to pack up their things. 'What do you think you're doing?' I shout. 'Sit back down. We're not finished!'

They look at each other incredulously. 'But Miss! You can't say that this time – the exam is in ten minutes!' cries Dreamer.

'Well then, that leaves us nine minutes to revise. Sit down.' They plump themselves down with a huff.

At eight fifty-five, Dreamer starts to head towards the door. 'Stop!' I shout. 'They cannot start the exam without us. So don't worry.' I hold my hand out. 'Just a couple more things . . .'

Dreamer spins round. 'Nah man, this is madness! Miss! You've lost it this time! We've got to go!'

Dreamer stamps his feet as Dopey looks back and forth between Dreamer and me, not sure what he should do. Deranged and Beautiful both look at the clock, worried. 'OK, OK.' I gather my stuff. 'You're right. Let's go everyone. Let's go get those "C"s!'

Dopey smiles, relieved at my display of sanity. 'Yes, Miss, we're gonna do it for you, you'll see.'

'Run, everyone, run!' shouts Dreamer. Deranged, Daring and the others head out the door.

I grab hold of Dopey's arm as we all stampede down the stairs rushing towards the exam hall. I ask him various questions about the set texts. Dopey answers dutifully and correctly. He grabs my hand. 'Don't worry, Miss. We're gonna do it!'

Like a tornado ripping into town, we tear into the peaceful exam hall. The children take their seats. The exam begins and I, closing my eyes and holding my breath, open up the exam paper to see if the gods have indeed been kind.

As Dopey works away, I stand at the front of the hall, not daring to walk past his desk to see his answers. If a 'D' it must be, then I will wait until 27 August to find out. Every now and then he looks up at me and nods, grinning, as if to say: 'Don't worry, Miss, we're doing it!'

I look to the skies and thank God for the paper. It is a good one. Please let him know what he's doing. Please let him double-check. Please let them all remember what we've learnt together. Please, God, give my kids a chance to come through on the other side with that 'C'.

Thursday 22 May

One more day till half-term. Thank God. I'm exhausted. It's been boiling hot all week and you can be sure that, come tomorrow, it'll start to rain. It always does for half-term.

Compassionate and I meet up for a coffee after work. She's looking huge now, radiant and happy. Looking at her, I wish I could look as together as she always does, and I promise myself to spend a little more time on myself from now on. We sit down at a small wooden table and settle in.

'Just a few weeks left now,' Compassionate says, contentedly. Her maternity leave starts soon.

'So I guess you and Bank will definitely send the kid to Wineaton after Bank's experience at my school. He must have been horrified.'

'Well, it's just that he hasn't seen that kind of thing before. You know, he went to a grammar school, and well . . . Anyway, we want what's best for our child. And not to mention, of course, that we only have to pay a third of the fees, as I work there.'

'Oh yes, I forgot. Yes, you couldn't possibly turn that down. But you need to tell Bank that some of the girls came and told me after his talk that they were going to set themselves some goals.

One of them wants to go into the police force and the other wants to be a beautician. Bank inspired them.'

'Really? I'll certainly tell him. He'll be pleased. Anyway, what about you and Liberal then? Aren't you going to have children soon?'

I blush. 'Yes, well, I suppose so. But I'm so busy and he's so busy, and I don't know how I could do my job and raise a child too.'

'Well, you would just do *less*. You'd have to. You'd have to do less is all.'

I think about Compassionate's suggestion about doing less and feel uneasy. How *can* I do less? That's just impossible.

'You need to be careful, Snuffy, working all the time. It isn't good for people's relationships. They say teaching is in the top five professions for the highest divorce rates.'

'I know, I know. There's this teacher at work – he teaches science – who is really amazing: he works so hard, he's in school from 7 a.m. to 8 p.m. every day, I swear to you, *every day*. And he still takes work home. He's superb with the kids – such a great teacher. I hear he's getting divorced. And I hear it's 'cause his wife couldn't take his work hours. She never sees him.'

'Exactly. Be careful, Snuffy. Most men want children. I'm certain Liberal wants them.'

But if I have children, how am I meant to do my job properly? And how can I be satisfied with only doing it partly well? Poor Liberal. What kind of a wife am I? What if he leaves me?

Half-term

It's half-term and Liberal and I have been invited to Bank's friends' country house in the middle of Gloucestershire for the weekend. Saturday afternoon, they take us to the village fete, and I note the sheep grazing in the next field. Families meander with their children amongst the various stalls, chatting, because, of course, they all know each other. Members of the families are in charge of the stalls, with homemade cakes on sale, potted plants and random kitchen items which have presumably been discovered in the cupboards of various villagers' kitchens. Often, it's the children running the stalls, collecting the 50 pence participation fee, and explaining the rules of the game to other children, who eagerly wait their turn.

How different this fete is to the one I went to in Regent's Park last year. There, no one knew each other, it was massive, with huge marquees, hired performers and lots of money backing every event. There are no roller coasters and bumper cars at this fete. Instead, one can play skittles or darts.

I grab three bean bags made out of stockings and dried beans and throw them at the homemade posts with coconuts on top. I hit one. It falls to the ground. I leap about happily because I've won. And what have I won? I've won the coconut. I wonder what my kids would say to that. How boring they would find this place, and how irritated would they be to win a coconut. I've known schools where they give out iPods as prizes.

Liberal and I return home on Sunday afternoon, me feeling satisfied that we've spent some quality time together. He hugs me from behind as I position my coconut prize in the middle of our front room's fireplace, giving it pride of place. 'Good weekend, eh?' he says.

'Yeah.' I smile. '*Great* weekend.'

Liberal swings me round to face him. 'Yeah, it was good to spend some time together.'

'I know. I'm trying to cut down. Have you noticed? I'm trying to work less.'

Liberal smiles as if he doesn't believe me. 'You'll have to, you know, when we have kids.'

'I know, I know . . . and that'll be soon, I know . . . and I want them to have what those kids had at that fete . . .'

Liberal heads towards the kitchen and I turn back round to face my coconut. As I gaze at it, I think about how unfair it is that my children have so much and, as a result, have so little. And I decide to always keep this coconut, to remind me that, in life, it is always the simplest of things that bring the greatest rewards.

Summer Term Part Two

Monday 2 June

Mr Goodheart clears his throat to get our attention at the briefing. 'OK, everyone. No phone call yet. The question is whether it will come now, so late in the year. We just don't know. So be ready. Ofsted could come knocking any minute.'

People start grumbling. The last half of summer term is meant to be a little easier, a bit of a cool-down after an exhausting year. The sun is out, the kids leave home and get home when it is still light out, they can play football and other sports after school, it is warm and everyone is generally happier. So to have Ofsted still hanging over our heads is the pits.

'You marked all your end-of-year exams over the holiday?' I ask Hadenough as we walk out of the staff room.

'Nah, most of them, but I still have two classes to do.'

'Hang in there, OK?'

Hadenough shakes his head, looking more fed up than ever as he walks away from me out of the hall.

Tuesday 3 June

Today I'm telling my Year 8s that we're going on a trip. They're excited and I have trouble calming them down. I explain that we'll be taking a bus and then a train and then the tube. And then I spend some time talking about what we are going to do, why we are doing it, what money to bring, where we will eat lunch, and so on. Finally I end with how we'll return on the tube and our time of arrival back at school.

As expected, when I finish talking, there are lots of questions. They cannot wait till next week. Neither can I. Dumbo, a white boy who isn't the sharpest tool in the toolbox, raises his hand to the sky, his eyes flickering madly behind his glasses. 'Yes, Dumbo?' I ask.

'Miss,' he asks, 'what's the tube?'

The rest of the class cackles with laughter. 'The *tube*? What's the *tube*?' They double over, some falling off their chairs. 'Don't you know? How can you not know? *Rah!!!*' Munchkin and Fifty laugh and laugh.

'That's enough, everyone,' I shout. Dumbo blinks even more, looking around at everyone, baffled by their reaction. I frown. 'There is no such thing as a silly question. Every question is a good question.' I smile, looking at Dumbo. 'The tube, Dumbo, well, it's the underground, you know?'

Dumbo looks at me uncomprehendingly and shakes his head. The rest of the class can barely contain their amazement. 'Rah! How can you not know? How can you not know?' Cent rolls his eyes. 'It's a train, Dumbo. It's a train that goes underground.'

'Yes, Dumbo, that's right,' I say, 'it's a train that goes under the ground.'

Dumbo looks frightened. 'Under the *ground*?'

I nod, moving towards him. 'Uh, huh, that's right: under the ground. But it's perfectly safe. You don't have to worry. We'll all be fine in it.' I smile. 'Have you never been on the underground before, Dumbo?'

Dumbo smacks his forehead. 'Oh yeah! Oh yeah! Once, on a school activity, I think maybe I went on it then.' He laughs.

'You see? That's great, Dumbo. I don't want you to drop out on me now. Remember what I said at lunch: I need you on this trip, you're going to be my assistant.' While the others are packing up their things, I whisper in Dumbo's ear. 'I'm counting on you, Dumbo. I need you to help with organizing everyone – telling them what to do. Do you think you can do that?'

Dumbo grins. 'Yes, Miss. Don't worry, Miss, I won't let you down.'

'Good.' I pat him on the shoulder. 'I knew I could count on you.'

'But, Miss,' he whispers back, 'why did you call it the *tube*?'

I shrug my shoulders. 'I don't know, Dumbo, I guess that's just what people call it.'

Mr Hadenough slumps into a chair in my office. 'Snuffy, I have some news.'

'Oh Hadenough, don't worry, we're nearly at the end of the year –'

'No, Snuffy, you don't understand.' He pauses. 'I've done it already.'

'Done what?'

'I saw Mr Goodheart before the end of half-term and I handed in my resignation.'

'You mean, you plan to leave this summer? You handed in your resignation and you never told me?'

'Look, I gave it in, but maybe I won't go. I had to give it in to catch the half-term deadline. But Mr Goodheart is trying to persuade me to stay.'

'Well, I knew you were having a tough time, but I thought you were managing to hang in there somehow. What changed?'

'You heard what happened to my phone, yeah?'

'No?'

'It went missing on Tuesday afternoon, from my lesson.'

'What is it with all these phones being stolen? Do you know who took it?'

'Nah. But I'm convinced it's Furious. The bloody bastard.'

'Furious? Why? You know Mr Cajole questioned Dreamer and him about it and he insists that he and Furious were not involved.' I sit on the edge of my chair, waiting to hear.

'Yeah, right! Like Dreamer would tell us the truth! Look, I was teaching his class period 5. I know the phone was in my bag half-way through period 5 because I took it out to make a point. I was trying to talk to the kids on their level, looking at the idea of comparison, and I took out my phone, asked Hip to take out his phone, and the kids had to vote on whose was better.'

'Ah.'

'So you see, they'd all seen my phone and they also saw exactly where I put it back in my bag. So then, when I went to dismiss the class at the end of period 5, I went to the door, and left the desk and my bag at the front of the class.'

'So you were standing by the door at the back of the classroom?'

'Yeah. And then suddenly Furious knocks a flower-pot off the desk.'

'Oh,' I say, figuring out what's happened. 'And he had to bend over to pick it up, I suppose?'

'Yeah. The perfect diversion. And everyone was moving towards the back of the room to leave, so no one was seeing what was happening, and it was too far away for me to see anything.'

'So you think he bent down and, while picking up the flower-pot, he stole the phone?'

'Yeah. There's no other explanation. But Ms Sensible says anyone could have taken it, that maybe the kids from my period 6 lesson took it. I didn't notice the phone was gone until after school. And then I cancelled it. So who knows? And I guess Ms Sensible's right. I have no proof. But I just know Furious took it.'

Oh my God. Suddenly it strikes me that maybe it was Furious who stole Adorable's phone that day. And then Ms Alternative's phone . . . Furious was with Dopey, who returned it to the office, after all. And when I fell over in the canteen that day and my phone went missing, Furious was also there . . . 'Have you had your phone statement yet?' I ask.

'No.'

'Well, maybe he did something with the phone after stealing it. Maybe he made a call.'

Hadenough stands up. 'Good thinking! I'll go call them right now and get a statement. I'm gonna get that kid.'

Friday 6 June

I'm running across the playground. Damn. I'm late. Just found two kids fighting. I couldn't really leave them to it. I had to break it up and get them to the office. It wasn't a bad one, but still: now I'm so bloody late!

I run up the stairs and throw open my classroom door: 'Miss, you're *late*!'

A chorus of 'Yeah, Miss!'; 'Yeah, Miss! You're LATE!'; 'Detention for you, Miss!' follows.

Fifty gets up and writes my name on the board. 'That's your whole breaktime gone!' He laughs.

'OK, yes, all of you. I'm sorry. I'm late. You're right. I deserve a detention.' I walk to the board and hold my hand out towards Fifty. He hands me the board pen. I put an X by my name – the sign for detention.

'*Yay!*' The class cheers. Some of them even clap.

'OK, OK.' I signal for them to calm down. 'Don't get so excited.' I pause, looking around at everyone. They're all sitting in the correct seats, bags on the floor, books out, ready to learn. 'And look at all of you! I'm so proud. You've organized yourselves so well. You would have thought a teacher was in here!'

Cent coughs. 'We're very responsible, Miss. Don't ya know that?'

'Well, you know . . . No, I don't think I did. But you've made me realize.' We all laugh. 'OK then, let me just get the lesson out on the whiteboard.'

The lesson goes very well. Bizarrely, no one misbehaves. They're all as good as gold. How lovely. In fact, they're so good, we get an enormous amount done. In spite of my lateness, we tear through everything I've planned.

I look at the clock. 'Oh my goodness! Is that the time already?' It's nearly ten forty-five, and that's when the lesson ends and break begins. 'OK, everyone, pack up. We've done really well today. Well done. Just look at how much we do when everyone is behaving themselves.'

The kids get up and start to pack their things away. They seem to do it at lightning speed. And without me asking or insisting, they go quiet and stand perfectly behind their chairs as I always ask them to do before they're dismissed.

I'm amazed. 'Wow! You all are on fire today, you're fantastic. Ready already? What's got into you?' I stand in front of them, and they face me in silence, looking at the clock. 'OK, everyone, let's just wait till we hear the bell.'

Tick tock, tick tock. They still stand in silence, waiting. But no bell. Flipping hell. I know this silence is going to break any second. They can't hold it for this long. And then I'll have to get angry with them. Damn. Where the hell is the bell?

Munchkin pushes his glasses up on his nose. 'Miss, there must be something wrong with the bell.'

I go to my classroom door, open it up and look down the corridor. The problem is that we're in a corridor which is tucked away, so the other kids won't be around this bit. Why on earth has the bell not gone yet?

Munchkin sighs. 'Miss, we've been *good* this lesson. Just let us go.'

I turn round. 'OK, then, yes. Off you go. Left side out first, as usual.' I hold the door wide open and they dash out down the corridor.

I return to my desk and start sorting out my things. The bell still hasn't gone. I look at the clock. It's ten fifty. I open the door again and look out. It's too silent. Where are the other kids?

I don't wear a watch. They make my skin itch. And by now I've turned off the computer so I can't check the time. I return to the computer and press the button to turn it back on. As it's chugging on, I hear some noise in the corridor. I pop my head out. It's Cent. 'Cent,' I shout after him, 'come here.' He runs up to me. 'What's going on? Are the other kids out for break?'

'No, Miss.'

I study his face. 'What have you all done?'

'We switched the clock, Miss. We put the time forward. It ain't break, Miss, we're still in lesson time.' He can't contain himself.

'What?' I start to charge down the corridor. '*What?*' I look round at Cent. 'I can't believe you've done this!' I shake my head, laughing. 'You really got me this time.'

Cent jumps about. 'Yeah! We got you, Miss! We got you, innit?'

I stop in my tracks, pointing my index finger at him. 'Look, you had better go and find everyone . . . and get them back here this instant.'

Cent leaps around. 'OK, Miss, I'll get 'em! I'll get 'em!' And he tears off down the corridor.

A minute later I hear laughter and stampeding outside. Then they pour into the class. 'We got you, Miss. We got you.' '*Rah!*' They are creasing up.

'Yeah, yeah.' I can't help but enjoy their amusement. 'You did. You certainly did.' They sit down. All of them are here. Funny, I think, how they've all come back. They've come back because they want to join in the laughter and the sense of satisfaction at having 'got me'. So on they go, giggling and joking, retelling the story over and over about how Fifty changed the clock, but Munchkin helped him reach it, how Adorable told them not to do it, but Cent persuaded her to play along. Finally the bell goes. 'OK,' I say. '*Now* you can go.'

They pour out the door. 'We got you, Miss. We got you!'

'Yes, I know! Now get outta here!'

Monday 9 June

Hadenough comes marching up to me in the playground brandishing a piece of paper. 'I've got it!' He has a big smile plastered across his face.

'What does it say?' I try to grab the paper from his hands, but he holds it up too high.

'Well, I think we've got him.'

'Really? Tell me! What does it say?'

Hadenough and I rush to the staff room. We look at the phone statement. There is no way Hadenough's period 6 class stole that phone because, during period 6, games were being downloaded on to the phone.

'Someone in that Year 10 class during period 5 took my phone,' he says, 'and I guarantee you it was Furious.'

I study the statement further, looking at the specific times of the downloaded games. We realize that the games started coming on to the phone about ten minutes into period 6 and then continued being downloaded for a period of no more than ten minutes.

'Why did he stop? Why did he only use the phone in that ten-minute window?'

Hadenough doesn't really have an answer. 'Maybe someone stopped him. He must have been in a lesson. Maybe the teacher saw him use the phone?'

'Oh my God, yes!' I run to the notice board where the full time-table is posted. 'That's it. He was in a lesson. We need to figure out where he was.' Both Hadenough and I start scanning the sheets on the wall. 'Let's see . . . Tuesday, period 6, 10B.' We draw our fingers along the different lines.

Oh, I hope he was with one of the better teachers. I hope he was with someone who will be able to remember what happened and who has some control of their classroom, enough control to remember Furious's exact movements. How is it possible anyway for a child to be in a lesson downloading games and the teacher not to notice? Some of us should be ashamed of ourselves.

My finger follows 10B's classes across: period 4, period 5, period 6 . . . Bingo. Mr Hadenough looks to where my finger is pointing. 'So? Who was it?'

Oh my God. Hadenough looks at me. I look at Hadenough. We both burst into laughter. 'I'm such an idiot,' I say. 'Furious has English with *me* on Tuesday, period 6.' I run and grab my planner. I have to remember exactly what we were doing last Tuesday –

Dring.

There goes the bell. God damn! Hadenough and the rest of the teachers go rushing out the staff-room door. I follow after them. I'll have to figure the mystery out later, when I have a moment to breathe.

Tuesday 10 June

I'm sitting with some of my Year 8s on the benches in the playground and the sun is beating down. Fifty, Cent and Munchkin have taken off their blazers and we're all parched. They want to write something to say at assembly next week as it's their tutor group's week to give assembly. I'm trying to help them. 'Well, remember all the work we did around speech writing in the autumn term?' I say, smiling. 'Just think, what would Churchill say?'

'Who?' Munchkin asks.

I laugh. 'You know, *Churchill*.'

Cent looks up. 'Oh, yeah . . . the *dog*!'

'No. Not the dog. Remember?' I stare at them. 'Not the dog, not the football manager . . . Who was Churchill?'

Fifty squeezes his eyes shut as if he were diving deep into his memory. Suddenly his eyes snap open. 'Was he our prime minister?'

'That's it, boys, you've got it – that's it! He was our prime minister.' And the three of them fall about laughing in wonder at my excitement.

Friday 13 June

I'm heading down to the high street at three thirty in search of some chocolate, which, thanks to the healthy-schools agenda, is banned in school, when I notice Cavalier lurking down one of the side streets nearby. I wave. 'Cavalier, hey! How are you?' I have to shout because he's only just about in earshot.

He waves back sheepishly and puts his hand in his pocket. I want to talk to him. I wonder how he is. I wonder how he's doing at the PRU. I move towards him. But as I do, Cavalier turns and walks the other way. 'Cavalier!' I shout again. 'Cavalier!' But he ignores me and walks quickly in the opposite direction. What's happened to the Cavalier I once knew?

The sun may be shining, but my feet feel heavy as I trudge along the road. Now I need that Kit-Kat more than ever.

Monday 16 June

Today, my invited speaker is Bobby. He's a black policeman. I'm hoping to build on Bank's and others' visits.

As I imagined, the students are horrified by Bobby. By definition, a black man cannot join the police force. Bobby talks about the issues facing black policemen which don't affect white policemen. He talks about racism in the police force and how difficult it is for a black policeman to climb the ranks. He talks about how black people call him names in the street, like 'traitor' or 'Uncle Tom', what it feels like, and the kind of resolve he needs to keep going. Interestingly, Beautiful, our aspiring policewoman, remains perfectly silent, but listens carefully to everything that Bobby says.

The children now have their turn to ask questions, and they are keen. So they put their hands up. Bobby makes one request. He insists that the children omit the words 'yeah', 'like' and 'innit' from their question. Simple enough. Or so you would think.

Dopey has his hand in the air. 'Yeah, so, Sir –' Dopey puts his hand over his mouth. 'Oops.'

Munchkin has his hand up. 'OK, so, like, what I wanna say is –' He puts his hand over his mouth too, realizing he's just committed another word crime.

Child after child, they begin to speak, and about three or four words into their sentence, sometimes fewer, they stop dead, realizing that they have failed at the task in hand: to ask a question without using the words 'innit', 'like' or 'yeah'. And then they try again, giggling, squeezing their eyes shut, trying really hard not to mess up. Some find the task so difficult they give up speaking altogether. Others get frustrated and end up shouting, 'You know what I mean!' because they are unable to obey the simple rule of speaking normal English.

As this fiasco continues, I look around at Mr Hadenough, who is standing next to me, also watching the children stumbling as if lost in the dark. We start to laugh. It's hilarious.

But we aren't laughing at the children. We're laughing at ourselves. Because, for the first time, we realize that we no longer hear these words. We don't flinch at them. We don't even notice them. It is simply the way our children speak.

I am reminded of that tale about the frog. If you throw a frog into a pan of boiling water, he will jump straight out. But if you put a frog into a pan of cold water and slowly turn up the heat, he will boil to death.

Tuesday 17 June

I sit down in Ms Sensible's office. 'Hi, Ms Sensible, I've figured out what happened with Hadenough's phone.'

'Well, I can't wait to hear it,' she says.

'Furious took the phone, as Hadenough says, when the flowerpot dropped. He pushed it off the desk to create a diversion and then the phone was his.' I pause. 'Then he came to my lesson. It was hot that day, really hot. And we were doing a test. Furious refused to sit still. He said he felt ill. He needed to get some water, he needed air. So I sent him outside to do exactly that.'

'Is that when he downloaded the games?'

'Yes, exactly. I sent him out a little way into period 6. This matches with what the phone statement says. And he was out of my lesson for about ten minutes. And during that time, no one was watching him. When I got him back into my lesson, the downloading stopped, because he couldn't do it any more with me watching him. And when I went to get him back in, he had a phone in his hand. He put it away when I told him to come in.'

Ms Sensible stands up. 'You're certain of this, Snuffy?'

'Yes, I'm absolutely certain.'

Ms Sensible immediately calls the head. 'Hello? Mr Goodheart? . . . Yes, well, I have Ms Snuffleupagus here. And I think we know who our phone thief is. It's Furious . . . Yes, we do . . .

Ms Snuffleupagus has proof that he took Mr Hadenough's phone.' She pauses. 'Yes, Sir. I'll be with you right away.'

I stand up. 'OK then, I'd better go.'

Ms Sensible smiles. 'Yes. I have to go speak to Mr Goodheart about it all and explain what you've said to me.' She points her finger at me. 'Make sure you write all of this up and add it to what we have from Mr Hadenough. Mr Goodheart may decide to go for permanent exclusion on the back of this. And we need our argument to be watertight.'

As I make my way down the corridor, away from Ms Sensible's office, the weight of what is happening makes its way to my shoulders. They feel heavy. Furious . . . permanent exclusion? Gosh. I haven't really thought this through. But he needs to go. Furious is a cancer in this school. And we need to cut him out.

Wednesday 18 June

Mr Hadenough grabs my arm as I walk towards the staff room. 'Briefing *today*? It's *Wednesday*. What the hell is going on?'

'What do you think?'

Hadenough's eyes flare wide. 'Ofsted?'

'Has to be. Why else would they call for an emergency meeting like this?'

Hadenough looks like he's seen a ghost. We walk into a buzzing staff room. Everyone is expecting the worst. Some staff are holding each other's hands. Others are squeezing the wooden arms of their battered armchairs so tightly that their knuckles have turned white. I look at Ms Magical and smile. How many times must she have been through this in her career? She shrugs, mouthing, 'What can you do?' in my direction. After a few minutes, which seem to last an eternity, Mr Goodheart takes centre stage.

'Uh hum,' he starts. Everyone goes quiet instantly and looks up at him, as a child looks up at its mother, waiting to be led. 'Good news, everyone, the dreaded time is finally here. We got the phone call too late yesterday for me to let you know then. The lovely

Ofsted will be with us tomorrow and Friday.' The room is absolutely silent. People look as if he's just told them he has a terminal disease. 'They'll be here all day Thursday and Friday morning. On Friday afternoon, they are likely to be feeding back to the senior team. But please don't count on that.'

Ms Sensible steps forward. 'Remember all the preparation we've done. Remember: plan your lessons – every lesson – carefully. Lesson plans are *not* required. Just put into practice everything we've talked about and prepared for. The inspector may pop in for as little as ten minutes. They are unlikely to stay for more than thirty minutes. There will probably be four or five inspectors. So we think that they'll see about twenty lessons or so during their two-day stint.'

Mr Hadenough nudges me. 'Well, at least we didn't get the call on Friday for a Monday or Tuesday visit. Then our whole weekend would have been ruined.'

Mr Goodheart nods. 'The school will be open tonight until 9 p.m. to allow you the opportunity to prepare as much as is necessary. I know we'll all give it our best shot. Good luck!'

The room erupts into chatter. People are texting on their mobiles to tell loved ones they won't see them till late tonight.

'Let's go and show them what we're made of, everyone,' Mr Sporty shouts from the corner.

'Yay!' the younger staff cheer. 'Come on, everyone.'

Hadenough squeezes my arm. 'Well, they're here . . . this is what we wanted.'

Thursday 19 June

It's 7 a.m. The staff room is packed. People are printing by the computers. People are photocopying at the photocopier. There is an odd silence. No one is chatting. No one is taking a break. The enemy is in our midst.

I worked till midnight last night. I'm exhausted already and we haven't even begun. I was making PowerPoint after PowerPoint for my lessons. I was cutting out bits of paper and stuffing them in envelopes to create interesting 'sort activities'. That took an age. And I have a full six-period day today. My God. How will I ever survive?

Lesson one is down, five to go. I am setting up for my period 2 class with my Year 10s when the interactive whiteboard suddenly goes black. 'The board, Miss, the board's gone off,' shouts Hip.

My heart starts to race. I fiddle around with some of the wires at the back of the computer. Hip stands and plays around with the projector. *Tick tock, tick tock.* I pull a wire out, push a wire in. Nothing. Damn. There is a knock at the door.

Gulp. My heart disappears into the pit of my stomach. Five minutes into the lesson and I haven't yet started. I'm dead. The class turns slowly to face the door.

In walks Furious. God damn you, Furious!

'Furious! Where have you been? You're five minutes late.'

I'm so stressed I can feel myself sweating. I turn to Wholesome. 'Go and get me a technician. Now! Tell him it's urgent.'

Wholesome runs to the door. He can see I'm about to pass out from the anxiety. Furious stands in such a way as to block the door, and Wholesome has to twist around him. 'Furious, you're late and now you're causing trouble. You know how much you're on the edge!'

Furious hisses at me. 'Yeah, well, you want me *out*, don't ya? You're gonna get it.'

'Just sit down, Furious. I don't have time for this. We have to get on with the lesson.'

I look at the door. Damn. Think of something. Do something. Why is Furious even here, anyway? Isn't he meant to have been excluded?

I decide to do an exercise which requires a little bit of physical activity to get us started. While we're doing it, Mr Fixit turns up, waves a magic wand and the whiteboard starts working again. As he's sorting it out, some of the kids are whispering to each other. 'Ofsted . . . Ofsted . . .'

'Oh my God, Miss, it's an inspector!' shouts Hip.

The class immediately jumps round in their seats. I look at the door. No inspector. Everyone bursts into laughter. So do I.

'OK, Hip, very funny.' I open up my lesson on the board. 'Let's get to it then.'

Friday 20 June

'Were you seen?'

'Nah.'

'Were you seen?'

'Nah.'

'Were you seen?'

'Yeah, she was in for twenty minutes.'

'Really? Mine only stayed for ten.'

'Was their feedback any good?'

'Yeah, some of what she said made sense.'

'Mine was a load of bollocks. An ex-art teacher watching my maths lesson. It was ridiculous.'

The staff room, before school, is explosive and packed. People are still printing and photocopying like there is no tomorrow. Most of us were in school until nine last night. I'm so tired I can barely see straight. I haven't been seen. Neither has Hadenough. He runs up to me.

'Well, if they didn't get us yesterday, they'll slam us today, won't they?'

I shrug. 'Yeah, maybe. I wish they'd seen me yesterday. I wish this thing were over and done with.'

'Just one more day. And then it's the weekend. We can do it.' Hadenough punches me in the arm. 'Come on.'

Ms Magical walks past me and I smile at her. 'Hey! Were you seen?'

'Yes!' She pouts and sits down in the corner. I slot myself down next to her.

'What happened?'

'They gave me a 3,' she says.

'Oh. I'm sorry. That's shit.' I give her arm a pat. 'But you know it's all bollocks. You know that you're amazing with these kids.'

'Yeah, but like we said before, it doesn't matter what I know, or what you know. All that matters is the grade that some stupid inspector gives you for one solitary fifteen minutes of a lesson out of a lifetime of lessons.'

'And not only that, but he's judging you by criteria which are a load of crap.'

Ms Magical nods. 'So now I'm a "satisfactory" teacher.'

'No! Don't you say that! You are one of the most extraordinary teachers I know. So many of us look at you and want to be just like you. Really. I'm not joking. The kids know it. The staff know it. You're outstanding. And if Ofsted don't know it, then they're a bunch of idiots.'

Ms Magical gets up. 'Yes, well, I have a full day today. Have to get out there. Maybe they'll drop by again. Who knows?' She turns around to go.

'Good luck! Remember to include some group work,' I call after her. As I do, I think about the absurdity of this system. How can it be that those teachers who are the most inspirational, the most dedicated, the most admired by both staff and students, get given a 3? Who are these failed teachers to tell us how to do our jobs? If they could do it, they'd still be doing it. To judge a lesson according to certain criteria (the *wrong* criteria at that) is easy and can be done in twenty minutes. But to judge a teacher takes weeks of analysis, of inner knowledge, of painstaking observation of more than just their lessons.

And *teachers*, not *lessons*, are what make a school what it is. Teachers (including the head) are what make a school outstanding or unsatisfactory. Teachers are the heart of any school, and two days of dropping into lessons tells you nothing about them and therefore tells you nothing about the school.

The staff-room door swings open. It's Ms Sensible. 'An inspector is coming this way.' She looks around nervously. 'Just giving you the heads up.' She looks at me. 'I think she may visit the English department this morning.'

I smile. Shit.

Saturday 21 June

Yesterday was the day of all days. I didn't get seen by the inspectors. All that work, all that time . . . all for nothing. At lunchtime, as predicted by Mr Goodheart, the inspectors retreat into a room to deliberate. We teachers continue on high alert, in a collective permanent panic. So no one notices when Cavalier makes his way into the school. He's wearing his uniform. He looks just like any other boy. As he's been excluded, he isn't allowed to be on the school premises, but no one realizes that he's there.

There I am in the playground towards the end of lunch, about to head towards my lesson, when I spot Cavalier by the bins. 'Cavalier?' I move towards him. 'Cavalier? Is that you?' I squint as the sun hits my eyes.

The boy pulls a hood over his head and runs behind the school. So I walk speedily after him. He's much faster than me and quickly disappears. By the time I get to the back of the school, he's gone. I figure he probably walked out the back entrance. Was it Cavalier? Or was I imagining things? Confused, but relieved – we don't want any nonsense happening today with those inspectors still here – I wander back to the side playground, where I was before.

I'm on my way, the playground still out of sight, when suddenly kids start screaming: 'Fight! Fight!' As I turn the corner, I catch sight of Cavalier, standing over Furious. Blows are going every which way – except that the blows are coming more from Cavalier, and Furious is on the ground, blocking Cavalier's fists. Cavalier has a bottle in his hand. There is blood everywhere. Cavalier throws his arm into the air, bottle in hand.

'No!' I shout, as I run towards them. 'Cavalier! *No!*'

Down comes his arm. I leap as far as I can towards them, trying to grab Cavalier's arm. I miss. Down comes the bottle, breaking across Furious's head.

'You wanna fuck with me? Chaa!' Cavalier is proud, grinning, blood all over his teeth and face. I fall to the side.

Mr Sporty appears and grabs hold of Cavalier, who allows himself to be hauled up. The damage is done. Furious is down for the count. Cavalier is satisfied.

'The inspectors,' I whisper to Mr Sporty. 'The inspectors!'

Mr Sporty nods. 'I'll get him to the office. I'll call the police and an ambulance.' He winks. 'They're in room 7 deliberating. Hopefully, they won't notice.'

I'm practically hysterical, throwing myself next to Furious, who is covered in blood. The broken bottle lies by his side. I can feel the tears build up in my eyes.

Oh my God. If the inspectors see this, we're dead. But room 7 is on the other side of the school, so maybe we'll be OK. I wonder if Cavalier timed this on purpose? Shit. Is Furious going to be OK?

I have to reassure him in any case. 'You're going to be OK, Furious. You're going to be OK. Mr Sporty has called for an ambulance. Just lie here, they'll come and get you. I promise. It'll all be OK.'

Furious slightly opens his eyes and looks at me through tears and blood. He tries to get up. 'Where is he?' he growls. 'Where the fuck is he?'

I push him back to the ground. 'He's gone. Just lie down. Let's wait for the ambulance.'

I grab hold of Furious's bloodied hand and squeeze it tight. He looks at me from the ground and, for a moment, I think I see a glimmer of gratitude in his eyes, and that makes me squeeze his hand just that little bit more.

Ms Sensible comes running over. 'OK, Snuffy, the ambulance is outside. We have them down by the side entrance.' She points. 'You know, to avoid you know who. The paramedics are coming in. They'll get Furious on a stretcher and get him to hospital.'

As I'm talking to Ms Sensible, I let go of Furious's hand. 'Miss, Miss . . .'

I look back down and see his hand, reaching. I take it in mine and squeeze it again, as hard as I can. 'It's going to be OK, Furious. I promise you. It's going to be OK.'

But is it? I have no idea.

Sunday 22 June

'Don't make me get up,' I squeal.

'It's noon!' Liberal throws the bedsheet off me. 'You have to get up!'

'But I'm so tired. I can't get up. I have to sleep. I just have to.' I groan. 'I never want to go back to school.'

Liberal bends over and kisses me on the forehead. 'OK, babe. I'm sorry. You sleep.'

I pull the bedsheet back over me, and Liberal turns to leave. I pop my head back out. 'Hey! Why don't you come lie down here with me?' He cuddles up next to me. I turn to him. 'Remind me again why I went into teaching?'

Liberal smiles. ''Cause you wanted to change the world.'

'Oh yeah, thanks.' I place my head on his shoulder and fall fast asleep.

Monday 23 June

I'm standing in the head's office, just before the briefing. The entire school is wondering what Ofsted's verdict was.

Mr Goodheart looks up. 'Thanks for popping in, Snuffy. I wanted to thank you for everything you did on Friday with the Furious–Cavalier incident.'

'That's OK, Sir. I was so worried about the inspectors. Was everything OK in the end?'

'Thanks to you, the inspectors didn't see any of what happened.'

'Oh, thank goodness. But what about our grading? Did we make it?'

'Well, I was going to break the news to you all together at the briefing . . .'

'Of course.'

'But I don't suppose it'll make any difference if I tell you now. What's done is done.'

My heart sinks. 'Oh. I see.'

'Yes.' There's a twinkle in his eye. 'We did it.'

'What?'

'A 2. We managed to retain our "good".'

I clap my hands together. 'Oh thank God for that!'

Mr Goodheart smiles. 'Yes, we even got "good with some outstanding features". Not bad at all. The official report will arrive in the next few days, of course, but for now, we at least know where we stand.'

I can't keep still. 'That's fantastic, Sir. That's brilliant. Everyone will be so pleased.' And then a thought stops me. 'And Cavalier and Furious? I know Furious is still in hospital, right? He's sent me a few texts saying he's OK, but nothing more.'

'Yes. He's lost a few teeth, and the gash on his head from the bottle is pretty bad. Looks like he'll be in the hospital for about a week.' He cups his chin in his hand. 'As for Cavalier . . . the police are dealing with him. I think Furious's parents may press charges.'

Ms Sensible sticks her head in the door. 'Briefing, you two!'

I turn around. 'We're coming,' I say.

And off we all go to tell the rest of the staff the news.

Tuesday 24 June

Munchkin is always in trouble these days: always sent out of lessons for disruption, always pushing other children around, always getting into fights. Because of Munchkin's general disaffection, I threatened to leave him at school when the rest of us were going on this trip. 'Please, Miss,' he pleaded. 'Please let me go. I promise to be good. I promise I won't be bad. Please, Miss, I promise.' He tugged at my heart strings and I gave in.

As I sit on the tube, towards the centre of a packed carriage, my gaze wanders over to the other side, to Cent, Fifty and Munchkin, sitting quietly, all engrossed in their PSPs. We pull into a station. The doors open. In walks a young Asian woman and, attached to her side, is her mother. Her mother is frail and wrinkled. Her head is covered and her hands shake. The old woman struggles to step on to the train. Her daughter leads her towards the pole, directing her mother's hand to grasp it for safety.

My boys are deep in modern-day Pac-Man-land. They don't see what's going on. I look on, from several seats away, fearing the old woman might lose her grip, that she might trip and fall. Suddenly Munchkin looks up. Before I can even think of what the right thing to do is, without hesitation, Munchkin stands. His seat snaps up and hits the back of the tube wall. Munchkin stands back, away from his seat, giving way. The young woman tries to lead her mother towards the seat, but she's struggling. The seat is pressed up against the tube wall. Munchkin notices the young woman trying to hold her mother upright while she reaches for the seat. He rushes forward. He pushes the seat down. And the old woman places her bottom squarely on it.

I watch on in amazement. My little Munchkin just helped that woman. No one asked him. No one told him what to do. We try to teach charm and manners at school, but more often than not, we fail miserably. It was as if, by instinct, he just knew what he should do. The other people in the tube look on at the spectacle. 'He's mine,' I want to cry out. 'Munchkin belongs to me.' My heart swells with pride.

As he moves away from the old woman, to take his position standing against the interconnecting door, he glances over at me. So instead of shouting at the crowd and claiming ownership of Munchkin, I look right at him, nod my head and smile. Munchkin grins. I know Munchkin, I know what that grin is saying. You made a promise and you have delivered. You promised me you'd be good, and you've gone far beyond that promise: you've been charming, gallant and decent. And, frankly, Munchkin, I am as proud as I could possibly ever be.

My father has been ringing every day since the Furious–Cavalier incident. Liberal told him about it, and he's worried. I've been avoiding his phone calls. Finally, though, he gets me.

'Snuffy, I heard about this incident last week with those boys. Liberal said that there was blood and an ambulance had to go to the school?'

'Yes, Daddy.'

'But is this really safe? I mean, should you really be teaching in this school?'

'Yes, Daddy, that's what I like, remember?'

I'm referring to the many conversations we used to have when I was finishing up university and my father assumed I would want to do something sensible like a law conversion course. Everyone was doing either that or going to work in management consultancy. I should do the same. Instead, I announced teaching was what I wanted to do. And so, having been a teacher himself, my father let me, assuming it was a phase I was going through and that, in a year or two, I would get over it and pursue a more sensible and well-respected career.

For about two years he used to tease me and say, 'Well, when you've finished with teaching and get on with *real* life,' and I would smile and ignore it. Then, over the years, I would tell my school stories and my mum and dad would listen. And slowly, they began to see how much I loved my job, and were reminded of why they were drawn to the work themselves. Eventually, my father stopped saying, 'When you've finished with teaching,' because he gradually came to accept that teaching was what made me happy. Once, he even commented, 'Snuffy, even though you work all the hours God sends, I don't know anyone who loves their job as much as you do.'

This time, though, my father is genuinely worried. 'Yes, I understand you like your job but this school sounds dangerous. Couldn't you find another school to teach in?'

'No, Daddy. I love Ordinary School. I don't know why. I just do.'

Friday 27 June

Mr Goodheart has summoned me to his office. I pop my head round his door. 'Ms Snuffleupagus,' he says. 'Good. Come in, come in. This Furious situation. Ms Sensible told me what you and Mr Hadenough figured out about his phone going missing. I want to see this phone statement. And I hope you've written all of this up?' I tell him I have.

'Right. On the back of the theft of Mr Hadenough's phone, I have decided to go for permanent exclusion.'

'No managed move?'

'No. Ms Desperate is refusing. I offered to make a deal with the head of Basic School and get Furious a place there, but she is so angry about the recent fight with Cavalier, she holds us responsible and she won't have any of it.'

'So what will happen?'

'It isn't going to be easy. They've hired a lawyer. They'll fight us every step of the way when we are in front of the panel. But we need to do what is right for the school.'

'Yes, Sir. I understand.'

'So I'm just letting you know what the plan of action is. I'll be in touch about what happens next. You'll have to put together a log, of course, all the incidents he has ever been involved in since Year 7. It will take you some time, so plan for a weekend to do it.'

'OK, Sir.' I back out of his office. 'Thanks, Sir.'

Furious, excluded? Lawyers? Panels? Oh my God. What have I done?

Saturday 28 June

There's a knock at the front door and Liberal goes to answer it. 'Hello, Hadenough. How are you? Come in. Want a drink?'

Hadenough shakes his head. 'Nah. Just wondered if I could have a quick word with Snuffy.'

I sit down next to him on the sofa as Liberal disappears into the kitchen. 'You OK?' I ask.

'Just thought I should let you know that I've finally done it. I'm out, and this time I'm not going back. That 3 from the Ofsted inspector was the last straw. My girlfriend wants to move out of London. Maybe I'll get a teaching job out of London somewhere. Or maybe I'll just quit teaching altogether. In the meantime, I can just do supply.'

I don't know what to say. Liberal walks in with a jug of lemonade. 'Look, man, I know it's none of my business, but you gotta do what's best for you. What's with all you teachers always talking about leaving?'

Hadenough laughs. 'Snuffy never talks about leaving. She's insane. All she wants is to work in a difficult inner-city school.' He nudges me in the side. 'Eh? What's wrong with you anyway?'

Liberal pours me a glass. 'Who knows? Snuffy's always been a little different. That's why we love her.'

I look at Hadenough. 'Come on, Hadenough, stay. Don't leave just yet.'

'No.' He shakes his head vigorously. 'My girlfriend . . . she's had enough. We can't afford a private school and we want kids, and so we have to move anyway. And Ofsted has sealed it for me.'

'Yeah, but what they say doesn't mean anything.'

'Easy for you to say. You weren't seen. I'm going. I'm sorry.' He gets up.

I stand up too. 'Well, you don't have to leave. Liberal and I were going to fix lunch. You're welcome to join us.'

'Nah. Thanks, guys.' Hadenough shakes Liberal's hand. 'Thanks. I have to go. My girlfriend is waiting for me at the flat.'

As Hadenough walks out the door, Liberal puts his arm around me and kisses me on the forehead.

Some of my Year 8s are in the classroom, settled in their seats, already on with their starter activity, while I'm writing something on the board with my back turned to them and to the door to the classroom. A few of them are out on a trip, so I'm not expecting them. I hear the door open, some scuffling, some whispering, and then the door closes back again. I do not turn around.

As my pen glides across the board, I clear my throat. 'Fifty, I suggest you get up from under that table and take your seat.' I smile to myself. There is absolute silence in the room. Then I hear a little scuffling. 'Fifty, I said get up out from under that table. You're wasting learning time.'

Munchkin takes a deep breath. 'But, Miss! Fifty's on the history trip. He's not here.'

I turn around and look at the desks, searching for whoever it was I could hear crawling on the floor. But they're too well hidden. I'm guessing it's Fifty. Fifty is silly like that, and the number-one character in this class, with the right combination of nerve and idiocy to be super-silly. 'Oh really, Munchkin? Fifty's out of school today, is he?'

Munchkin nods while fixing his glasses on his nose. Adorable looks at me sheepishly. I hear a little rummage.

'Fifty! Come out, come out, wherever you are!' I sing in my best voice, trying hard to sound like Glinda, the good witch of the North. 'Come out, come out, wherever you are . . . and meet the young teacher who fell from a star . . .'

Fifty pops his head out from under the table. 'Young? You isn't *young*, Miss!'

The others giggle at Fifty's sudden appearance, and I wag my finger in Munchkin's direction to tell him off for fibbing. 'Charming!' I shoo him away, laughing. 'Now take your seat! I *knew* it was you. And how did I know it was you?'

Adorable giggles. ''Cause it's always Fifty, Miss. It's always him! Anyway, I think you're young, Miss.'

I glance at Adorable and smile. 'That's very kind of you, Adorable, but I'm afraid that Fifty is right. I'm not young like you, with your lives in front of you . . . so much promise, so much excitement ahead . . .'

Fifty throws himself down in his seat. 'Yeah, but like, you is all right, Miss . . . I mean, you is all right, even though you're old, yuh know?'

'Thank you, Fifty . . . I think. Now, back to work, everyone.'

That's the thing about working with children: you constantly feel like a grandmother.

Thursday 3 July

Polish and Adorable come tearing down the playground and halt in front of me. The sun is out today and the girls are carrying their blazers. 'Miss! He just called her – he just called her –' Adorable yells at me.

'Yeah, yeah, yeah, he just said, yeah . . .' Polish can't put her words together.

'Yeah, Miss, I mean, I don't wanna swear, but . . .'

'Yeah, Miss, he just called me . . .'

They're acting crazy. I hold my hand up. 'OK, girls, what's happened?'

'Yeah, well, Miss, yeah, I don't wanna swear, but what's the "c" word mean?'

Don't they know? I mean, they have to know. Are they just trying to get me to say it? But they're behaving so wildly that I can't figure it out just by looking at them. 'It's a bad word, girls,' I say. 'It isn't very nice.'

'Yeah, yeah, but what does it mean?' shouts Polish.

Adorable jumps in. 'I mean, yeah, Miss, I mean, we don't wanna put you in a difficult position, but he just called me it and we wanna know what it means.'

'OK, girls. It's a body part.'

The girls are agitated, and confused. 'Whuaaa? What's that mean?'

'Body part?'

'What body part?'

I lean in, whispering. 'It's a body part that only girls have.'

'Raaaaaah!' They look at each other, screeching. 'He called you *that*!'

'He called me *that*! *Raaaaaah!*'

Suddenly they take off. They run away, no doubt in the direction of the boy in question. Heh, heh, I think, I'd hate to be that boy right now. Innocence. Isn't it lovely?

Monday 7 July

Mishap is outside the office, waiting to say hello to me. I'm excited to see her. I wonder how the business studies course is going at college. I quickly tie up my meeting and head down to see her with a skip in my step.

The skip soon becomes a standstill when I see Mishap standing next to a stroller. She's still got on those same old earrings. 'Hello, Mishap. How are you?' I give her a quick hug.

'Hello, Miss, I'm fine.' She bends down to put something in the stroller.

I'm a little confused. I mean, this baby cannot possibly be hers. She's only seventeen or eighteen after all. She only left school last year. 'So whose baby is this, then?' I probe, dreading the answer.

'Mine, Miss,' she announces proudly.

I'm stunned. The usual 'Congratulations' doesn't drop off my lips. Instead, I stand there, struggling for something to say. Quickly and awkwardly, I paint a smile on my face, trying desperately to look happy. 'Well, I can tell you one thing, Mishap, you beat me to it!' I chuckle, and so does she. Just at this point, Adorable and Polish wander past.

'Hi, Miss.' They wave at me and look at Mishap and her baby, smiling.

'Hi, Adorable. Hi, Polish.' I find myself trying to stand in front of Mishap, in order to block their view. Don't look at her! Don't be like her! Just turn away!

Suddenly seized with shame, I look back at Mishap and grin. 'See you again soon, I hope, Mishap,' I manage. I literally run down the corridor, needing to go and teach but grateful for the excuse to get away. I just don't know what to say to her. Will Mishap ever make anything of herself, the way I had hoped? Doubtful. I guess you win some, you lose some. Mishap is definitely one that I lost. I cannot help but think that Seething, with her 23-year-old boyfriend, is going to follow a similar route.

As I get round the corner, I stop to catch my breath. I lean against the wall. I feel sick. My head sinks into my hands. Mishap . . . Jesus. I want to crumple into tears, but I have a lesson to teach.

Funny how, in some settings, strollers are a sign of happiness. In my neck of the woods, strollers only signify defeat.

Wednesday 9 July

I'm holding the whole of my Year 8 class in at lunch for a ten-minute detention. One isn't meant to give class detentions. It isn't fair on the kids who weren't misbehaving. But as I know they were all chatting, bar maybe one or two, I'm keeping them. Adorable will just have to forgive me.

I use the time to try and talk some sense into them. I explain that the more they chat, the more they fall behind. I try to make them see the bigger picture by mentioning other classes and drawing the school up into a kind of race, saying that they are now ten minutes behind everyone else. They listen but, ultimately, they don't really care.

'You don't understand what you're competing with. You don't know what the kids are like at other schools,' I say.

Munchkin squints behind his glasses. 'What do you mean, Miss?'

'I mean that you've never been inside Wineaton, for example. You don't know what their lessons are like, how everyone is quiet all the time so the teacher is able to plan and manages to teach so much more. You don't know how much they get done every lesson and how hard their homework is. You only have each other to compare yourselves to.'

Fifty scowls. 'Ha! Homework! Why would we want homework that's hard?'

'Because hard work makes you into successes. You shouldn't always want to pursue what's easy. You think they're all studying media studies and drama at Wineaton?'

I pause from my shouting, taking a breath, realizing what I'm saying, hoping the kids won't go back and tell my colleagues what I just said. 'You want to keep your doors open. You want to keep on succeeding so that, as you pass each step, more and more doors open for you. You don't want your decisions to close doors, you want to get to university.'

Cent's eyes open wide. 'So where'd you go then, Miss? To university?'

'I went to Cambridge.'

The class goes quiet. Munchkin pushes his glasses up on his nose. 'You mean you went to *the* Cambridge, Miss?'

'Yes, I went to *the* Cambridge. What other sort of Cambridge is there?'

Adorable smiles. 'Miss was clever at school.'

I point my index finger at them. 'But that's the point! I was no more clever than any of you. It's just that I worked hard, I didn't talk when I was told to be silent and I did the best that I could. So I kept doors open for my future.'

Munchkin winces. 'Yo, Miss, that makes no sense. If your doors were open, then why you teaching *us*?'

I sigh, dropping my arms down by my side. 'Why do you kids always say that to me when I tell you where I went to university? Why don't you get that I *want* to work here? I *chose* this job.'

The entire class looks confused. Cent frowns. 'But who would want to teach *here*?'

My eyes nearly pop out of my head. 'I do!'

Fifty's hand is up in the air, gangster style. 'Gimme some, Miss!'

I throw my hand out in his direction, not quite sure of what to do, and he takes it, does some weird handshake, and then gives me back my hand. The class is buzzing with excitement. Imagine that. Miss *chose* to be here.

Thursday 10 July

We have interviews for a maths post today, to replace Mr Had-enough, who leaves for good at the end of term. So I've helped Ms Joyful organize for the candidates to teach a lesson. Six candidates. Mr Cajole, Ms Sensible, Ms Joyful and me, we're all observing. And then, of course, there are the kids who observe too. They even do a 45-minute panel interview in the library.

After the lessons, Ms Joyful and I meet with Mr Cajole and Ms Sensible to discuss the lessons they've seen. Mr Cajole preferred candidate 2 over candidate 1. Ms Sensible preferred candidate 3 over candidate 4. And Ms Joyful and I preferred candidate 5 over candidate 6. And what did the kids say? In each case, they preferred the lesser candidate. That's always the way. We always ask the students' opinions, and they generally get it wrong. Why did they prefer candidate 1? Because she threw a ball around. Why did they prefer candidate 4? Because he played several games. Why did they prefer candidate 6? Because he was a little more 'street' in his manner and the kids liked his cool style.

So who should we choose? Do *I* teach a lesson that the teachers will like or that the kids will like? More importantly, if children believe that they are the ones who choose their teachers, what does this tell them about where they are in the pecking order? Does it not suggest that they are on top?

Everyone thinks that, because they've been to school, they know how to teach. In fact, according to current practice, judging teachers and knowing who is the better teacher at interview is so easy that even thirteen-year-olds can do it.

Friday 11 July

Inset day today: that means training. No kids in school. Mr Hadenough nudges me as I pour some hot water into a mug in the staff room. 'God, it felt so nice coming into school this morning,' he says. 'Not only is it great weather, but there was none of that dread.'

I chuckle. 'Yeah, I know what you mean. You feel a sense of calm coming in, don't you? I mean, it isn't dread that we feel normally, just a little anxiety and a need for pumped-up energy.'

'Well, this morning, there was none of that. I knew I was coming to work, not going to war.'

I laugh. 'Yeah. Even though we'll be working all day, it feels like a day off when the kids aren't around.'

'And you know, Snuffy, that's how most other people feel every day.' Mr Hadenough heads towards the door. 'I just want to have a life, you know?'

Saturday 12 July

Liberal looks up from his newspaper and puts his coffee down on the table.

'Great news about Compassionate and Bank, eh?'

'Yeah. I know she secretly wanted a boy, so yes.'

'When we have kids, you're never going to want to send them to a state school, are you?' Liberal sighs.

I put my pen down from my marking 'Well . . . no, not really. I'm sorry. It's just that I know what goes on in schools in London. I just couldn't do it.'

Liberal frowns. 'But I'm not sure I could send my kids to a private school.'

'I know, I know. But we can't move out of London, and even if we did, we'd have to live in some tiny village to find a half-decent state school. Your work is here, and I really love working with inner-city kids. A state school in London is too much of risk.'

'Is it?'

'You hear all my stories. You know what Ordinary is like. Do you really want our kids to end up like Cavalier? Or Furious?'

'Of course not. But is that inevitable? I'm sure there are lots of kids who go through the system who are just fine.'

'Yeah, there are. But do you want to take that risk? And is being "fine" really what you want for *our* kids? Don't we want them to be extraordinary? Don't we want to give them the best possible chance at life? Don't we want them to be Nobel Prize winners, space explorers, cancer curers, revolutionaries who can change the world for the better?'

'That's exactly what I want! But how can we afford it?'

'I don't know. I guess it means we won't be able to have more than one kid. The Chinese people who run the little takeaway down the road, they're not rich, but they send their one child to private school 'cause he's their pride and joy . . . You didn't struggle at Cambridge like I did. You didn't have to spend night after night trying to catch up and never really managing it.' I get up from the armchair and sit next to him on the sofa. Liberal puts his arm around me and I smile. 'Don't you remember how you used to have to help me with my work?'

'But a private education isn't everything. Just look at *me* . . .'

'Exactly. Look at you. You've had every door open to you. You're confident, clever, well balanced. Even though Stoic might be OK academically, what kind of human being is he going to be *socially*?' I rub Liberal's hand. 'I just want our kid to have what you had.'

'I guess maybe you're right.' He hangs his head.

I jump on his lap. 'Wow! You think maybe I'm *right*?'

He nods reluctantly. 'Yeah, you're right, OK? Maybe you're right.'

I laugh as he kisses me on the forehead. 'Oh my God! We have to get this on tape.' I hold his head in my hands. 'Ah, babe,' I mur-mur. 'I'm sorry. I so wish I were wrong.'

Monday 14 July

It's after school, and I'm sitting with Mr Goodheart in his office. 'OK, Snuffy, I just want to talk you through what to expect tomorrow, seeing as you haven't been in an exclusion meeting before.' I nod obediently. 'So, first thing to remember is: don't say anything more than is necessary. The lawyer they've hired will try to trick you into saying what he wants.'

OK: don't say anything more than is necessary. I'll remember. I repeat the instruction over in my head.

'So watch out for that. I know this guy and he's ruthless. He'll do and say whatever is necessary to prove his case.'

'OK,' I say.

'Always back what I say, whatever he tries to get you to say. Remember what I've said and keep repeating it, whatever it is. Never stray from the issues at hand. OK?'

'OK.'

'There will be a panel of three governors. Ultimately, remem-ber, they will back us if we have a watertight argument. The log should be enough.' He flips his fingers through a pack of stapled papers which I put together at his request, listing every incident Furious has ever been involved in at school since Year 7: the date, the details, the crime. 'Good work with this. Although there are a few issues . . .'

Mr Goodheart talks me through the possible sticky bits of the log, where there wasn't a write-up from a teacher, where every detail wasn't noted, where we didn't get witness statements from other students. Anything that he thinks will be an area that the lawyer will use to prove that we're incompetent, he highlights to me. Always: where is the proof? It is our word against Furious's. The fact that we are not only adults, but professionals, means nothing.

I must look like a rabbit in headlights. Mr Goodheart notices. 'Look, don't worry, he adds. 'We'll be fine. Just stick with me. Remember, we're a team. United, we win.'

'Yes, Sir, I know. United, we win. You can count on me.'

As I walk out of his office, I swallow hard. United we win. I can do this.

Tuesday 15 July

Furious, his foster parents and their lawyer sit opposite us in the foyer. Furious's arm and head are still bandaged up, and his face looks sore and bruised. We want him out. They want him in. And the governors are to decide.

We march towards the room, and I feel my heart disappear into the pit of my stomach. My instinct is to walk with Furious, ask him how he is, if he is in pain. But I can't. I walk with the head, and Furious walks with his parents. We are enemies. All I can think of is Ms Desperate standing over my desk, pleading: '*Save my boy . . .*'

Mr Goodheart leans over to me as we walk in the door. 'Damn, he looks good. He'll get the governors' sympathy looking all beat up like that.'

We begin. To my surprise, the lawyer isn't that clever and I feel equipped to perform appropriately for what is to become five hours of hell, going late into the night. No food, only water, and a five-minute loo break is all the relief any of us gets. Furious himself seems unconcerned by this procedure. Does he understand its magnitude? I don't know. He looks more bored than anything else, looking around the room, yawning and tapping his fingers on the table. Has he grasped that if the governors uphold the head's decision to exclude, that this will basically be his first step on that slippery slope to prison? No, I don't think he has. Goddammit, Furious. Why did he never listen to me?

Mr Inevitable and Ms Desperate know all too well what will happen to him. And when they speak with heart-wrenching honesty of their attempts to try to keep their adopted boy in line, my heart sinks a little lower. But I remember the head's wise advice: never say anything more than is necessary. United, we win; united, we win.

Mr Inevitable is clearly upset. 'It isn't that we haven't worked hard for Furious, you know. We took him in when he was three years old. His mother abandoned him. And we've given him everything.' Ms Desperate nods as he continues. 'Furious isn't the best-behaved boy in the world, but he had a very hard first three years. He doesn't even know his real father.'

Our lawyer is looking annoyed, but Mr Inevitable isn't stopping for anyone. 'Don't you see? He's a good boy really, but he didn't have the right start in life and we've tried, we really have.'

Our lawyer clears his throat. 'Well, Mr Inevitable, no one is saying you haven't done a good job raising Furious. The matter in hand is the theft of the phone.'

I feel sick with stress. Furious keeps looking at me. I try to divert his gaze, but every now and then our eyes cross paths and I feel like running over to him and giving him a massive hug. United, we win; united, we win. We battle it out politely, and, eventually, the five hours of hell come to an end and we all leave, exhausted, drained and defeated from the emotional turmoil of it all.

I sit in Mr Goodheart's office. 'So, how do you think it went?'

He shrugs. 'We'll hear tonight. Go home. I'll ring you as soon as I know.'

I sit at home in my front room, windows open, late into the evening, waiting for the phone call from Mr Goodheart to tell me whether our decision has been upheld.

'Are you OK, babe?' Liberal is worried about me. 'It's ten o'clock. Why don't we go to bed?'

'I can't. I have to wait for the phone call. They're taking ages in deciding. What does that mean?'

Liberal shrugs. 'I don't know how these things work.'

'The worst bit of it is that I don't know what result I want. I mean, Furious is bad and he should go, but –'

Liberal pats me on the head. 'You're only human, babe.'

The wait seems to take for ever. And then, finally . . . it comes: 'Ms Snuffleupagus, I'm sorry to ring so late. But I know you would want to know . . .'

'Hello, Sir. Yes. I've been waiting by the phone. What did the governors say?'

Mr Goodheart sighs. 'You'll be happy to know that the governors have upheld our decision for permanent exclusion. We have *won*.'

I put the phone down and tell Liberal. He hugs me and I start to cry. Furious is gone. Finally, he's out. Mr Goodheart was right. United, we win. United, we win. Too bad I cannot help but feel, united, too, we fall. I turn to Liberal as he puts his arm around me and he wipes the tears as they fall down my cheeks.

Wednesday 16 July

This morning, Furious and his foster parents have returned to the school to be told the governors' decision. It's a brief meeting, and when it's over we all get up to go. As Furious's father, Mr Inevitable, is leaving, he turns to me. 'You made a mistake, you know.'

Mr Goodheart passes in front and whispers to me, 'Just keep walking. Don't engage with him. Follow me.'

But I find my feet are stuck to the ground. I cannot obey the instruction. I have known Mr Inevitable for five years. I know him to be a kind, hard-working man. Because of me, his family's future has been altered irrevocably. His eyes contain a mixture of hurt and anger. He hates me. 'Sorry, Sir?' I blink. 'I made a mistake?'

'My son isn't a thief.'

'Sorry?'

'I'm not saying you're lying. You just made a mistake. My son didn't take that phone.'

Furious stands next to his father, looking at the ground. He doesn't look at me, not once. Mr Inevitable puts his arm around his shoulders. 'Come on, son,' he says. It occurs to me that this is the first time I've ever heard him call Furious 'son'.

As I wander down the corridor, the seed of doubt starts to sprout. Did I make a mistake? Was it the right day? Did Furious steal that phone? Have I just excluded a child for nothing?

I run to Mr Goodheart and explain. He reminds me that Furious isn't being excluded for the theft on its own. The theft is merely the last of a long list of incidents. The boy needed to go. And even if I did make a mistake, we *know* he took the phone, just as we *know* he stole a bunch of other phones in various other incidents. He reminds me of all the different incidents Furious has been involved in – disrupting learning, throwing a stone at Mr Hadenough, the harassment of Beautiful. He reminds me of the several children who have been bullied by Furious. The boy needed to go.

But what if I made a mistake? What if he didn't take this particular phone? Do the ends justify the means? The boy needed to go, it's true. So why do I feel so bad about it?

Thursday 17 July

I feel like I've been in a boxing ring. Is teaching meant to be like this? What's going to happen to Furious? And to Cavalier? What of little Munchkin?

I'm sitting in front of the TV, zoning out, when Liberal hands me some vanilla caramel brownie ice cream and sits next to me. 'Hey, you look like you need this,' he says kindly.

'Thank you.' I kiss him on the cheek. 'I don't know why I do any of this. Why did I choose this damn career? Why did I decide to throw away any hope of a normal life? And why on earth do you put up with me?' I look up at him and start to cry.

He kisses me. 'Hey, come on now. Where's my soldier girl? Look at how much difference you make to these kids.'

I shake my head. 'I don't do anything. I jump through Ofsted hoops just like everyone else. I stuff my lessons full of games and cut them up into tiny pieces so that the kids don't have to develop any kind of concentration span.' I wipe the tears off my face. 'I'm so crap that I couldn't save Furious – and look at Cavalier. I should have seen that coming. I should have been able to stop it.'

Liberal starts to raise his voice. 'No, soldier girl. You're wrong. What about Stoic? What about Munchkin? What about Seething? And what about that young woman who went to Oxford and then became a teacher because of you?'

I look at him and wonder how he knows their names, how he remembers about that Oxford girl, and I realize that he really does listen to me, even if sometimes he doesn't agree.

'Yeah, I guess, but we're still losing the battle.'

'No, you're not. What you do is remarkable. I could never do what you do. You're like no one I've ever known . . . crazy as you are.'

I smile. 'I wouldn't be able to do any of it without you.'

Liberal grins. 'I know, babe. I know.'

Friday 18 July

Every morning, an old man sits at the bus stop in front of Ordinary School. He is tall and wide, with a full head of white hair, crumpled white skin, and he walks with a noticeable limp. Standing next to him is his smiling ten-year-old grandson, always in an impeccable school uniform, complete with cap and knee-high socks.

Today I see him sitting on a wall nearby and approach. We talk for a while about his grandson and the old man beams with pride as he sings the boy's successes. Next year he'll be going to secondary school, he tells me.

'So where do you hope to send your grandson?' I probe.

'Well, dear, his primary school is excellent, and most of the children tend to go to Basic School, so I suppose he'll go there.'

My heart sinks. He doesn't know the excruciating web of

madness that is the secondary-school system. He doesn't know that, in a few years, his sweet grandson will be unrecognizable.

Some people are lucky enough to live in areas where state schools are a real choice. He is not one of them. There is no advice I can give this man. So we chat a little longer about how my school has improved over the years, as has Basic School. Like so many people, he really has no idea what an inner-city school is like, but I nod, and smile, and do my best not to shatter his image of his grandson's future. 'Well, I must run now,' I say eventually, holding out my hand. 'It was a pleasure to finally meet you.'

'Oh yes, dear,' he stammers. 'Thank you for saying hello, dear.'

As I walk back towards school, I catch site of Cavalier down the road. 'Cavalier!' I call.

He turns around and comes towards me. He looks at the ground. 'Hi, Miss.'

'Hi, Cavalier. How are you? Are you OK? What are you doing now?'

'Nothin',' he says. 'I'm not doing nothin'.'

'I take it they didn't press charges then?'

He shakes his head. 'No.'

I squeeze his arm. 'I'm sure it will all work out, Cavalier. Listen to your mother, OK? Just listen to your mother.' I hear the bell go and I know I need to get inside. 'I need to go, Cavalier.'

'Yeah, sure, Miss.' He stuffs his hands in his pockets, and I walk towards the school gates. I twist the lock and walk in. As I do, Cavalier calls out. 'Miss!'

I look around. 'Yes?'

'Thanks!' And with that, he disappears down the street.

Tuesday 22 July

Cent missed his detention with me yesterday and we're trying to make it up while I'm on break duty. The trees are full with leaves, dappling the street with shadow. Cent comes and stands by my side on the asphalt step. He's small and almost frail-looking, standing on his own without his mates around him. Even though he's a terror around the school, he's only thirteen after all. His dark skin shines in the sunlight. 'Hey Miss, man, I'm here,' he says.

'Hi, Cent. Great. While we're here, just the two of us, I've been wondering, where is your family from?'

'From Nigeria. Lagos.'

'And how long have you been here?' I can still hear a hint of an accent in his speech.

'Three years innit.'

'All this bad behaviour of yours. I'm guessing you would never have behaved in Nigeria the way you do here, right?'

'No, Miss,' he answers, hanging his head.

'So why is that?'

'It's Africa, Miss. That's how it is there. Yeah? It's like a family. It isn't like here.'

'I don't understand.'

Cent has trouble answering the question. He keeps saying that the environment is different, that it's impossible to explain, that I would have to go there to see why children simply don't misbehave in Nigeria. Eventually he laughs. 'It's 'cause you'll get beaten bad in Nigeria, Miss, man, teachers and parents. Everyone beats ya.'

'And you think being beaten is the only reason you behave? I mean, if we beat you here, would you behave?'

Cent's eyes look straight at me. 'Yeah, yeah, yeah.'

'And is that the only difference then? Between school in Nigeria and school in London?'

Cent shakes his head. 'Nah, that ain't it. It's Africa, man, it's like a family.'

'What do you mean by "it's like a family"?'

''Cause there's too much violence in London, man! Nigeria is a safe place. Look at all 'em stabbings!'

Leaving aside the very bizarre conclusion that Lagos is less violent than London, I'm still confused. 'You mean to say that the stabbings out there' – I gesture towards the open air and the world beyond the school – 'are the reason you misbehave in *here*?'

Cent shakes his head. 'Nah nah, I mean that you have to be seen to be "in" with the bad ones here, otherwise yuh get robbed, man, or yuh get beat. They need to know your face as one of 'em.'

'You mean that, if they know who you are, they'll leave you alone?'

'Yeah, so they knows your face, yuh know? Yuh gotta be one of them. Yuh gotta blend, so then when you pass 'em, they knows yuh.' Cent pushes his chin forward. 'And yuh don't get robbed.'

I smile, as if the penny is dropping. 'And there isn't that outside pressure to be bad in Nigeria?'

Cent shakes his head. 'Nah, Miss, it's like a family.'

'So where would you rather be then, Cent, here, or Nigeria?'

'Well, both, Miss. Here, 'cause it's a rich country, there is more opportunities like, but Africa, 'cause it's Africa, 'cause my friends and family are there.'

'Don't you have any friends here?'

'Yeah, but they isn't friends like in Nigeria, people you can count on. Like, they is just people I know.'

'What do you mean? Don't you have anyone who you would call a friend here?'

'Fifty. That's it. He's the only one I'd call a friend. You nuh understand, Miss. Remember what happened to Cavalier? Wholesome knew it was gonna happen. They all knew. No one did anything to stop it, yeah. That wouldn't happen in Africa. Africa is like a family.'

I smile. Yeah, I get it. Africa is like a family. What's London like then? I look at my watch. 'Nearly time to go in, Cent. What're you doing this summer?'

Cent shrugs. 'Nuffin'. Just hanging out.'

'Will you try not to forget what life is like in Africa, this summer, while you're hanging out?'

Cent nods. 'Yeah, sure, Miss. If it makes you happy . . . sure.'

Wednesday 23 July

I open my office door and find a card under the door.

Dear Snuffy,

What can I say? I can't believe I am actually going. I am really going through with it. It is going to be strange, leaving the madness of Ordinary. You have been truly inspirational. You have been supportive and encouraging – always helping me to take on new ideas and challenges. I very much doubt that I will ever have a colleague like you again in my life and I hope that I can use what I have learnt from you in my future career. You have been a wonderful leader and friend. Thanks for everything. All the best for the future, and please stay in touch!

Hadenough x

Bloody hell. Even after all our conversations, I still thought he would decide to stay. Hadenough is my friend. He gets it. What am I going to do without him?

He appears at my door, grinning, holding a photo that he took of Dreamer, Dopey and me one lunchtime in the playground. He hands it to me. 'Here you go, another photo for that kitchen wall of yours.'

'Thanks, Hadenough.' And I throw my arms around him and hug him as tight as my arms will go.

Thursday 24 July

'OK, you lot, last lesson before the summer holidays!'

My Year 8s cheer. Munchkin and Cent are sitting together at the back for the game that I've planned. The little Munchkin with squidgy cheeks of yesteryear is long gone.

'Boys, concentrate, please.' They sit up straight in their chairs and listen. We play our game. And when it's over, I ask them all what their plans are for the summer. They explain to me that they don't have any. They aren't going anywhere, they aren't doing anything. They're going to spend the summer watching TV and playing on their PSPs.

Something occurs to me. I rummage in my desk drawers. Ah, there it is. 'Remember how I went to China last year?'

'Yeah, I remember. You brought us back those Chinese skittles.' It's Adorable who speaks.

'That's right. Well, this is what one of the girls at the school I visited in China gave to me.' I hold up a letter. And then I read it aloud to them:

To Miss, with love:

'Nothing is impossible if you put your heart into it.' I always think the saying is good. Because I hoped that I could talk to foreigner many years ago. And now the dream comes true. Finally I can. Because of this dream. I like English. I like speaking. Now, I can speak English 'well'. Everywhere in China is beautiful. I heard that England is a beautiful place too. I hope I can study there. I can visit England some day. I am a girl. A girl who has dream, and she will work hard for dream. She never gives up until the dream comes true.

A Chinese girl

I read them the letter and they listen in absolute silence. It's amazing how still they are. When I finish, Cent lets out a gasp. 'Wow, Miss, they really want to work hard in China, don't they?'

'Rah!' They all laugh. 'Glad we don't live there!'

'Oh, for goodness' sake!' I burst into laughter and pretend to throw the letter at them. 'What are you like! Aargghhh! Try to pick up a book this summer,' I shout.

'Rah!'

I have to laugh too. They're so funny. I do love them. 'See you in September then, everyone. Have a good summer!'

'Yeah! You too Miss, man! You too!'

They wave to me as they head towards the door. Munchkin, the last to leave, turns back. 'Yo, Miss!'

'Yes, Munchkin?'

He looks up at me from the ground and, for a moment, I see the sweet, squidgy-cheeked boy I once knew. A wide grin breaks out on his face. 'Thanks, Miss.'

I wink at him. 'Have a good holiday, Munchkin.' And off he goes.

Friday 25 July

Today is the best day of the year for all teachers: the last day of summer term. The long summer holiday is just about to start. There is no marking to catch up on during this holiday. There is no planning of lessons, really, that one can do. Six whole weeks. OK, yes, one may be in school here and there, but an oasis of calm lies ahead.

Somehow, the kids go home without a hitch. 'See you in September, Miss,' they shout as they run out the gates at midday, having spent the morning watching videos and eating sweets.

The departing teachers give their goodbye speeches, and we hand them presents and give them lots of hugs. At the end of it, Hadenough approaches. 'You coming to the pub after?'

'Yeah, maybe.' I nudge him. 'What're you going to do now then?'

'Not sure for the moment. Like I said, my girlfriend and I will probably move out of London. We're going to figure it out this summer.'

'But we'll still be friends. We'll keep in touch.'

'Yeah, of course we will.'

Mr Goodheart approaches. 'Will you be in for the exam days, Snuffy?'

'Yes, of course I will, Sir. Have to see whether Dopey gets that "C"!'

Mr Goodheart winks at me. 'Yes . . . I'm counting on it!'

My heart sinks. Jesus. Come on, Dopey, don't let me down.

Summer Holidays

Friday 1 August

We've had Year 6s with us for a week at school. 'Summer school', they call it. Lots of very small children out of uniform doing 'fun learning', and getting to know the secondary school they will join in September.

I watch them at lunch today, wandering around the grounds. How ordered and polite they are, how kind to each other, how well behaved and obedient . . . how delightful. I peer at them. What drugs are these children taking? What's made them so much like the way children are meant to be?

These children are just as poor and rich as our children in Years 7 through to 13. They are just as doughnut-like, and just as bright. They come from the same families: a mixture of broken homes and happy 2.5 white-picket-fence fantasy. Indeed, last year, at summer school, our current Year 7 were just the same. And the year before that, our current Year 8 were delightful too. Fifty, Munchkin, Cent . . . they were all lovely once. So what happens to them?

There is the point about age, of course: as children move through puberty, they become increasingly difficult. Thirteen, fourteen, fifteen are the most difficult, and when they come out on the other side, their challenging status decreases with age. This aside, though, there are two main reasons for their obedience and good manners. They are in the unfamiliar, and they are frightened.

These Year 6 children have been told just how strict secondary school is going to be. They have been read lists of rules and consequences by several different people. They have been told how lucky they are to be at this school, and they know that they should be grateful. They don't want to jeopardize their places at this wonderful school, which they and their parents fought so hard to get into.

Come September, these children will still behave angelically, for about four to six weeks. Over that time, though, reality will slowly dawn on them. They will begin to notice that while school *says* that X is expected, in reality, it is not. While school *says* that X behaviour will result in one losing one's place at the school, in reality, rarely, if ever, does a child get permanently excluded.

Why should these Year 6s, in a small space of time, completely transform? Because they will eventually realize that the school – that *we* – are lying to them.

The reality is that they have nothing to fear at all.

Wednesday 27 August

And so finally, after waiting an eternity, 27 August is here. The sun is beaming high in the sky. Walking into school, I run into Mr Goodheart. I'm late. 'Sorry I'm late, Sir. I was held up.'

He smiles. 'I have some good news for you.'

'You know my results? Did –'

'No, no,' he interrupts me. 'About Furious.'

'What about him?'

'His mother decided to take your advice. They've sent him to Nigeria. He's starting school there in September.'

'Really?' I clap my hands. 'Oh thank God for that. Maybe he'll turn it all around.'

'Yeah, we'll see. Now get up there and do your job!'

I go straight to it, without looking at the results in the office, and stand behind my table, handing out the GCSE exam envelopes. I have no idea how my lovely Year 11s have done.

In walk Deranged, Beautiful, Seething and Psycho, dressed in tight jeans and slinky tops. 'Hi, Miss,' they chorus.

'Hi there, girls. Good to see you.' I look through my pile of envelopes and hand them over. 'Here you go. Good luck.'

They walk over to the side and rip open their envelopes. I hand out a few more. Eventually there's a bit of a lull and I hurry over to the girls. 'So? How'd you do?'

'Yeah, yeah, OK, Miss.' They nod as they chomp on their chewing gum.

'And how'd you do in English?' I shout.

Deranged grins. 'Yeah, a "C", Miss. Beautiful got a "C" and Psycho too.'

'Brilliant! Well done, girls! What about you, Seething?'

'A "D", Miss . . . I'm sorry. It's a "D" innit.' She makes a face.

I tilt my head to the side. 'Hey, it's OK. You can try to retake this year. And how about your other subjects? How'd you do?' She explains how she has two 'C's – one of them in history – but the rest are 'D's, 'E's and a couple of 'F's. I listen, trying to look as positive as possible. 'And you, Deranged, how about the other grades?'

'Got the five "C"s, Miss: beauty college here I come!'

'Well done, that's great news, Deranged. And Beautiful?' I pull her over to the side, whispering, 'Did you break up with him?'

'Yeah, Miss, I did it, I did it! And seeing how's he's going Nigeria, it's, like, over, innit?'

'Good for you, Beautiful. That's great – well done!' As I'm grinning madly, I notice Dreamer, Daring and Dopey walk in the door. 'See you later, girls.' I rush towards the door. 'Boys! Boys!'

'Miss, man!' Dopey runs up to me and throws his arms open. As he reaches me, he realizes what he's doing and immediately drops his arms to the side. 'Yeah, Miss, yeah, we come for our results, yuh know.'

'Yes, boys. Come over here, I'll find you your envelopes.' I move to the table and sift through. Finding them, I nervously hand them over. I catch Mr Goodheart looking at me from the other side of the room. I glance in his direction and smile. He holds his hand up in the air, crossing his fingers. I look at Dreamer, Daring and Dopey as I place the envelopes in their hands. 'Good luck, boys.'

They walk to the other side of the room together. As they do, I find myself starting to pray. Please, God. Please, dear God, let him get that 'C'. If anyone deserves one, it's Dopey. That boy gave it his all. That boy did more than any kid I have ever known. He just has to get a 'C'. He just *has* to.

Dreamer begins to open his envelope first. Dopey seems too scared to open his. He watches Dreamer. I am frozen still, watching them, no longer capable of doing my job of handing out envelopes. Out come Dreamer's certificates. He looks down and reads them as Dopey looks on. I can't read his face . . . a mixture of pleasure and disappointment. I can't tell what he's thinking. Eventually I march over to them and ask what Dreamer got. He grins. 'A "C", Miss. I got it!'

I'm relieved. 'Well done, Dreamer. Fantastic news! Your brother will be proud.' I pat him on the arm. 'And the other grades?' Dreamer lists a bunch of 'C's, 'D's and 'E's. I nod, remaining positive. I look at Daring, who, by now, has got his envelope open. He hangs his head.

'Sorry, Miss. It's a "D".'

'That's OK, Daring, that's OK. How'd you do elsewhere?'

He nods. 'Three "C"s. That ain't bad, right?'

'It's great, Daring. Don't worry. You've done well.' I stroke his arm as I speak. I look to Dopey. 'And you, Dopey?' I point to the envelope in his hands. 'Aren't you going to look?'

Dopey shakes his head. 'I'm scared, Miss.'

'Come on, Dopey, you have to open it sometime. Let's see what you got.'

Dopey nods, draws a deep breath and rips open the envelope. I stand back, giving him some privacy. Dopey looks down at his certificates. He looks upset. He frowns. Oh no. Dopey . . . He looks up at me. Then grins. 'I told ya, Miss, I told ya I'd do it!' He rushes towards me. ' "Choo choo!" A "C", Miss! A "C"!' He throws his arms open and grabs me. I throw my arms around him.

'Wahey! You did it! You did it!' I jump around with Dopey holding on to me. 'He did it, Mr Goodheart!' I shout. 'Dopey did it! He did it!'

Mr Goodheart smiles, pointing his thumb to the ceiling and mouthing 'I know' in my direction. I look at the rest of Dopey's certificates. He has a beautiful array of 'D', 'E', 'F' and 'G' grades. He got a 'G' in maths. Ms Joyful will be happy. Except, within the bunch of failing grades, Dopey has defied the odds, he has turned water into wine, he has secured our 100 per cent. Dopey has one 'C'.

The little engine has arrived at the top. My darling Dopey got there. My head has his 100 per cent, Dopey has his 'C', and I have the memory of a boy who managed to do the unthinkable, who managed to surprise even me – a boy who with determination and sheer hard work put his hand in mine and allowed me to lead him to the top of the hill. It's a memory that I will cherish for ever.

Thursday 28 August

In term time, every morning, before the bell, before I run out on to the battlefield, I read the poster on my wall. It's a quote from the Obama election campaign:

I will never forget that the only reason that I'm standing here today is because somebody, somewhere stood up for me when it was risky. Stood up when it was hard. Stood up when it wasn't popular. And because that somebody stood up, a few more stood up. And then a few thousand stood up. And then a few million stood up. And standing up, with courage and clear purpose, they somehow managed to change the world.

No one hears the voices of my children. No one listens to my colleagues when they shout about the shocking behaviour, the dumbing-down or the chaotic leadership of our education system.

September is around the corner. A new year lies ahead. Let's make it a better one.